MEASURING SUICIDAL BEHAVIOR AND RISK IN CHILDREN AND ADOLESCENTS

Measurement and Instrumentation in Psychology

Measuring Suicidal Behavior and Risk in Children and Adolescents

David B. Goldston

AMERICAN PSYCHOLOGICAL ASSOCIATION
WASHINGTON, DC

Published by
American Psychological Association
750 First Street, NE
Washington, DC 20002
www.apa.org

To order
APA Order Department
P.O. Box 92984
Washington, DC 20090-2984

Tel: (800) 374-2721; Direct: (202) 336-5510
Fax: (202) 336-5502; TDD/TTY: (202) 336-6123
Online: www.apa.org/books/
E-mail: order@apa.org

In the U.K., Europe, Africa, and the Middle East, copies may be ordered from
American Psychological Association
3 Henrietta Street
Covent Garden, London
WC2E 8LU England

Typeset in New Baskerville by World Composition Services, Inc., Sterling, VA

Printer: United Book Press, Inc., Baltimore, MD
Cover Designer: Berg Design, Albany, NY
Technical/Production Editor: Rosemary Moulton

The opinions and statements published are the responsibility of the author, and such opinions and statements do not necessarily represent the policies of the American Psychological Association.

Library of Congress Cataloging-in-Publication Data
Goldston, David B.
  Measuring suicidal behavior and risk in children and adolescents / David B. Goldston.
    p. cm.
Includes bibliographical references and index.
  ISBN 1-59147-008-0 (alk. paper)
  1. Children—Suicidal behavior—Diagnosis.   2. Teenagers–Suicidal behavior—Diagnosis.   3. Children—Suicidal behavior—Psychological testing.   4. Teenagers—Suicidal behavior—Psychological testing.   5. Psychological tests for children—Evaluation.   6. Youth—Psychological testing—Evaluation.   I. Title.

  RJ506.S9G65 2003
  618.92′858445075—dc21   2003005155

British Library Cataloguing-in-Publication Data
A CIP record is available from the British Library.

Printed in the United States of America
First Edition

Contents

List of Measures

Chapter 5. Self-Report Inventories and Behavior Checklists

Chapter 6. Survey Screening Items for Suicidal Behaviors

Chapter 7. Assessing Risk of Suicidal Behaviors: Self-Report Questionnaires and Clinician Rating Scales

Chapter 8. Assessing Risk of Suicidal Behaviors: Multitiered Screening Assessments

Acknowledgments

Preparation of an earlier version of this book was supported by National Institute of Mental Health (NIMH) Contract No. 263-MD-909995 and NIMH Grant MH48762.

I am appreciative of the numerous researchers and members of the American Association of Suicidology who took the time to send materials and respond to correspondence and phone calls in preparation of this book. I would also like to thank colleagues, staff, and volunteer assistants (Ali A. Asharali, Stephanie Sergent Daniel, Patricia Frazier, Ashley Kirkman, Laura Longino, Joseph Manno, Beth Reboussin, and Lyn Treadway) who assisted in the preparation of and provided feedback on the book. Lastly, I am appreciative of the experts in this area (Greg Brown, Lucy Davidson, David Jobes, Cheryl King, Peter Lewinsohn, Eve Moscicki, Edith Nottelmann, and Jane Pearson) who provided feedback on this book.

Any errors or omissions in the book are the sole responsibility of the author.

Part I

Overview

Introduction:
Measuring Suicidal
Behaviors and Risk

Suicide is the third leading cause of death among adolescents, exceeded only by homicide and accidents (Miniño, Arias, Kochanek, Murphy, & Smith, 2002). Despite a decrease in the rate of completed suicides from 1994 to 2000, the suicide rate for youths is still considerably higher (10.4 per 100,000 in 2000 for 15- to 24-year-olds; Miniño et al., 2002) than it was several decades ago (4.5 per 100,000 for 15- to 24-year-olds in 1950; National Center for Health Statistics, 2000). Suicide is a major source of preventable death in this age group, and a recent study estimated that in the year 2000, approximately 3 million teenagers (almost 15%) in the United States either attempted suicide or seriously considered suicide (Substance Abuse and Mental Health Services Administration [SAMHSA], 2002).

Suicidal ideation and behavior are a major reason for psychiatric emergencies and psychiatric hospitalization (Peterson, Zhang, Santa Lucia, King, & Lewis, 1996) and often reflect associated psychiatric problems and difficulties with coping. Indeed, studies of samples from communities and clinical settings suggest that the great majority of suicidal behaviors occur in the context of diagnosable psychiatric disorders (Gould et al., 1998; Kovacs, Goldston, & Gatsonis, 1993; Shaffer, Gould et al., 1996; Shafi, Steltz-Lenarsky, Derrick, Beckner, & Whittinghill, 1988). The most common psychiatric disorders associated with suicidal behaviors are affective disorders (Brent, Perper, Moritz, Allman, et al., 1993; Goldston et al., 1998; Gould et al., 1998; Kovacs et al., 1993; Shaffer, Gould et al., 1996), but a considerable proportion of suicidal behaviors occur in the presence of other disorders as well (Goldston et al., 1998; Gould et al., 1998; Shaffer, Gould et al., 1996). Suicidal behavior among youths often is accompanied by higher rates of other high-risk behaviors, including substance abuse (Burge, Felts, Chenier,

& Parrillo, 1995; Felts, Chenier, & Barnes, 1992; Garofalo, Wolf, Wissow, Woods, & Goodman, 1999; Woods et al., 1997), weapon carrying (Durant, Krowchuk, Kreiter, Sinal, & Woods, 1999; Orpinas, Basen-Engquist, Grunbaum, & Parcel, 1995; Woods et al., 1997), physical fighting (Garofalo et al., 1999; Garrison, McKeown, Valois, & Vincent, 1993; Woods et al., 1997), and sexual behavior (Burge et al., 1995; Nelson, Higginson, & Grant-Worley, 1994). Youths with repeated suicidal behavior are at particularly high risk. Compared with youths who are not suicidal or youths who have made only single suicide attempts, youths with recurrent suicidal behavior have been noted to have more functional impairment, greater family violence or substance abuse, and greater family history of mental illness (Walrath et al., 2001). Suicidal behavior among adolescents and adults often portends greater risk for later difficulties, including additional subsequent attempts and completed suicide (Goldston et al., 1999; Leon, Friedman, Sweeney, Brown, & Mann, 1990; Lonnqvist & Ostano, 1991; Tejedor, Diaz, Castillon, & Pericay, 1999).

Justifiably, then, suicide and suicidal behaviors among youths have garnered increasing attention over the last several decades. To illustrate, a search of the PsycINFO database for journal articles focused on children or adolescents and the key words *suicide* or *suicidal* yielded 209 articles published during the years 1972 to 1981. In the next decade, 1982 to 1991, the number of articles published in this area increased to 814. For the decade of 1992 to 2001, the number of articles increased again to 1,737, an increase of a factor of eightfold relative to two decades earlier.

The Surgeon General of the United States (U.S. Public Health Service, 1999) in his Call to Action to Prevent Suicide has called for greater understanding, prevention, and treatment of suicidal behaviors. In the National Strategy for Suicide Prevention (U.S. Public Health Service, 2001), concern about suicidal behaviors has been translated into a concrete action plan of steps toward increased recognition, prevention, and treatment of suicidal behaviors. The Institute of Medicine's report *Reducing Suicide: A National Imperative* has further underscored the importance of continuing efforts to understand, monitor, prevent, and treat the suicidal behaviors of youths and young adults (Goldsmith, Pellmar, Kleinman, & Bunney, 2002). Moreover, the U.S. Department of Health and Human Services (1998) decided to include suicide as one of the leading indicators of health status in the national health promotion and disease prevention initiative Healthy People 2010.

To the practicing clinician, the suicidal behavior of clients is often a major source of concern and anxiety. Decisions about whether, when, or how to intervene with suicidal behavior or the potential for suicidal behavior quite literally can have life-or-death consequences. Unfortunately, there have been few controlled prevention and treatment trials for suicidal behaviors among youths. Particularly in the absence of data regarding the best evidence-based practices, careful and systematic assessment can aid the clinician and provide concrete data and documentation regarding whether interventions are working. However, such systematic assessment is often not used.

Despite the needs of clinicians and the high public health interest in suicidal behaviors, there has been surprising lack of consensus in the field regarding the most appropriate instruments for assessing suicidal behaviors and suicidal risk. There also have been disagreements among researchers and clinicians regarding the best way of defining or conceptualizing suicidal behaviors. Such inconsistencies in approach have made it more difficult for clinicians, researchers, and educators alike to reach conclusions about risk factors and the best strategies for identifying risk and for preventing and treating juvenile suicidal behaviors. Peter Lewinsohn and associates (Lewinsohn, Garrison, Langhinrichsen, & Marsteller, 1989) identified this as a central problem as early as 1987 in a National Institute of Mental Health (NIMH) workshop on Suicidal Behaviors in Adolescents and Young Adults:

> Perhaps the most salient conclusion that emerged . . . was that the data reported in the scientific literature (and subsequently in the popular press) were very difficult to interpret because they were collected employing different definitions of critical items, and used disparate instruments with unknown validity and reliability in non-comparable populations. (p. 1)

Purposes and Rationale of This Book

Because of this concern about the state of the art a decade ago, Lewinsohn and his colleagues were commissioned by NIMH to critically review the literature on the assessment of suicidal behaviors among children and adolescents (Garrison, Lewinsohn, Marsteller, Langhinrichsen, & Lann, 1991; Lewinsohn et al., 1989). Their review was a major contribution to the field but became outdated as the years passed and the knowledge base accumulated. By the late 1990s, two workshops ("Suicidality in Youth: Developing the Knowledge Base for Youth at Risk" sponsored by NIMH and "Treatment Research With Suicidal Patients" sponsored by NIMH, the National Institutes of Health (NIH) Office of Rare Diseases, and the American Foundation for Suicide Prevention) concluded that an update of the Lewinsohn et al. (1989) review would be important for advancement in our understanding of suicidal behaviors. In that context, NIMH commissioned a technical report (Goldston, 2000) reviewing the literature on the assessment of suicidal behavior and risk in the decade since Lewinsohn et al.'s review.

The current book expands and updates the NIMH technical report and is designed to be "user-friendly." It is intended to reach a broad audience—mental health treatment providers, graduate students, individuals interested in prevention efforts, and researchers studying juvenile suicidal behaviors. A number of excellent books have been published that describe the process of assessing suicidal behavior and risk (e.g., Berman & Jobes, 1991; Jacobs, 1999; Shea, 1999). What this book offers is different: This volume is intended primarily as a critical and comprehensive reference book of available instruments that can be used for screening purposes or as adjuncts in the assessment of suicidal behaviors and risk among children and adolescents. In this book, I have attempted to review as many as possible of the available instruments for detecting, describing, or estimating the risk of suicidal behavior available at the time of this printing. In the context of this critical review, I have highlighted gaps in the research knowledge and promising areas for new research in suicidal behaviors and risk assessment. At the end of several chapters are tables to assist the reader in comparing and contrasting instruments. In the Appendix, a series of decision rules are presented to assist the reader in choosing among the different instruments for various purposes.

Intended Audience

As mentioned, this book has been written for a broad audience of individuals interested in the assessment of suicidal behaviors—practitioners, researchers, and students alike. It is often useful for the clinical practitioner to elicit information about areas of concern using different formats, methods, and informants. This book should provide information regarding possible alternative ways of assessing suicidal behaviors. Moreover, it has been shown that information obtained from an unstructured clinical assessment is often less reliable than information obtained in more "objective" formats for decision making (Dawes, Faust, & Meehl, 1989). Although results obtained with assessment instruments should never supplant clinical judgment, if used properly, such data can complement and extend the evaluative process. In clinical settings, assessment instruments can be used to help identify individuals with past or current suicidal behaviors, to aid in the estimation of risk, or to monitor patients thought to be "at risk." Standardized assessment of suicidal behaviors and risk factors can assist in identifying needs or targets for intervention (e.g., the reduction of hopelessness) and assessment of whether the intervention is working as intended (and therein, whether additional or alternative therapeutic steps need to be taken).

In schools and other settings for prevention efforts, assessment instruments can be used for screening purposes. Unfortunately, suicide prevention efforts in the schools that are widely targeted have on occasion been thought to be associated with unintended undesirable effects (Shaffer, Garland, Vieland, Underwood, & Busner, 1991). In this context, assessment instruments can be used to screen for individuals thought to be at higher risk for targeted or individualized prevention efforts, or they can be used to identify students who have already made or contemplated suicide attempts. Depending on the setting and need, assessment instruments for screening purposes can be used by themselves or as part of a multifaceted or tiered assessment strategy. In the latter scenario, individuals thought to be at risk on the basis of responses to questionnaire data are typically assessed more thoroughly with standardized interview-based assessment instruments in a second level of screening for suicide risk (e.g., Eggert, Thompson, & Herting, 1994; Reynolds, 1991; Shaffer & Craft, 1999).

Whether widely targeted or specifically tailored toward youths identified as being at risk, there are scant data documenting the effectiveness of school-based prevention programs. Evaluation of the effectiveness of prevention programs is the first step toward determining which programs have the strongest effects and should be widely disseminated. Careful and systematic evaluation of prevention and treatment programs and improved "assessment of and recognition of the mental health needs in children" in educational, pediatric, and other settings are public health goals that have been articulated by the Surgeon General (U.S. Public Health Service, 2000).

Standardized assessment instruments of course are indispensable in clinical research. Self-report questionnaires and standardized interviews for assessing suicidal behaviors provide a systematic means of selecting samples, or describing and characterizing participants in studies. Such instruments also provide outcome measures with which to gauge the effectiveness and efficacy of suicide interventions. In addition to aiding in the selection of appropriate research instruments, the critical review of the literature on suicidal behavior and risk assessment helps shed light on gaps or needs in this area as well as unverified assumptions about the nature of suicidal behaviors and purported risk factors for suicidal behavior. Research needs often include the further development and refinement of assessment instruments, demonstration of instruments' use in differentiating between suicidal and nonsuicidal individuals, and examination of instruments' ability to predict future suicidal behaviors in different settings and in different population groups.

Selection of Instruments

This book focuses on instruments that have been used to evaluate suicidal behaviors in children and adolescents since 1989, the date when Lewinsohn et al.'s review was published. The present volume covers both instruments developed since 1989 and instruments developed before 1989 but used subsequently. Instruments are included in this book if they focus on suicidal behaviors or include questions that can be used for assessing risk of suicidality. Several groups of suicidal behavior instruments are reviewed: (a) instruments for assessing the presence of suicidal behaviors, (b) instruments for assessing risk or propensity for suicidal behaviors, (c) instruments for assessing the intentionality and medical lethality of suicidal behaviors, and (d) other instruments (including instruments assessing exposure to suicidal behavior). Both instruments focusing specifically on suicidal behaviors (narrow-band instruments) and instruments focusing on a wider range of behaviors but including questions about suicidal behaviors (broadband instruments) are reviewed. Instruments reviewed include both interview (structured and semistructured) instruments and self-report inventories.

For inclusion in the book, instruments must have been used or described in published articles or chapters (peer reviewed as well as not peer reviewed) or specifically marketed as useful for assessing suicidality in youths since 1989. There are several classes of instruments that are not reviewed in this volume. First, there have been numerous studies in which questions about suicidal behavior have been included in "needs surveys" or one-time high school screenings. As a rule, such instruments are not reviewed unless they (a) have been used in large or multisite studies or (b) focus on specific understudied populations such as American Indians or gay, lesbian, or bisexual youths.

Second, a large number of variables have been found to be related to increased risk for suicidal behaviors, particularly in general population samples characterized by low levels of distress. Instruments assessing constructs such as general psychopathology or distress, or even severity of depression or anxiety, are generally not reviewed unless they contain items directly assessing suicidal behaviors or assess constructs specifically described as having presumed or theoretical importance in understanding suicidal behavior (e.g., hopelessness or reasons for living).

Third, various projective and objective personality tests (e.g., Minnesota Multiphasic Personality Inventory–A; Butcher et al., 1992) have been used in the assessment of *suicidal risk*. Such instruments are generally not reviewed unless they have specific indices or scales for assessing suicidal behaviors or the risk of suicidal behaviors (e.g., the Suicidal Tendencies Scale of the Millon Adolescent Clinical Inventory; Millon, 1993). A review by Johnson, Lall, Bongar, and Norlund (1999) concluded that objective personality inventories by themselves tend to have limited use in the assessment of risk and prediction of suicidal behavior.

Last, Lewinsohn et al.'s review (Garrison, Lewinsohn, et al., 1991; Lewinsohn et al., 1989) included instruments used with college students and instruments used only with adults that showed promise with youths. In contrast, the present volume focuses only on instruments that have been used with children and adolescents up to the age of 18. Instruments used with college student populations are included in a review of adult suicide behavior assessment instruments written under contract from NIMH by Gregory Brown at the University of Pennsylvania (Brown, 2001).

Within the confines of these parameters, I have attempted to identify as many as possible of the available and currently used instruments for assessing suicidal behaviors and risk among youths. Several methods were used to identify instruments for inclusion in this book. The starting point for this effort was the review by Lewinsohn et al. Social Science Citation Abstracts, PsycLIT, and Medline computerized database searches were conducted to determine whether instruments described in the earlier review had been cited or used since 1989. PsycLIT and Medline searches as well as the catalogs of major publishers of psychological tests also were used to identify new instruments. In addition, a letter was sent to all recipients of NIH funding (identified from the CRISP database) who may have published findings regarding suicidal behavior or used instruments for assessing suicidality with youths. A similar letter was sent to members of the Research Division of the American Association of Suicidology. Follow-up contacts were made to researchers known to have published findings regarding juvenile suicidality who failed to respond to earlier mailings or contacts.

Organization of This Book

The four sections of this book focus on (a) issues important in the evaluation of suicidal behavior and risk, (b) instruments used for detecting the presence or severity of suicidal behavior, (c) instruments used in estimating the risk or describing the clinical characteristics of suicidal behavior, and (d) clinical considerations in the choice of instruments and future directions for research in the assessment of suicidal behavior and risk. These four sections are followed by an Appendix that is intended to help the reader make decisions about which suicide assessment instruments are most appropriate for specific needs.

This book is organized in part by the type of instrument: (a) instruments for assessing or detecting the presence of suicidality, (b) instruments for assessing risk for suicidal behaviors, (c) instruments for assessing intent and lethality of suicidal behaviors, and (d) other instruments. Instruments are described in terms of the definitions of suicidal behaviors used (when appropriate), the psychometric characteristics of the instrument, and the populations for which the instrument has demonstrated utility.

Part I of the book introduces the topic area of suicidal behaviors and risk and overarching issues important in evaluating and comparing various assessment instruments. In this vein, chapter 1 (this chapter) provides an overview of the problem of suicidal behaviors among children and adolescents, as well as an overview of the intended audience and potential use of this book. Chapter 2 focuses on issues regarding nomenclature and definitions of suicidal behaviors. Several questions are posed for evaluating the adequacy of various assessment instruments in inquiring about suicidal behaviors in a manner consistent with the operational definitions proposed by O'Carroll et al. (1996). There also is a discussion of psychometric issues relevant to instruments for assessing suicidal behaviors and risk. Specifically reviewed are issues of reliability, internal consistency, dimensionality, concurrent validity, and predictive validity. Other factors related to past demonstrated use of instruments are also reviewed, including the populations or settings within which instruments have been used and whether instruments have been used in treatment studies. The last section of this chapter focuses on the topic of respondent bias and how it may affect the usefulness or validity of suicide assessment measures.

Part II of this book focuses on instruments for evaluating the presence or absence or the severity of suicidal behaviors (detection instruments). In this context, chapter 3 is a review of the adequacy and use of psychiatric diagnostic interviews for assessing suicidal behaviors. Specifically described are both structured interviews (interviews that are designed to be administered exactly as written) and semistructured interviews (interviews that are more flexible than structured interviews but require more clinical judgment). In chapter 4, interviews and clinician-rating scales developed specifically for assessing suicidal behaviors are reviewed. Chapter 5 provides an overview of the use of depression and self-report inventories and behavior checklists for assessing or screening for the presence of suicidal behavior. In chapter 6, several survey screening items for suicidal behavior are reviewed. Surveys are reviewed that have been developed for several specific populations, including Native American youths, runaway and homeless youths, and gay, lesbian, and bisexual youths.

Part III of this book focuses on suicide-related instruments that are not primarily detection instruments. Chapter 7 is a critical review of self-report instruments and clinician-rating scales that have been developed for or marketed as being useful in the assessment of risk for suicidal behavior. Some of these risk assessment instruments are grounded in theory, whereas others have been developed with more of an atheoretical, empirical approach. In chapter 8, multi-tiered risk screening assessment batteries and clinician-rated indices of risk are reviewed. With these assessment batteries, a first-stage screening is often used to screen or determine whether someone is in a high-risk group. Later assessments are typically used to determine severity of risk or to assess the question of whether respondents are in imminent danger of harming themselves or are in need of treatment. Chapter 9 focuses on instruments used to assess the clinical characteristics of suicidal behavior, such as subjective intent and medical lethality. In chapter 10, I describe several instruments that are not classified elsewhere. These include instruments used to assess attitudes about suicide, exposure to suicidal behaviors and death, and the "pain" often associated with suicidal behavior.

Part IV (and chap. 11) of this book provides a summary, outlines the clinical considerations in the choice of instruments, and makes recommendations for future research in this area. The Appendix provides a set of decision rules to help readers choose those instruments that meet their specific needs.

Conceptual and Definitional Issues

Mental health professionals have used differing terminology or classification schemes to refer to similar suicidal behaviors, and conversely, have used identical terms to refer to different suicidal behaviors. Such multiple uses of terminology and differing definitions of key terms contribute not only to a lack of precision in our vocabulary but also to differences in estimates of the prevalence of suicidal behaviors (Meehan, Lamb, Saltzman, & O'Carroll, 1992); in some cases, they contribute to misconceptions about suicidal behavior. One of the clearest examples of a term that has been used in multiple ways is that of *suicide gesture.* The term suicide gesture has been used variously to refer to suicidal behavior of low medical lethality, suicidal behavior of low stated intent, suicidal behavior for which the ultimate goal is at least partially something other than death, and nonsuicidal self-destructive behavior (behavior without any intent to die; e.g., cutting to produce relief or tension reduction). The term *suicidal gesture* also has been pejoratively used to refer to suicidal behavior thought to be "manipulative" or evidenced by difficult-to-treat patients.

The problems engendered by the multiple uses of the term suicide gesture should be self-evident. In children and adolescents, there is mixed evidence pertaining to whether medical lethality and "intent" are substantially correlated (DeMaso, Ross, & Beardslee, 1994; Lewinsohn, Rohde, & Seeley, 1996; Nasser & Overholser, 1999; Plutchik, van Praag, Picard, Conte, & Korn, 1989). To use the same term to refer to both suicidal behavior of low medical lethality and suicidal behavior of low intent ignores the fact that the two sets of behaviors are not always identical. Moreover, arbitrarily trying to distinguish between "genuine suicide attempts" and less serious suicide gestures makes little sense against the backdrop of a literature suggesting that the great majority of all suicidal behavior is associated with mixed motives and varying degrees of ambivalence (Shneidman, 1986). Labeling suicidal behaviors as manipulative is a dangerous practice insofar as it promotes the notion that some suicidal behavior can be treated in a dismissive manner. Hence, imprecision in labeling or describing behavior can contribute to a lack of clarity, if not misinformation about, the phenomenon we are trying to understand.

In 1994, a workshop sponsored by the National Institute of Mental Health and the Center for Mental Health Services was held to discuss the problems in communication engendered by the different ways in which terms and definitions have been used in the suicide literature. As a result of this workshop, a standardized nomenclature was proposed (O'Carroll et al., 1996). In the definitional system proposed by O'Carroll et al. (1996, pp. 246–247), the term *suicide* refers to "death from injury, poisoning, or suffocation where there is evidence (either explicit or implicit) that the injury was self-inflicted and that the decedent intended to kill himself/herself." The term *suicide attempt* refers to "a potentially self-injurious behavior with a nonfatal outcome, for which there is evidence (either explicit or implicit) that the person intended at some (nonzero) level to kill himself/herself. A suicide attempt may or may not result in injuries." *Suicidal ideation* refers to "any self-reported thoughts of engaging in suicide-related behavior."

Although there are debates regarding the adequacy of any classification scheme, this particular scheme does offer the advantage of being straightforward and minimizing theoretical or clinical speculation regarding the "meaning" of various suicidal behaviors. The proposed definitions of suicide attempt and suicide were eventually adopted by the World Health Organization and provide a common metric against which the suicide assessment instruments in this book can be evaluated.

Definitional or classification schemes regarding suicidal behaviors are reflected in the queries used in instruments to assess suicidal behaviors and risk. The adoption of a similar approach for classifying or describing suicidal behaviors can engender greater consistency in how suicidal behavior is assessed across instruments. Using a particular approach for eliciting information about suicidal behaviors of course does not ensure that respondents will always respond to test items in the manner intended. However, grounding the queries and research in a single definitional system at least ensures a degree of consistency in approach, thereby enhancing communication among researchers and clinicians. Lack of consistency in the past has likely contributed to the lack of progress in research on suicidal behaviors and, more specifically, has likely contributed to inconsistencies among research studies and among different clinicians in their characterization of, and approaches to, working with suicidal patients. With this consideration, each of the detection instruments in this book is evaluated with regard to how closely the inquiries about suicidal behaviors correspond to the operational definitions proposed by O'Carroll et al. (1996). Specifically, four sets of questions are typically raised.

1. *Do the suicidal ideation questions specifically focus on thoughts of wanting to kill oneself, rather than being so inclusive as to include thoughts of death or thoughts of wanting to die? Alternatively, are there separate items in the instrument for thoughts of death and suicidal thoughts?* Within the nomenclature proposed by O'Carroll et al. (1996), thoughts of death or wanting to die without specific thoughts of killing oneself are not considered to be suicidal ideation (although they may provide important clinical information).

2. *Are the items for detecting the presence or absence of suicide attempts confounded with the clinical characteristics of the attempt? For example, do questions for assessing the presence or absence of suicidal behavior ask only about suicide attempts with "serious" intent, attempts that are near-lethal, or attempts that require medical attention?* According to O'Carroll et al.'s (1996) nomenclature, suicide attempts only need be associated with some ("nonzero") intent to kill oneself. This can be ascertained by inquiring whether the individual had any wish or expectation of death, or whether he or she thought that death was a possibility when engaging in the self-harm behavior.

3. *Is it implicit or explicit in the suicide attempt detection items that the behaviors of interest were associated with some "nonzero" intent to kill oneself?* Suicide behavior detection items should not be worded so broadly as to potentially elicit information about behaviors that are self-endangering but are not associated with any intent to die (e.g., self-mutilation for relieving stress, risk-taking behaviors, etc).

4. *Are the suicide attempt detection items confounded with questions of whether the behaviors resulted in identifiable injury or required medical attention?* According to the operational definitions proposed by O'Carroll et al. (1996), suicidal behaviors should be *potentially* self-injurious, but the completed act need not be associated with identifiable injury or need for medical attention. Suicide attempts with injuries are considered to be a subset of all suicide attempts.

Psychometric Issues and the Use of Measures of Suicidal Behaviors and Risk

Judgments about whether measures of suicidal behavior conform to a particular standard such as the suggested nomenclature and operational definitions of O'Carroll et al. (1996) are in actuality judgments about the face or content validity of the scales or assessment items. The instruments in this book are also evaluated with respect to more quantifiable psychometric characteristics, such as their test–retest or interrater reliability, internal consistency, dimensionality, concurrent validity, and predictive validity. I also describe the demonstrated use of the measures as reflected in the populations in which they have been used previously as well as the use of the instruments as outcome measures in controlled treatment studies. More information on the rationale for evaluating the instruments in each of these areas is provided below.

Populations Studied

Assessment instruments have been used in a variety of settings to assess the presence or the risk of suicidal behaviors—outpatient psychiatry clinics, inpatient psychiatric units, residential treatment settings, hospital emergency departments, juvenile detention centers, pediatric clinics or inpatient settings, and schools. Because of different base rates of both suicidal behaviors and risk factors for suicidality in different population groups, instruments that may have use in identifying at-risk individuals in one population may not be as useful in identifying at-risk individuals in another population (a point discussed by Meehl & Rosen, 1955). For example, factors found to be associated with risk for suicidal behavior in high school or community epidemiologic samples, in which most respondents are not distressed, may not be similarly associated with greater suicidal behavior in clinical samples or high-risk populations, in which there often is by definition a greater degree of distress or impairment.

In addition to their use in different settings, suicide assessment instruments also have been used with different population groups, including American Indians, Latinos (including newly immigrant youths), African Americans, inner-city youths, substance-abusing youths, and runaway youths. In this context, assessment instruments may differ in their cultural sensitivity or their relevance to suicidal behaviors in different contexts. Hence, I describe the use of instruments in evaluating suicidal behavior in different settings and also with different population groups.

Reliability

For purposes of this book, the term *reliability* is used to refer to the "reproducibility" of responses to a question or scale. Instruments are described and evaluated with regard to test–retest reliability (or stability over time) and interrater reliability (when appropriate). Reliability data (and any other psychometric characteristics) for specific cultural and ethnic groups are described when available. It is important to note that questions or scales may be "reliable" or yield reproducible responses without necessarily being "valid" or accurate measures of what it is they really purport to assess.

Internal Consistency

The degree to which people respond in a consistent manner to all of the items in a scale is referred to as *internal consistency*. As such, internal consistency reflects the degree to which items in a scale or a group of items purporting to measure a particular construct are interrelated. Internal consistency is primarily an issue when there are several items or a separate scale devoted to assessing a single construct such as suicide risk. Internal consistency generally is not an issue when there are single queries assessing suicide risk, (e.g., an item assessing whether youths recently made a suicide attempt).

Dimensionality

The results of factor-analytic studies with instruments also are described. Specifically, I describe instruments in terms of whether they measure single or multiple intercorrelated constructs (factors), the degree to which these factors dovetail with what would be predicted by the developers of the scale, and the consistency of factor-analytic results across differing studies. Dimensionality is primarily an issue when the developers of scales have posited that scale items measure a single construct or dimension or have suggested that a scale has a particular composition of specific interrelated constructs. Similar to internal consistency, dimensionality is generally not an issue when only single items are used to assess constructs (e.g., presence of suicidal ideation).

Concurrent Validity

Instruments are evaluated with regard to the *concurrent validity* or the degree to which they correlate with other indices of suicidal behavior and related constructs (at the same point in time). When information is available (and it usually is not), instruments also are evaluated with regard to their discriminant validity (the degree to which the measures do not correlate with theoretically unrelated constructs).

Predictive Validity

A number of instruments are described as useful for identifying youths "at high risk" for suicidal behaviors. Nonetheless, the true test of whether individuals are at risk is not the ability of an index or measure to differentiate between individuals with different histories but rather the ability of the index to predict *future* behavior. Hence, instruments (particularly those designed for determining risk or propensity for suicidal behavior) are evaluated with regard to their ability to predict future behavior.

Treatment Studies

Unlike the adult suicide literature in which a number of different treatment studies have yielded data about which instruments are best suited for assessing outcomes and ascertaining samples, precious few studies have focused on the treatment of suicidal behaviors in children and adolescents. To the extent that such data are available, information is presented regarding the use of the suicide assessment instruments in treatment studies.

Definitions of Evaluative Terms

A number of terms are sometimes used in this book to describe a test's relationship with future or already observed behavior. When individuals are predicted by an instrument as having an outcome, and they actually have that outcome, they are referred to as *true positives*. When the test or instrument predicts that individuals do not have an outcome, and indeed they do not have that outcome, the individuals are referred to as *true negatives*. When the assessment instrument predicts that individuals have or will have an outcome, and they in fact do not, the cases are referred to as *false positives*. When instruments predict that an outcome will not occur, but the outcome does occur, the cases are referred to as *false negatives*.

In different population groups, differences in the base rates of individuals identified at risk and of individuals actually evidencing the outcome of interest (e.g., suicidal behavior) can affect estimates of the proportions of false positives and false negatives. Additional descriptive terms refer to the performance of a test after consideration of the base rates of the outcome of interest. The term *sensitivity* refers to the proportion of individuals with the outcome of interest (e.g., suicide attempts) who have a positive test result (or who have been classified as high risk). *Specificity* refers to the proportion of individuals without the outcome of interest who have a negative test result (or who have not been classified as high risk). *Positive predictive value* refers to the proportion of individuals classified as high risk on the test that actually have the outcome of interest. *Negative predictive value* refers to the proportion of individuals classified as not being high risk who in fact do not have the outcome of interest.

In the study of suicidal behaviors, the consequences of missing cases (false negatives) are straightforward and dire: Opportunities may be missed for intervening with individuals who attempt or complete suicide. Hence, sensitivity is often regarded as more important in suicide risk assessment instruments than specificity. However, assessment instruments that over-identify individuals thought to be at risk (false positives) can be problematic if the number of individuals identified is so large that it becomes impractical to provide intervention or further assessment to all identified cases. Maximizing the proportion of true positives identified out of the total sample of individuals identified as being at risk is an issue of the positive predictive value of an instrument.

Kappa is a statistical term that refers to the agreement between two observers, or between a test and an outcome, while controlling for chance agreement given the base rate of the outcome. The following is a rough guide used in the interpretation of kappa (Altman, 1991):

> Agreement is poor < .20
> Agreement is fair = .21 to .40
> Agreement is moderate = .41 to .60
> Agreement is good = .61 to .80
> Agreement is very good = .81 to 1.00

Informant and Reporting Bias

Informant and reporting bias can influence the usefulness and the validity of suicide assessment instruments. Most of the instruments in this book are self-report or addressed to the child or adolescent. Others are addressed to the parents or other adult informants. In general, information collected from different reporters or informants or using multiple methods is likely to generate greater information than that collected from a single respondent or with a single instrument. However, in the case of discrepant reports from youths and parents, the question is raised about which report is more accurate or valid. Several studies have demonstrated that adolescents themselves typically report more suicidal behaviors than their parents (Breton, Tousignant, Bergeron, & Berthiaume, 2002; Klimes-Dougan, 1998; Velez & Cohen, 1988; Walker, Moreau, & Weissman, 1990). Although this could represent a social desirability bias with parents' reports, or a failure to interpret youths' self-destructive behavior as serious, such discrepant reporting is more often interpreted as parents' lack of awareness of their sons' or daughters' behaviors.

Of course, there also are occasions in which the report (or lack thereof) of suicidal behavior by the adolescent is intentionally misleading. In my experience, however, most children and adolescents in clinical and research settings are forthright in their reporting of suicidal behavior if sufficient rapport has been established. Those situations in which suicidal behavior is questionably reported as present or not present are typically situations in which consequences are linked to the reports of suicidality. For example, it is not uncommon for an adolescent to be brought into an emergency department for an evaluation following a suicide attempt only to deny that he or she was ever suicidal ("I took the 100 aspirin because I had a headache and wanted to go to sleep"). The adolescent may be in personal denial or ashamed of the attention paid to the suicide attempt; he or she may also be trying either to avoid talking about problems or to avoid hospitalization. In such cases, various methods and instruments for assessing suicidal behavior may be useful, but they should never supplant clinical judgment and other pertinent data (such as the adolescents' past history of attempts, access to a method of attempting suicide, adolescents' ability to engage in alternative ways of solving the problems that precipitated the suicidal crisis, presence of support persons, etc.).

In other situations, the adolescent may report suicidal ideation or suicidal behavior that may be questionable. Again, these situations are often associated with identifiable consequences (e.g., they may be partially an effort to forestall arguments with parents, to avoid a breakup in a relationship, etc.). Nonetheless, just because reports of suicidal ideation or behavior appear to be partially instrumental in their intent does not preclude the possibility that an adolescent is indeed at risk of engaging in suicidal behavior and may not care whether he or she lives. For this reason, it behooves the clinician or researcher to be exceedingly careful and cautious about dismissing the reports of suicidal ideation or behavior, regardless of whether the information has been obtained with specific suicide assessment instruments or through discussion with the youths.

Part II

Detection Instruments

Structured and Semistructured Psychiatric Diagnostic Interviews

Detection instruments are used for identifying either the presence or absence of current or past suicidal behaviors (if suicidal behaviors are conceptualized as discrete entities) or the degree of suicidality (if suicidal behaviors are conceptualized as being along a continuum). These instruments can be used in clinical practice to identify or monitor suicidal behaviors. They can be used in research studies to estimate the prevalence of suicidal behaviors or to study their phenomenology, contextual factors, precipitants, and course. Detection instruments are different from instruments that are used to estimate risk or propensity for suicidal behaviors. These latter instruments often assess constructs thought to be related to risk for suicidality, such as hopelessness or reasons for living, and may or may not include questions about past or current suicidality.

With adult patients, the use of semistructured detection instruments has been found to increase the identification of current and past suicidal behavior in relation to usual clinical practice (Malone, Szanto, Corbitt, & Mann, 1995). This first chapter on detection instruments focuses on psychiatric diagnostic interview instruments. Psychiatric diagnostic instruments can be structured or semistructured in format. Individuals administering structured interviews (e.g., the Diagnostic Interview Schedule for Children and Adolescents—IV (Shaffer, Fisher, Lucas, Dulcan, and Schwab-Stone, 1996) and the Children's Interview for Psychiatric Syndromes (Weller, Weller, Fristad, Rooney, & Schechter, 2000) are supposed to ask questions verbatim. Hence, these interviews are highly standardized, typically can be administered by lay interviewers, and do not require or allow for clinical judgment. Individuals administering semistructured interviews (e.g., the Interview

Schedule for Children and Adolescents [Sherrill & Kovacs, 2000], versions of the Longitudinal Interval Follow-Up Evaluation [Keller, 1993; Keller & Nielsen, 1998], and all of the school-age versions of the Schedule for Affective Disorders and Schizophrenia [Ambrosini, 2000]) can reword questions or ask additional questions to clarify responses. These interviews therefore are not as highly structured, allow for more clinical judgment and clarification, and are typically administered by individuals with diagnostic and clinical experience. The distinction between structured and semistructured diagnostic interviews is one of degree, and indeed, some interviews (e.g., the Child and Adolescent Psychiatric Assessment, Angold & Costello; and the Diagnostic Interview for Children and Adolescents, Reich, 2000) have characteristics of both structured and semistructured instruments.

The interviews vary considerably in the degree to which their assessment of suicidality has been demonstrated to be reliable or predictive of future suicidal ideation or behavior. The instruments also differ in the degree to which the queries are consistent with O'Carroll et al.'s (1996) definitions of suicidal ideation and behavior.

Most of the queries in these instruments are meant to stand alone; that is, they are not meant to be combined into a multi-item scale measuring suicidality. The inquiries of the Schedule for Affective Disorders and Schizophrenia, School-Age Epidemiologic Version (K–SADS–E; Orvaschel, 1994) are an exception, as these items can be been combined to form a continuous screening measure. With the exception of internal consistency information provided for the K–SADS–E screener, then, information about internal consistency and dimensionality is not reported for the diagnostic instruments.

The psychiatric diagnostic interviews differ in several other practical respects that are not the focus of the current book but that should be considered in the choice of instrument. For example, the interviews differ in cost, the amount of time required for assessment of symptomatic and symptom-free patients and participants, ease of administration, and the amount of time required to train new interviewers to criterion. The interviews also differ in terms of whether they are designed for the assessment of psychiatric diagnoses (and include "skip-outs" when youths or informants fail to report key symptoms) or require assessment of each symptom (i.e., are symptom-oriented rather than diagnosis-oriented).[1]

---

1. For more information about some of these practical aspects of the most common diagnostic interviews, the reader is referred to Volume 39, Issue 1, of the *Journal of the American Academy of Child and Adolescent Psychiatry* (published in January 2000).

Child and Adolescent Psychiatric Assessment

Description

The Child and Adolescent Psychiatric Assessment (CAPA) is a psychiatric diagnostic instrument that combines elements of both semistructured and structured interviews (Angold & Costello, 2000; Angold, Cox, Prendergast, Rutter, & Simonoff, 1995; Angold, Prendergast, et al., 1995). The CAPA is designed to be administered by trained lay interviewers or experienced clinicians to both children (ages 8 to 18) and parents/informants. Accompanying the CAPA is an extensive and well-documented glossary explaining coding rules and rationales. The CAPA not only has sections for assessing psychiatric symptoms and incapacity or functional impairment but also includes sections focusing on life events, family functioning, peer relationships, and school functioning. The CAPA has been used in epidemiologic and services related research, including community-based longitudinal studies (Costello, Angold, Burns, Erkanli, et al., 1996; Costello, Angold, Burns, Stangl, et al., 1996). Two companion instruments, the Child and Adolescent Impact Assessment (CAIA; Angold, Patrick, Burns, & Costello, 1996) and the Child and Adolescent Services Assessment (CASA; Ascher, Farmer, Burns, & Angold, 1996; Burns, Angold, Magruder-Habib, Costello, & Patrick, 1996), have been designed to assist in the assessment of burden associated with psychiatric illness, services use, attitudes toward service use, and barriers to service use. Spanish and computer-assisted versions of the CAPA are currently under development (Angold & Costello, 2000).

Populations Studied

The CAPA has not been used in published studies specifically focusing on suicidality, although studies of suicidality using the CAPA are in progress.

Assessment and Definitions of Suicidal Behaviors

The suicidal behaviors section of the CAPA includes a screen section asking generally about suicidal and self-injurious behaviors; specific questions about thoughts of wanting to die, suicidal ideation, plans, and attempts; a section regarding intent and lethality associated with suicide attempts (reviewed separately in Chapter 9 of this book); and questions regarding nonsuicidal physically self-damaging behavior.

The items regarding suicidal ideation and suicide attempts are consistent with the proposed definitions of O'Carroll et al. (1996). For example, in the CAPA's glossary (Angold, Cox, et al., 1995), *suicide attempts* are defined as "episodes of deliberate self-harmful behavior, or potentially self-harmful behavior, involving some intention to die at the time of the attempt." *Suicidal thoughts* refer to "thinking specifically about killing oneself, by whatever means." The CAPA items regarding suicide attempts focus on both the number of attempts in the last 3 months and the total number of (lifetime) attempts. There are also separate items for assessing thoughts of death and nonsuicidal self-damaging acts.

Reliability

Interrater agreement for depressive diagnoses on the CAPA (computed as κ) ranged from .85 to .90 (Angold & Costello, 1995). Interrater agreement for the suicidal behavior items was not reported separately.

Concurrent Validity

No published data were located.

Predictive Validity

No published data were located.

Treatment Studies

No treatment studies focusing on suicidal or related behaviors have been published.

Summary and Evaluation

The CAPA has an excellent set of questions for assessing suicidal behaviors and is complemented by two instruments, the CAIA and the CASA, assessing the impact of psychiatric problems and service use. However, to date, the CAPA has not been used in studies of suicidal behaviors.

Where to Obtain the Instrument

Adrian Angold, MRCPsych, Developmental Epidemiology Program, Department of Psychiatry and Behavioral Sciences, Duke University Medical Center, DUMC Box 3454, Durham, NC 27710

Children's Interview for Psychiatric Syndromes

Description

The Children's Interview for Psychiatric Syndromes (ChIPS) is a structured psychiatric diagnostic interview intended to assist in the *Diagnostic and Statistical Manual of Mental Disorders* (4th ed., *DSM–IV*; American Psychiatric-Association, 1994) diagnosis of disorders among youths (Fristad, Cummins, et al. 1998; Fristad, Glickman, et al., 1998; Fristad, Teare, Weller, Weller, & Salmon, 1998; Rooney, Fristad, Weller, & Weller, 1999; Teare, Fristad, Weller, Weller, & Salmon, 1998a, 1998b; Weller, Weller, Fristad, Rooney, & Schecter, 2000; Weller, Weller, Rooney, & Fristad, 1999a, 1999b). The ChIPS was originally developed for children ages 6 to 12 but was later expanded so that it could be used with youths up to the age of 18. For the youngest of participants, careful attention was paid in the development of the ChIPS to vocabulary used and the length of questions. The ChIPS can be administered by trained lay interviewers and, as such, is appropriate for epidemiologic studies and screening surveys. The ChIPS does not assess gradations of severity of clinically significant symptoms.

Populations Studied

The ChIPS can be used to assess children's suicidal behaviors but apparently has not been used in published studies of suicidal youths.

Assessment and Definitions of Suicidal Behaviors

The "morbid/suicidal thoughts" questions of the ChIPS are in the section assessing symptoms of major depression and dysthymia. Unlike other symptoms of depression, questions regarding suicidal behaviors are asked of youths even when they do not report dysphoric mood or anhedonia.

In the ChIPS, there are separate questions regarding thoughts of death/ wishing to be dead and suicidal ideation. The question regarding suicidal ideation (whether children ever thought of suicide or killing themselves) is straightforward and conforms to the definition proposed by O'Carroll et al. (1996). The question regarding suicidal attempts (whether children have ever tried to kill themselves) is straightforward, implies nonzero intent to die, and does not confound clinical characteristics of the suicidal behavior with the rating of whether the suicidal behavior occurred. There are no separate questions for assessing nonsuicidal self-harm behavior or total number of lifetime suicide attempts.

Reliability

No published data were located.

Concurrent Validity

No published data were located.

Predictive Validity

No published data were located.

Treatment Studies

No published data were located.

Summary and Evaluation

The ChIPS is a new diagnostic instrument. Questions regarding suicidal behaviors are in the section for assessing symptoms of major depression. Because of its easy-to-understand queries, the ChIPS may be particularly useful with younger children, but the questions regarding suicidal behavior are limited in scope. Reliability and validity data for the suicidal ideation/behavior items are also not available. To date, the ChIPS has not been used in published studies of suicidal behaviors.

Where to Obtain

American Psychiatric Press, Inc., 1400 K Street, NW, Washington, DC 20005

Diagnostic Interview for Children and Adolescents

Description

The Diagnostic Interview for Children and Adolescents (DICA) is generally a highly structured interview, but interviewers do have the latitude to "go off-interview" to clarify responses or rephrase questions, similar to semistructured interviews (Reich, 2000). As with the CAPA, the DICA is glossary or manual based and can be administered by trained lay interviewers. As such, the interview is appropriate for epidemiologic or screening surveys. As described later, the DICA also has been used in clinical research studies and longitudinal studies. Similar to the Diagnostic Interview Schedule for Children (DISC), which is reviewed next, the DICA was originally modeled after the Diagnostic Interview Schedule (DIS) for adults. The DICA yields current or lifetime diagnoses, and the latest version of the DICA is compatible with both *DSM–III–R* (American Psychiatric Association, 1987) and *DSM–IV* (American Psychiatric Association, 1994) diagnostic systems. The DICA has separate versions for children, adolescents, and parents. A computerized-assisted version of the DICA (which also can be self-administered) is also available.

Populations Studied

The DICA has been used in studies comparing suicide-bereaved children and other children experiencing loss of a parent (Cerel, Fristad, Weller, & Weller, 1999). The DICA also has been used to examine suicidal behaviors among children of depressed and well mothers (Klimes-Dougan, 1998; Klimes-Dougan et al., 1999) and children with posttraumatic stress disorder (Famularo, Fenton, Kinscherff, & Augustyn, 1996).

Assessment and Definitions of Suicidal Behaviors

In the latest version of the DICA (Child, Adolescent, and Parent), the section on suicidal behaviors includes queries about hopelessness, thoughts of death, thoughts of wishing to be dead, suicidal ideation, suicide plan, and suicide attempts in the last month and lifetime (worst episode). In a separate section of the DICA, adolescents are asked additional questions regarding age at first suicidal ideation, age at time of first suicide plan, lifetime suicide attempts, age at first attempt, and medical attention and degree of intent during "most serious suicide attempt."

The questions about suicidal ideation (whether children thought about killing themselves) and attempts (whether children tried to kill themselves) are straightforward and consistent with O'Carroll et al.'s (1996) recommendation regarding definitions of suicidal behaviors.

Reliability

In a study of 60 children and 60 adolescents (ascertained by means of birth records in the state of Missouri) as well as 60 of their parents (W. Reich, personal communication, December 1999), interrater reliability of the DICA question for current suicidal ideation was very good (children: $\kappa = .91$, adolescents: $\kappa = .93$, parents: $\kappa = .91$). In a study of adolescents being treated for depression in which the adolescents and parents were administered the DICA approximately 7 to 10 days apart, test–retest agreement for the (current) suicidal ideation item was moderate to good (adolescents: $\kappa = .79$, parents: $\kappa = .51$; W. Reich, personal communication, December 1999).

In a longitudinal study of youths of depressed and well mothers, lifetime reports of suicidal behaviors obtained with the DICA were compared with the data generated from four repeated assessments 3 years apart (Klimes-Dougan, 1998). There was moderate agreement between the two methods of assessment ($\kappa = .42$ for younger children, $\kappa = .60$ for older youths). Nineteen percent of youths who reported suicidal ideation at one of the follow-up assessments did not report suicidal thoughts in the lifetime assessment.

Agreement between children or adolescents and their parents regarding the youths' suicidal behavior was poor ($\kappa = .15$ for the younger children, $\kappa = .16$ for the older children; Klimes-Dougan, 1998). As described in chapter 2, such disagreement is not uncommon (e.g., Breton et al., 2002; Klimes-Dougan, 1998; Velez & Cohen, 1988; Walker et al., 1990). It is interesting to note that mothers who disagreed with their children's reports of suicidal behaviors tended to have a history of suicide attempts themselves (Klimes-Dougan, 1998).

Concurrent Validity

In a sample of children of well mothers and mothers with affective disorders (Klimes-Dougan, 1998), lifetime reports of suicidal content obtained from youths with the DICA were related, but not strongly related, to reports of suicidality from self-report measures ($\kappa = .20$ for the younger cohort, $\kappa = .35$ for the older cohort). Suicidal ideation and behavior (assessed with both the DICA and the Children's Assessment Schedule and conceptualized on a continuum) were related to the presence of hypomania and to having a mother who also had made a suicide attempt (Klimes-Dougan et al., 1999). In a sample of children with alleged abuse, youths with posttraumatic stress disorder had a higher rate of DICA assessed suicidal ideation than the other abused youths (Famularo et al., 1996).

Predictive Validity

In a longitudinal study of children of well and affectively disordered mothers, it was found that between 15% and 22% of youths reporting suicidal ideation at an earlier assessment made later suicide attempts (Klimes-Dougan et al., 1999). However, of the 13 youths attempting suicide, 77% reported suicidal ideation in a prior assessment period (Klimes-Dougan et al., 1999).

Treatment Studies

The DICA apparently has not been used in a published treatment study of suicidal youths. However, the DICA was used along with the Schedule for Affective Disorders and Schizophrenia for School-Age Children (K–SADS) to determine whether children and adolescents met *DSM–III–R* criteria for major depression (American Psychiatric Association, 1987) at two points in time as required for participating in a placebo-controlled trial of fluoxetine in the treatment of juvenile-onset depression (Emslie, Rush, Weinberg, Kowatch et al., 1997).

Summary and Evaluation

The DICA has been used in several studies of suicidal behaviors. The suicidal ideation/behavior queries are straightforward and well suited for research. Suicidal ideation has some sensitivity (but low positive predictive value) as a predictor of later suicide attempts (i.e., 77% of youths who attempted suicide in a prospective study reported suicidal ideation at an earlier assessment, but most youths with suicidal ideation at the earlier assessment did not go on to make later attempts).

Where to Obtain

Computerized and paper-and-pencil versions: Multi Health Systems (MHS), P.O. Box 950, North Tonawanda, NY 14120-0950 (www.mhs.com) or Wendy Reich, PhD, Washington University School of Medicine, Division of Child Psychiatry, 40 N. Kingshighway, Suite 4, St. Louis, MO 63108

Diagnostic Interview Schedule for Children

Description

The Diagnostic Interview Schedule for Children (DISC) is a structured psychiatric diagnostic interview for children and adolescents ages 6 to 18 and their parents (Shaffer, Fisher, Lucas, Dulcan, & Schwab-Stone, 2000).

The DISC was originally developed to be comparable with the Diagnostic Interview Schedule (DIS) used with adult populations (Shaffer et al., 2000). As its name implies, the most recent revision of the DISC (NIMH [National Institute of Mental Health] DISC–IV) is based on *DSM–IV* diagnostic criteria. However, an earlier version of the DISC, the NIMH DISC–2.3, is also in use and can be used to diagnose disorders in accordance with *DSM–III–R* criteria (Schwab-Stone et al., 1996; Shaffer, Fisher et al., 1996). The NIMH DISC can be administered by trained lay interviewers who are instructed to administer the queries exactly as written. As such, the DISC was primarily developed for epidemiologic studies and screening surveys. The majority of DISC questions have been worded so that they can be answered "yes," "no," "somewhat," or "sometimes."

A computer-assisted version of the DISC, the C–DISC, has been developed to aid in administration (Shaffer et al., 2000). In addition to the English language version, Spanish (Ribera et al., 1996), French (Breton, Bergeron, Valla, Berthiaume, & St-Georges, 1998), and Xhosa (Robertson, Ensink, Parry, & Chalton, 1999) versions of the NIMH DISC have been developed.

On the basis of the DISC–2.3, the self-report DSM Scale for Depression (DSD) was developed; this instrument is reviewed separately in the section on survey and survey screening items, this volume; see also Roberts, Roberts, & Chen, 1998). In addition, a suicidality scale (a Guttman scale) derived from the items on an earlier version of the DISC assessing suicidal behaviors also was developed (Brent et al., 1986). However, no reports could be located regarding whether a suicidality scale based on more recent versions of the DISC had been developed or evaluated.

Populations Studied

Versions of the DISC have been used to examine suicidal behaviors in incarcerated adolescents (Kempton & Forehand, 1992), clinically ascertained children and adolescents (Borst, Noam, & Bartok, 1991; Brent et al., 1986; Campbell, Milling, Laughlin, & Bush, 1993; King, Katz et al., 1997; Milling, Campbell, Bush, & Laughlin, 1992), and community and school-based samples of children and adolescents (Gould et al., 1998; D. Shaffer, personal communication, October 1999).

Assessment and Definitions of Suicidal Behaviors

The NIMH DISC–2.3 has separate inquiries about thoughts of death, suicidal ideation, the presence of a suicide plan, and whether these thoughts were associated with dysphoria. These questions reference the 2 weeks and the 6 months preceding the interview. The queries of the NIMH DISC–IV are similar and reference the 2 weeks, 4 weeks, and the year preceding the interview. These queries occur in the context of the depressive disorders section but are asked of all interviewees.

The NIMH DISC–2.3 also inquires about lifetime suicide attempts, number of suicide attempts, age at first suicide attempt, suicide attempts within the last 6 months, suicide attempts when dysphoric, and methods of suicide attempts. The inquiries of the NIMH DISC–IV are again similar but focus on lifetime attempts as well as attempts in the 4 weeks and in the last year preceding the interview. The question about age of first suicide attempt (in the NIMH DISC–2.3) was not included in the NIMH DISC–IV. However, a question about whether the suicide attempts required medical attention was added. Neither version of the DISC has an item assessing nonsuicidal self-harm behaviors.

The stem query regarding suicidal ideation in both the Parent and Youth versions of the DISC–IV and the Child version of the DISC–2.3 are likely to elicit a conservative estimate of suicidal ideation because of the word *seriously* used in the query. Without being explicitly defined, the word *seriously* can be interpreted in various ways by respondents. The queries regarding suicide attempts (whether the child tried to kill himself or herself or made a suicide attempt) are consistent with recommendations by O'Carroll et al. (1996).

Reliability

In a sample of child psychiatric outpatients clinically diagnosed as having "common" *DSM–IV* disorders (and their parents), the NIMH DISC–IV was administered twice at approximately a 1-week interval (D. Shaffer, personal communication, October 1999). Test–retest agreement for whether children met criteria for the *DSM–IV* major depression symptom of recurrent thoughts of death, suicidal ideation without a specific plan, suicide attempt, or specific plan was good ($\kappa = .79$ for parents, $\kappa = .67$ for youths). Indices of agreement were also computed for the individual questions to youths and parents on the NIMH DISC–IV regarding suicidality. Indices of agreement (κ) are summarized by question and informant in Table 3.1.

G. Canino (personal communication, November 1999) conducted a test–retest study of the Spanish version of the DISC–IV in Puerto Rico. The test–retest interval for the DISC–IV administrations was approximately 12

Table 3.1

Test–Retest Reliability of the NIMH DISC–IV Queries Regarding Thoughts of Death and Suicidal Behaviors

Question	Adult	Youth
Q21. Seriously thought about killing self during last year	.78	.66
Q21A. Thought about killing self many times during last year	.69	.67
Q21B. Plan for suicide during last year	.58	.77
Q22D. Seriously thought about killing self during last 4 weeks	.55	
Q22. Ever (in whole life) tried to kill self	.85	.77
Q22B. Tried to kill self in last year	.92	.78
Q22E. Medical attention for suicide attempt	.74	.74

Note. From D. Shaffer (personal communication, October 1999).
NIMH DISC–IV = National Institute of Mental Health Diagnostic Interview Schedule for Children Version IV.

days. Indices of agreement (κ) are summarized by question and informant in Table 3.2.

In a sample of child and parent pairs from a multisite community sample (half of whom were thought to meet diagnostic criteria for *DSM–IV* disorders), the NIMH DISC–2.3 was administered twice, 1 to 15 days apart (D. Shaffer, personal communication, October 1999). Indices of agreement

Table 3.2

Test–Retest Reliability of the Queries Regarding Thoughts of Death and Suicidal Behaviors in the Spanish Version of the DISC

Question	Adult	Youth
Q21. Seriously thought about killing self during last year	.68	.35
Q21a. Thought about killing self many times during last year	.23	.40
Q21b. Plan for suicide during last year	.21	1.0
Q22. Ever (in whole life) tried to kill self	.92	.80

Note. From G. Canino (personal communication, November 1999).
DISC = Diagnostic Interview Schedule for Children.

were computed for the individual questions to children and parents on the NIMH DISC–2.3 regarding suicidality. Indices of agreement (κ) are summarized by question and informant in Table 3.3.

Concurrent Validity

In a sample of juvenile delinquents, suicide attempts assessed with the DISC–2 were related to number of depressive symptoms in Caucasian adolescents but not African American adolescents (Kempton & Forehand, 1992). In a community sample, suicidal ideation and attempts assessed with the DISC–2.3 were found to be associated with elevated rates of almost all psychiatric disorders relative to nonsuicidal youths (Gould et al., 1998). Consistent with the other reports (Garrison et al., 1993; Kandell, 1988), suicide attempts were more strongly related to substance use disorders than suicidal ideation (Gould et al., 1998).

In an inpatient psychiatric setting, adolescent reports of suicide attempts in response to the DISC were moderately related (κ = .53) to clinicians' assessment of suicidality (Prinstein, Nock, Spirito, & Grapentine, 2001). Adolescent reports of suicidal ideation as assessed with the DISC were in fair agreement (κ = .32) with clinician ratings of suicidality and were in moderate agreement (κ = .49) with "caseness," as defined by being above the 70th percentile on the Suicidal Ideation Questionnaire (SIQ) or Suicidal Ideation Questionnaire—Junior (SIQ–JR; Prinstein et al., 2001).

Table 3.3

Test–Retest Reliability of the DISC–2.3 Queries Regarding Thoughts of Death and Suicidal Behaviors

Question	Adult	Youth
Q27. Thought about killing self during last 6 months	.75	.60
Q27A. Thought about suicide (when depressed or equivalent)	.65	.52
Q27B. Thought about suicide a lot of time for at least 2 weeks		.39
Q27C. Plan for suicide	.59	.52
Q28. Ever tried to kill self	.39	.67
Q29. Tried to kill self in last 6 months	.28	.32

Note. From D. Shaffer (personal communication, October 1999).
DISC–2.3 = an earlier version of the Diagnostic Interview Schedule for Children.

In a second study, adolescent inpatients who reported thoughts of wanting to die or suicidality as assessed with the DISC similarly were more likely to score above the cutoff on the SIQ–JR than other inpatient youths (King, Katz et al., 1997). DISC-assessed suicidal ideation and lifetime suicide attempts also were associated with Spectrum of Suicidal Behavior (SSB) scores (King, Katz et al., 1997).

Predictive Validity

In one study pertinent to predictive validity (D. Shaffer, personal communication, October 1999), a large number of high school students were screened with several measures including the DISC. A portion of the students, approximately half of whom were thought to be at risk because of their responses to another instrument (the Columbia Teen Screen), were followed up approximately 3 to 4 years later. Reports of current suicidal ideation (as assessed with the DISC at the initial screening) had 38% sensitivity and 78% specificity in predicting later DISC-assessed suicidal thoughts. Reports of lifetime suicide attempts yielded 31% sensitivity and 88% specificity in predicting later ideation. Reports of attempts in the last 6 months yielded only 7% sensitivity and 98% specificity in the prediction of later suicidal thoughts.

In this same study (D. Shaffer, personal communication, October 1999), reports of current ideation (on the DISC) at the initial screen had 50% sensitivity and 81% specificity in predicting suicide attempts over the next 3 to 4 years. Reports of lifetime attempts yielded 47% sensitivity and 90% specificity in the prediction of later attempts. Reports of suicide attempts within 6 months of the initial screening yielded only 18% sensitivity and 99% specificity in the prediction of later attempts.

Treatment Studies

No published treatment studies of suicidality using the DISC were located.

Summary and Evaluation

The DISC is perhaps the most widely used structured psychiatric diagnostic interview in studies of suicidal behavior and is well designed for epidemiologic research. Responses to the NIMH DISC–IV stem suicidal ideation items are likely to yield conservative estimates of the prevalence of suicidal thoughts but have been shown to have predictive validity. The test–retest reliability of the query assessing lifetime suicide attempts in the NIMH DISC–IV is considerably higher than the reliability of the item assessing lifetime attempts in an earlier version of the DISC, the DISC–2.3. For researchers or clinicians using the Spanish version of the DISC–IV, it should be noted that the test–retest reliability of the stem item regarding suicidal ideation was not high for youths. Similarly, the test–retest reliability of the follow-up questions for suicidal ideation (in the Spanish version of the DISC–IV) was not high for parents. In one study in the New York area, responses to the questions regarding suicide attempts within the last 6 months had poor sensitivity (perhaps because of low base rate of the predictor variable) in predicting later suicidal ideation and attempts; the questions regarding lifetime suicide attempts were more sensitive predictors of later suicidal ideation and attempts.

Where to Obtain

English language and computerized versions: Division of Child and Adolescent Psychiatry, Columbia University—New York State Psychiatric Institute, 1051 Riverside Drive, New York, NY 10032

French version: Jean-Jacques Breton, MD, MS, Riviere-des-Prairies Hospital, Research Department, 7070 Perras Boulevard, Montreal, Quebec, Canada H1E 1A4

Spanish language version: Glorisa Canino, PhD, Professor and Director, Behavioral Science Research Institute, Medical Sciences Campus, University of Puerto Rico, P.O. Box 365067, San Juan, Puerto Rico 00936-5067

Dominic–R and Dominic Interactive

Description

The Dominic–R is a structured and picture-accompanied interview instrument designed for use with 6- to 11-year olds (Valla, Bergeron, Bidaut-Russell, St-Georges, & Gaudet, 1997; Valla, Bergeron, & Smolla, 2000). The Dominic–R was developed as an assessment tool for selected psychiatric disorders and can be administered by trained lay interviewers, either in paper form or via computer. The computerized version of Dominic–R (the Dominic Interactive) can be used to assess *DSM–IV* disorders; the paper version can be used to assess *DSM–III–R* disorders. Dominic–R is introduced to children as a game (the "Dominic game"). For each set of inquiries in the Dominic–R, children are presented with one to three visually engaging pictures portraying the symptom or behavior of interest. Children are told that "all kinds of things happen to Dominic" and are then asked a series of questions about whether they feel or have engaged in behaviors like the character Dominic. Children simply respond "yes" or "no" to the queries (the authors chose not to attempt to elicit information about gradations of severity given the age of the youths for whom the instrument is intended). Symptoms inquired about with the Dominic–R are not grouped according to diagnosis; queries inquiring about symptoms are also intermixed with questions asking about normal behaviors. Unlike some of the other psychiatric diagnostic instruments, there is not a parallel form of the Dominic–R for eliciting information from adult informants; that is, this is an interview for use strictly with children. Because of the age of the target population, no attempt is made in the Dominic to assess duration or onsets of symptoms. The Dominic has been translated into Spanish, German, and French. A different version of this instrument, called the Terry, has been developed for use with African American youths and features a person of color as the main character (Bidaut-Russell, Valla, Thomas, Bergeron, & Lawson, 1998). The Terry has been translated into French. The authors note that the Dominic "was intended for clinical and epidemiological purposes and as a screener in school" (Valla et al., 2000, p. 88).

Populations Studied

The Dominic–R has not been used in studies focused specifically on suicidality.

Assessment and Definitions of Suicidal Behaviors

In the Dominic–R, there are two screening questions for suicidality that assess whether the children often think about death or about killing themselves and whether they often think about death and dying, like the character Dominic. The wording of the first question is such that it may elicit information not only about thoughts of suicide but also about thoughts of death in general. The second question does not specifically inquire about suicidal ideation.

It is difficult to evaluate the queries of the Dominic–R simply on the basis of the words that are used (because so much of the experience is visual). In this regard, the first screening question is accompanied by a progressive series of three pictures. In these pictures, a boy is depicted as sad, thinking of himself at the edge of the bridge looking into the water, and then imagining the act of jumping off the bridge itself. Clearly then, even though the question asks about thoughts of death in addition to suicidal ideation, the visual cue "pulls" for thoughts of suicide. The second query regarding thoughts of death is accompanied by a single picture of a boy imagining himself in a coffin.

The effects of using visual stimuli to assess suicidality with younger children have not been well studied. Researchers do not know whether the use of pictures portraying suicide helps children to understand queries about this symptom or whether there is any deleterious effect of showing a boy thinking of killing himself with a specific method. To their credit (given the potential suggestibility of younger children), the authors portray a means of killing oneself that is not as lethal as many (although jumping does appear to be one of the more common methods of suicide attempts for preadolescents; Pfeffer, Conte, Plutchik, & Jerrett, 1979).

There is no screen for suicide attempts in the Dominic–R. However, if a child responds positively to one of the two questions already mentioned, the clinician is alerted when the protocol is scored that the child's risk of suicidality needs to be further evaluated. Sample questions are provided for inquiring further about thoughts of death (frequency and duration), suicidal ideation, and suicide attempts/self-endangering behaviors. As sample questions, these are not scored in any formal way.

Reliability

The reliability of the two Dominic–R questions assessing suicidality was assessed in a sample of community children 7 to 12 days apart. In a sample of 290 youths, κ for the suicidal ideation question was .57, and κ for the thoughts of death question was .58 (Valla, 2002).

Concurrent Validity

In the development of the Dominic–Interactive, the criterion-rated validity of items (including the two suicide items) was assessed by comparing the clinicians' judgments of children's explanations of their responses to the actual yes/no responses given by children (Valla, 2002). In this sample of both English- and French-speaking children, both referred for treatment and nonreferred, agreement between judges for one item inquiring about thoughts of death or dying was in the moderate range (average κ = .56). Agreement between judges for another item inquiring about thoughts of death or of killing themselves was in the good range (average κ = .76).

Predictive Validity

The predictive validity of the Dominic–R suicidal behavior questions has not been evaluated.

Treatment Studies

The Dominic–R has not been used in treatment studies of suicidal youths.

Summary and Evaluation

The Dominic–R is a structured psychiatric diagnostic interview for children. Information is not elicited from parents or adult informants. In the Dominic–R, children are not only asked questions verbally but also are presented with visually engaging pictures portraying the symptoms or behaviors that are the subject of inquiry. There are two screening items on the Dominic–R assessing thoughts of death and suicidal ideation. However, the Dominic–R to date has not been used in studies of suicidal behaviors, and the effects of assessing suicidal behavior by using visual cues have not been evaluated.

Where to Obtain:

Jean-Pierre Valla, MD, MSc, Riviere-des-Prairies Hospital, Research Department, 7070 Perras Blvd., Montreal, Quebec H1E 1A4, Canada (http://www.dominicinteractive.com)

Interview Schedule for Children and Adolescents

Description

The Interview Schedule for Children and Adolescents (ISCA) is a semistructured symptom-oriented psychiatric interview (Kovacs, 1997; Sherrill & Kovacs, 2000). The ISCA can be used with youths from ages 8 to 17; the Follow-Up Interview Schedule for Adults (FISA) was developed as a forward extension of the ISCA for assessing youths followed into adulthood in longitudinal studies. There are currently two complementary versions of the ISCA: a version for assessing current and lifetime symptomatology and a version for assessing current and interim symptomatology (since the last follow-up assessment in prospective studies). In both versions of the ISCA, psychiatric symptoms are rated in severity (on 0–8 or 0–3 rating scales) over the 2 weeks or over the 6 months preceding the interview depending on the symptom. Versions of the ISCA with simplified (0–3) severity ratings also have been developed.

The interview is administered to both youths and parents or guardians. Because the interview is oriented toward symptoms rather than toward specific psychiatric disorders, all symptoms in the main interview are administered; the results from the interview can be used with multiple diagnostic systems. For each symptom assessed with the ISCA, operational criteria specify the severity levels with which symptoms are considered to be "clinically significant." Only symptoms that are clinically significant in terms of duration, severity, and functional impairment contribute to the operational diagnostic criteria for psychiatric diagnoses. The ISCA was designed to be administered by experienced, trained clinicians. As the authors note, "the ISCA is of particular value in clinical research requiring detailed but flexible assessments" and "There is encouraging evidence that follow-up versions of the schedule are useful tools in research focusing on developmental psychopathology in a longitudinal setting" (Sherrill & Kovacs, 2000, p. 75).

Populations Studied

The ISCA has been used to examine suicidal behaviors among youths in inpatient and outpatient psychiatric settings (Goldston et al., 1996, 1998, 1999, 2001; Kovacs et al., 1993) and with medically ill youths (Goldston et al., 1997; Goldston, Kovacs, Ho, Parrone, & Stiffler, 1994).

Assessment and Definitions of Suicidal Behaviors

There are separate questions in the ISCA corresponding to thoughts of dying or death, suicidal ideation/threats, contemplated methods for suicide, "idea" or "purpose" associated with suicidal ideation, recurrent thoughts about wanting to die/suicidal ideation/suicide threats, suicide attempts, number of past attempts, medical attention for suicide attempts, intoxication at the time of attempts, and intent associated with the attempts. There is an item regarding nonsuicidal deliberate self-harm in the latest version of the ISCA.

The queries regarding suicide attempts and suicidal ideation are consistent with those proposed by O'Carroll et al. (1996). The definitions used in the ISCA were specifically developed to be compatible with recommendations regarding the assessment of suicidal behavior from an NIMH Task

Force (Resnik & Hathorne, 1973). In the ISCA, a *suicide attempt* is defined as "an executed, completed behavior which has the potential, no matter how remote, of resulting in bodily harm." Behavior is considered to be suicidal if volitional and self-precipitated, and associated with at least some intent to die. In the ISCA, behaviors that are not completed (i.e., suicide attempts that are interrupted in the preparation stages, before their execution) are considered to be suicidal ideation, not suicide attempts; *suicidal ideation* is defined simply as thoughts of killing oneself. There are separate items for assessing suicidal ideation and recurrent thoughts of death.

Because the ISCA is a symptom-oriented interview, the suicidal ideation and suicide attempt items are asked of all participants. That is, unlike some other diagnostic interviews, there is no skip-out rule if participants do not report key symptoms associated with depressive disorders.

Reliability

Data obtained from an interrater trial of 46 cases indicated that agreement for the ISCA items regarding suicidal ideation and suicide attempts was high (κ = .95 and 1.00, respectively, Kovacs, 1981). A separate interrater comparison was conducted by Goldston et al. (2001). Two raters examined transcribed interviewer notes regarding suicidal behaviors for 40 clinically ascertained adolescents participating in a longitudinal study who were initially rated as having either suicidal ideation or suicide attempts. The raters (who did not conduct the original interviews and were blind to participants' identities and any additional information contained in the relevant interviews) independently determined whether participants had experienced suicidal ideation or made a suicide attempt. Interrater agreement in classifications of suicidal ideation and attempts was 95% (κ = .90).

Concurrent Validity

ISCA-rated suicidal ideation and suicide attempts have been found to be associated with diagnoses of depressive disorders (Goldston et al., 1998; Kovacs et al., 1993). ISCA-rated suicidal ideation has also been found to be associated with serious noncompliance with the medical regimen among diabetic youths (Goldston et al., 1994, 1997). Adolescents rated on the ISCA as having multiple past suicide attempts were found to have different clinical characteristics than adolescents rated as having only a single prior attempt or no prior attempt (Goldston et al., 1996, 1998).

Predictive Validity

Prior suicide attempts as assessed with the ISCA have been found to be among the most potent predictors of subsequent suicide attempts among depressed youths and among adolescents who have been psychiatrically hospitalized (Goldston et al., 1999; Kovacs et al., 1993). Moreover, affective disorders, severity of depressive symptoms, hopelessness, and survival and coping beliefs have been found to be differentially related to likelihood of later suicide attempts depending on prior history of ISCA-assessed suicide attempts (Goldston et al., 1999, 2001).

Treatment Studies

No published treatment studies of suicidal youths were located.

Summary and Evaluation

The ISCA is the only symptom-oriented (rather than diagnosis-specific) semistructured psychiatric diagnostic interview reviewed and one of the few semistructured instruments specifically developed for longitudinal study. The ISCA has been used with clinically ascertained youths and medically ill youths but not with epidemiologic samples. The ISCA queries are excellent and have been shown to have predictive validity in two different clinical samples.

Where to Obtain

Maria Kovacs, PhD, Western Psychiatric Institute and Clinic, University of Pittsburgh School of Medicine, 3811 O'Hara Street, Pittsburgh, PA 15213

Kiddie—Longitudinal Interval Follow-Up Evaluation and Adolescent—Longitudinal Interval Follow-Up Evaluation

Description

The Kiddie—Longitudinal Interval Follow-Up Evaluation (K–LIFE; Keller & Nielsen, 1988) is a psychiatric diagnostic interview designed for longitudinal and treatment studies. The K–LIFE is a downward extension of the adult Longitudinal Interval Follow-Up Evaluation (LIFE; Keller et al., 1997), which was used in the Collaborative Treatment Study of Depression. The K–LIFE can be used to assess the course of psychopathology over 6 months according to *DSM–III–R* and Research Diagnostic Criteria (RDC) depending on the symptom. The K–LIFE can be used with either children or adolescents.

An adolescent version of this instrument, the Adolescent—Longitudinal Interval Follow-Up Evaluation (A–LIFE; Keller, 1993), has been developed but has not been used in published research. The original A–LIFE was designed for use with *DSM–III–R*, but adaptations of the instrument have been developed for use with *DSM–IV* and for follow-up intervals over 6 months. The LIFE instruments are appropriate for clinical research and were developed specifically for use in longitudinal studies.

Populations Studied

The K–LIFE and A–LIFE apparently have not been used in published studies to examine suicidal ideation or behavior in youths.

Assessment and Definitions of Suicidal Behaviors

There are two suicidal behavior assessment sections in the K–LIFE and A–LIFE. The first assessment section occurs in the context of symptoms of major depressive disorder. This section includes questions about thoughts of self-harm, thoughts of not wanting to live, and suicide attempts and plans.

Some of the queries in both versions of the LIFE are so broad as to likely initially elicit not only information about suicidal ideation but also thoughts about wanting to die and thoughts regarding nonsuicidal self-harm. However, the instructions in the A–LIFE explicitly state that the symptom is *not* to be considered clinically significant if it involves only "self-mutilation without suicidal intent."

The K–LIFE and the A–LIFE also have a second section titled "Suicidal Gestures and Attempts" in which participants are asked whether there have been times when they have tried to hurt themselves. Follow-up questions include questions about the total number of attempts/gestures; the date, intent, and medical lethality associated with each attempt/gesture; and whether participants were intoxicated, on medication, delusional, hallucinating, confused, or disorganized when the gesture/attempt occurred.

The stem query of this section is so broadly worded as to potentially elicit responses about nonsuicidal self-harm in addition to suicidal thoughts/behavior. This query therefore does not appear to conform to the recommendations by O'Carroll et al. (1996).

Reliability

No published data were located.

Concurrent Validity

No published data were located.

Predictive Validity

No published data were located.

Treatment

The K–LIFE has been used in controlled treatment trials for adolescent depression (Emslie, Rush, Weinberg, Kowatch, et al., 1997) and in a naturalistic follow-up of depressed adolescents who had been psychiatrically hospitalized (Emslie, Rush, Weinberg, Gullion, et al., 1997). However, the K–LIFE and A–LIFE have not been used in a published controlled treatment trial of suicidal youths.

Summary and Evaluation

The parent instrument of the K–LIFE and A–LIFE (the LIFE) was used in the Collaborative Treatment Study of Depression with adults. The K–LIFE and A–LIFE, like the parent instrument, were developed specifically for longitudinal study. Nonetheless, little reliability or validity data have been published regarding the child and adolescent versions of the LIFE. Additionally, the K–LIFE and A–LIFE queries regarding suicidal ideation and behavior are not consistent with the nomenclature for suicidal behavior suggested by O'Carroll et al. (1996).

Where to Obtain

Martin B. Keller, MD, Butler Hospital, 345 Blackstone Blvd., Providence RI 02906

Schedule for Affective Disorders and Schizophrenia, School-Age Epidemiologic Version

Description

The Schedule for Affective Disorders and Schizophrenia, School-Age Version, or K–SADS, is a semistructured interview designed to assess psychiatric disorders in children and adolescents from the ages of 6 to 18. There are at least four versions of the K–SADS currently in use: the Schedule for Affective Disorders and Schizophrenia, School-Age Present State Version (K–SADS–P IVR); the Schedule for Affective Disorders and Schizophrenia, School-Age Lifetime Version (K–SADS–L); the Schedule for Affective Disorders and Schizophrenia, School-Age Present and Lifetime Version (K–SADS–PL); and the Schedule for Affective Disorders and Schizophrenia, School-Age Epidemiologic Version (K–SADS–E). The similarities, differences, and historical development of these versions of the K–SADS have been described by Ambrosini (2000). All currently used versions of the K–SADS are designed to be administered separately to parents and youths for the purpose of assessing psychiatric disorders, defined in accordance with *DSM–IV* criteria. The K–SADS should be administered by clinicians who have been trained in the diagnostic assessment of children and adolescents and are familiar with *DSM–IV*. The K–SADS versions are appropriate for clinical research and have been used in community-based and longitudinal studies.

The K–SADS–E (Orvaschel, 1994) focuses on both current symptomatology and the severity of symptoms during the most severe past episode. Symptoms associated with past episodes are rated as present/absent; current symptoms are rated as mild, moderate, or severe (but the format of present/absent ratings can be retained at the discretion of the interviewer). The K–SADS–E is appropriate for both children and adolescents.

In several studies (e.g., Brent et al., 1992, 1997; Brent, Perper, Moritz, Baugher et al., 1994; Brent, Perper, Moritz, Liotus et al., 1994; Lewinsohn, Rohde, & Seeley, 1993, 1994, 1996; Renaud, Brent, Birmaher, Chiappeta, & Bridge, 1999), the K–SADS–E has been used in conjunction with the K–SADS–P. In some cases, this strategy may have been used because earlier versions of the K–SADS–P had more detailed current symptom rating scales than the K–SADS–E but were not designed to assess lifetime psychopathology. The most recent version of the K–SADS–E (Orvaschel, 1994) has finer gradations in symptom ratings for current psychiatric symptoms, just as the most recent version of the K–SADS Present State Version (the K–SADS–P IVR) has a scoring sheet for lifetime psychiatric disorders.

Populations Studied

The K–SADS–E (often in conjunction with the K–SADS–P) has been used in suicide autopsy studies to assess past history of suicidal behavior among individuals who completed suicide and history of suicidal behavior among community or clinically referred control participants (Brent et al.,

1988; Brent, Perper, Moritz, Allman, et al., 1993; Brent, Perper, Moritz, Baugher, & Allman, 1993). The K–SADS–E also has been used to assess youths who have been exposed to suicide (Brent et al., 1992; Brent, Perper, Moritz, Liotus, et al., 1993; Brent, Perper, Moritz, Liotus et al., 1994) and has been used in studies of suicidal behavior in community epidemiologic and longitudinal samples (e.g., Lewinsohn et al., 1993, 1994, 1996) and among incarcerated youths (Rohde, Mace, & Seeley, 1997). The K–SADS–E also has been used to assess psychiatric outpatient adolescents participating in a treatment study of depression (Brent et al., 1997, 1998).

Assessment and Definition of Suicidal Behaviors

Unlike some versions of the K–SADS, the K–SADS–E has separate queries for recurrent thoughts of wanting to die, suicidal ideation, the presence of a plan for suicide, and suicide attempts in the major depression section. These items are rated both for the current episode of disorder and for the greatest severity in the past.

The item regarding suicidal ideation (whether the participants thought about hurting or killing themselves) is likely to elicit responses both about suicidal ideation and ruminations about nonsuicidal self-injury (e.g., cutting oneself to relieve tension). The item regarding suicide attempts (whether the participants ever tried to kill themselves) is straightforward and implies nonzero intent to die. There is a question assessing total number of past suicide attempts in the K–SADS–E. There is one question regarding non-suicidal, physically self-damaging behaviors.

Similar to other versions of the K–SADS, the suicide behavior questions in the major depression section of the K–SADS–E might be skipped alto-gether if researchers choose to use skip-outs when participants do not answer positively to stem items regarding dysphoric mood or anhedonia. For this reason, the K–SADS–E also includes separate suicide assessment questions at the end of the interview that are asked of all participants. These questions ask about the presence of a suicide plan and the presence (and number) of suicide attempts. The query regarding suicide attempts (whether the participants ever tried to kill themselves or did anything that could have killed themselves) may elicit initial answers about nonsuicidal risk-taking suicidal behaviors (in addition to suicide attempts), requiring further clarification.

Reliability

In Table 3.4, interrater reliability data are presented from interviewers in training for the suicidal behavior items of the K–SADS–E (H. Orvaschel,

Table 3.4

Interrater Reliability Data for K–SADS–E Queries Regarding Thoughts of Death and Suicidal Behaviors

Item	Parent	Child	Summary
Thoughts of death	.80	.77	.74
Suicide ideation	.74	.83	.70
Suicide plan	.62	.81	.78
Suicide attempt	.88	.50	.56

Note. Data reported as correlation coefficients. From H. Orvaschel (personal communication, November 1999). K–SADS–E = Schedule for Affective Disorders and Schizophrenia, School-Age Epidemiologic Version.

personal communication, November 1999). In Table 3.5, interrater agreement for the suicide assessment items (see Table 1 of Lewinsohn et al., 1996, for items) in a sample of 213 adolescents of a modified version of the K–SADS–E is presented (P. Lewinsohn, personal communication, September 1999).

In a sample of 281 adolescents and parents, P. Lewinsohn (personal communication, September 1999) found poor to moderate parent–child agreement for the modified K–SADS–E items (see Table 3.6). However, as noted previously (Breton et al., 2002; Klimes-Dougan, 1998; Velez & Cohen, 1988; Walker et al., 1990), parents are often unaware of their children's suicidal behaviors.

Table 3.5

Interrater Agreement for Queries Regarding Thoughts of Death and Suicidal Behaviors From a Modified Version of the K–SADS–E

Item	Current	Past
Thoughts of death	.85	.71
Wishing to be dead	.70	.69
Suicidal ideation	.88	.78
Suicide plan		.74
Suicide attempt		.95

Note. Data reported as kappas. From P. Lewinsohn (personal communication, September 1999). K–SADS–E = Schedule for Affective Disorders and Schizophrenia, School-Age Epidemiologic Version.

Table 3.6

Parent–Child Agreement in Responses to Modified K–SADS–E Queries About Thoughts of Death and Suicidal Behaviors

Item	Current	Past
Thoughts of death	.17	.40
Wishing to be dead	.01	.40
Suicidal ideation		.39
Suicide plan		.32
Suicide attempt		.50

Note. Data reported as kappas. From P. Lewinsohn (personal communication, September 1999). K–SADS–E = Schedule for Affective Disorders and Schizophrenia, School-Age Epidemiologic Version.

Asarnow and Guthrie (1989) developed a classification of suicidal behavior based on reports to the K–SADS–E, the Depression Self-Rating Scale, and information in medical charts (0 = *absent, no report of suicidal ideation or attempts;* 1 = *suicidal ideation only, some documentation of suicidal ideation but no report of suicide attempts;* 2 = *evidence of a suicide attempt*). In a sample of child psychiatric inpatients, interrater reliability was found to be good ($\kappa = .77$ for ratings of suicidality status on the 3-point scale, $\kappa = .72$ for presence/absence of suicidal ideation, $\kappa = 1.0$ for presence/absence of suicide attempt).

Internal Consistency of a Screener Composed of K–SADS–E Items

Lewinsohn et al. (1996) found that a scale composed of five modified K–SADS–E items (the questions regarding thoughts of death and suicidal ideation from the K–SADS–E depression section, a modification of the K–SADS–E depression question regarding suicide plans, the question regarding suicide attempts at the end of the K–SADS–E asked of all participants, and one additional question regarding wishing to be dead; see Table 1 of Lewinsohn et al., 1996, for actual items) was internally consistent and fit a Guttman scale of increasing severity and frequency.

Concurrent Validity

Adolescents in the community with history of suicide attempts assessed with a modified K–SADS–E were found to have greater current and lifetime suicidal ideation, more pessimism, more negative attributions, a greater likelihood of depressive disorders, disruptive behavior disorders, substance use diagnoses, lower self-esteem, poorer coping skills, poorer health, more use of medications, and more parental dissatisfaction with grades than youths without a history of attempts (Lewinsohn et al., 1993). Among incarcerated adolescents, current and lifetime suicide attempts assessed with the K–SADS–E have been found to be associated with a greater likelihood of major depression, dysthymia, and anxiety disorders (Rohde, Mace, & Seeley, 1997).

Using a combination of the K–SADS–E and the Present State version of the K–SADS in a psychological autopsy study, Renaud et al. (1999) found that suicide completers had a greater history of nonlethal suicide attempts than matched community controls. Lewinsohn et al. (1996) found that the answers to the adapted K–SADS–E questions regarding thoughts of death and suicidal behavior (as described earlier; see Table 1 of Lewinsohn et al., 1996, for actual items) loaded on a single factor in a principal-components analysis with scores from another suicide screening instrument (developed as an addition to the Center for Epidemiologic Studies Depression Scale).

Predictive Validity

Lewinsohn et al. (1994) found prior history of attempts assessed with a modification of the K–SADS–E to be one of the strongest predictors of later attempts (increasing the risk 18-fold). Using past history of suicide attempts assessed with the K–SADS as a screener for future suicidality in a community sample of adolescents would have yielded 54% sensitivity, 94% specificity, 14% positive predictive value, and 99% negative predictive value (Lewinsohn et al., 1996).

Treatment Studies

The K–SADS–E does not appear to have been used in a treatment study specifically targeting youths' suicidal behaviors. However, the K–SADS–P and K–SADS–E have been used together in a treatment study of depressed youths (Barbe, Bridge, Birmaher, Kolko, & Brent, 2001; Brent et al., 1997, 1998). In this study, adolescents with a current or past history of suicidal ideation when they entered the study were more likely to drop out of the clinical trial than adolescents without such histories. In addition, although suicidal ideation status did not predict treatment response if youths participated in cognitive therapy or family therapy, the adolescents with current or past suicidal ideation did respond more poorly to the nonspecific supportive therapy than youths without such histories (Barbe et al., 2001).

Summary and Evaluation

The K–SADS–E (often in conjunction with the K–SADS–P) is probably the most widely used semistructured psychiatric diagnostic interview used in studies of suicidal behavior. The K–SADS–E has more specific questions regarding suicidal ideation/behaviors and much more psychometric data regarding the suicidal ideation/behaviors items than other versions of the K–SADS. The K–SADS–E has been used in a treatment study of depression and has demonstrated predictive validity.

Where to Obtain

Helen Orvaschel, PhD, Center for Psychological Studies, Nova Southeastern University, 3301 College Avenue, Ft. Lauderdale, FL 33314

Schedule for Affective Disorders and Schizophrenia, School-Age Lifetime Version

Description

The Schedule for Affective Disorders and Schizophrenia, School-Age Lifetime Version, or K–SADS–L (Klein, 1994), is a semistructured diagnostic instrument that has been used primarily in industry-sponsored clinical trials (Ambrosini, 2000). Unlike the other versions of the K–SADS, which can be used with children as well as with adolescents, the K–SADS–L is specifically recommended for use with adolescents. As the name implies, this version of the K–SADS was designed to assess lifetime psychopathology; however, symptoms are rated both for lifetime occurrence and for occurrence during the last 2 weeks or current episode of disorder. The symptom severity rating scales differ depending on the symptom, but most symptoms are rated on a 0–4, 0–6, or 0–7 rating scale. Similar to the K–SADS–P IVR, the K–SADS–L is a modification of earlier versions of the K–SADS–P.

Populations Studied

The K–SADS–L has been used with suicidal psychiatric inpatients (Joiner, Rudd, Rouleau, & Wagner, 2000).

Assessment and Definitions of Suicidal Behaviors

Suicidal ideation and behavior in the K–SADS–L are rated according to their most severe level during the lifetime and according to their most severe level during the preceding 2 weeks or current episode of the disorder. There are no separate items assessing thoughts of death and suicidal ideation in the K–SADS–L. Indeed, thoughts of death, suicidal ideation, and suicide attempts are rated on a single 0 (*not at all*) to 7 (*very extreme: suicidal attempt with definite intent to die or potentially medially harmful*) rating scale. The continuous rating scale of severity reflects the perspective of some researchers that thoughts of wanting to die, suicidal ideation, suicide attempts, and suicide completions all fall along a single continuum (e.g., Lewinsohn et al., 1996).

Using a cutoff of 4 (moderate) for clinical significance (recommended by R. Klein, personal communication, November 1999) indicates that the participant "thinks of suicide and has thought of a specific method." This cutoff is consistent with the *DSM–IV* diagnostic criteria for major depression. However, this cutoff is more stringent than the definition of suicidal ideation proposed by O'Carroll et al. (1996) because of the requirement that a specific method of suicide attempt be considered. Hence, a cutoff of 4 on this item would yield a conservative estimate of the prevalence of suicidal ideation.

The continuous rating scale also confounds questions about the presence/absence of suicidal behavior with the clinical characteristics of the behavior. For example, suicidal behavior of a *primarily communicative* type (a question of intent) is rated as less severe than suicidal behavior that is *potentially medically harmful* (a question of medical lethality). This is problematic because suicidal intent and medical lethality are not always correlated in juvenile populations.

There is one item in the K–SADS–L inquiring about total number of discrete suicidal acts within the present episode of illness and during the lifetime. Additional questions in the K–SADS–L focus on medical lethality and intent associated with suicide attempts (and are reviewed separately) and on nonsuicidal physical self-damaging acts.

Reliability

No data regarding the reliability of suicidal ideation/attempts items are available (R. Klein, personal communication, November 1999)

Concurrent Validity

Multiple suicide attempters (as determined with the K–SADS–L) were found to have higher scores on the Children's Depression Inventory than other suicidal youths (Joiner et al., 2000).

Predictive Validity

No published data were located.

Treatment Studies

The K–SADS–L apparently has not been used in a treatment study of suicidal youths. However, items of the K–SADS–L have been used to determine whether youths were suicidal and hence ineligible to participate in a multisite pharmacotherapy treatment study for depression (R. Klein, personal communication, November 1999).

Summary and Evaluation

The suicidal ideation/behavior queries of the K–SADS–L are not as specific as those of the K–SADS–E. The K–SADS–L suicidal ideation/behavior items have also not been evaluated psychometrically as thoroughly as those from the K–SADS–E.

Where to Obtain

Rachel G. Klein, PhD, Department of Psychiatry, New York State Psychiatric Institute, 1051 Riverside Drive, New York, NY 10032

Schedule for Affective Disorders and Schizophrenia, School-Age Present State Version

Description

The latest Schedule for Affective Disorders and Schizophrenia, School-Age Present State Version IVR, or K–SADS–P IVR (Ambrosini, 2000; Ambrosini & Dixon, 1996), was developed primarily for the assessment of current psychopathology. Severity ratings range from 0 to 4 or 0 to 6 depending on the symptom. A scoring sheet for recording lifetime diagnoses has been developed, but its validity has not been tested. The K–SADS–P IVR has three "mini-SADS" modules (M–SADS for Affective Disorders, A–SADS for Anxiety Disorders, B–SADS for behavioral disorders) that can be administered in lieu of the entire K–SADS if researchers so choose (e.g., if the purpose of a clinical trial is to study the effects of an intervention on a specific disorder).

In addition, unlike other versions of the K–SADS, items from the Hamilton Depression Rating Scale (HAM–D) using the Structured Interview

Guide for the HAM–D (Williams, 1988) have been incorporated into the latest version of the K–SADS–P. These items were included to facilitate comparisons between child and adult research. The use and limitations of the HAM–D for assessing suicidal behavior is described in the next chapter. An earlier version of the K–SADS–P has been translated into Hebrew (Apter, Orvaschel, Laseg, Moses, & Tyano, 1989).

Populations Studied

The K–SADS–P, the predecessor of the K–SADS–P IVR, has been used in conjunction with other versions of the K–SADS in suicide autopsy studies to assess past history of suicidal behavior among individuals who completed suicide and history of suicidal behavior among community or clinically referred controls (Brent et al., 1988; Brent, Perper, Moritz, Allman, et al., 1993; Brent, Perper, Moritz, Baugher, & Allman, 1993). The K–SADS–P also has been used to study suicidal behaviors in community epidemiological and longitudinal samples (e.g., Garrison, Jackson, Addy, McKeown, & Waller, 1991; Lewinsohn et al., 1993, 1994, 1996; McKeown et al., 1998), with psychiatric outpatients and inpatients (e.g., Apter et al., 1995; Myers, McCauley, Calderon, Mitchell, et al., 1991; Myers, McCauley, Calderon, & Treder, 1991; Strauss et al., 2000), and with adolescent psychiatric outpatients participating in a treatment study (Brent et al., 1997, 1998).

Assessment and Definitions of Suicidal Behaviors

The K–SADS–P IVR has several detection items regarding suicidal behaviors. The first is actually the suicide item from the HAM–D. This suicide item should not be considered separately from the other items of the HAM–D included in the K–SADS–P IVR, and if done so, would be problematic for reasons that are detailed in the next chapter.

The second detection item of the K–SADS–P IVR focuses on suicidal ideation. As with most other non-HAM–D items on the K–SADS–P IVR, this item is rated twice, both for the worst level of severity during the last year or present episode of illness and for the level of severity for the last week. Similar to the K–SADS–L, suicidal ideation and behavior are rated on a single 1–7 continuous rating scale.

Unlike the K–SADS–L, a cutoff of 3 on this scale (*mild: sometimes has thoughts of suicide but has not thought of a specific method*) corresponds only to suicidal ideation and not thoughts of death. A cutoff of 4 on this scale (*moderate: often thinks of suicide and has thought of a specific method*) would yield a conservative estimate of the prevalence of suicidal ideation/behavior. (Note that even *DSM–IV* does not require *both* recurrent suicidal ideation and suicidal ideation with a plan for the symptom to count toward a diagnosis of major depression; rather, *DSM–IV* requires *either* recurrent suicidal ideation *or* suicidal ideation with a plan). Similar to the K–SADS–L, the continuous rating scale is also problematic because it confounds the definition of suicidal behavior with the clinical characteristics of suicidal behavior.

A third detection item in the K–SADS–P IVR focuses specifically on the number of discrete suicidal acts during the last year or during the present episode. This latter item can be used to determine history of suicide attempts separately from ideation. However, only suicide attempts during the last year are rated with this item. This may be problematic for clinicians and researchers, in that data from both adolescents and adults have suggested that a history of suicide attempts not in the recent past may have the same prognostic value as attempts that are more proximal (Clark, Gibbons, Fawcett, & Scheftner, 1989; Goldston et al., 1999).

The K–SADS–P IVR also has queries about the medical lethality and intent associated with suicidal behavior; these last questions are reviewed separately in chap. 9. In addition, the K–SADS–P IVR has a question asking specifically about nonsuicidal self-damaging physical acts.

Reliability

Interrater and test–retest reliability data for psychiatric diagnoses assessed with different versions of the K–SADS–P have been reported (Ambrosini, 2000), but reliability data specifically for the suicidal behavior items have not been reported.

Internal Consistency of K–SADS Screener

The internal consistency of the summed scores of suicide items from a modification of both the K–SADS–P and K–SADS–E has been described by Lewinsohn et al. (1996). These data are described in the K–SADS–E section (because the questions used by Lewinsohn et al. more closely resemble the suicidality items in the K–SADS–E than the K–SADS–P).

Concurrent Validity

In a mixed sample of child and adolescent outpatients and inpatients, Myers, McCauley, Calderon, Mitchell, et al. (1991) found suicidality (as rated on the 7-point K–SADS–P continuous scale) to be positively correlated with severity of depressive symptoms and hopelessness and negatively correlated with self-esteem. In addition, adolescent psychiatric inpatients with affective disorders and a history of suicide attempts had earlier and longer duration of affective disorder, greater self-rated depression, more cognitive distortion, and greater likelihood of exposure to suicidality than similar but nonsuicidal youths (Brent, Kolko, Allan, & Brown, 1990).

Predictive Validity

Myers, McCauley, Calderon, and Treder (1991) found severity of suicidality rated from the K–SADS–P 7-point rating scale at baseline to be predictive of suicidal ideation and behavior over the 3-year follow-up. Additionally, in a longitudinal study of young adolescents in the community, McKeown et al. (1998) found any K–SADS rated suicidal behavior (ideation, plans, or attempts) within the last year to be predictive of suicide plans 1 year later. There was a strong but statistically nonsignificant trend for prior suicidal behavior to be predictive of suicide attempts over the next year and a weaker trend for prior suicidal behavior to be related to later suicidal ideation.

Treatment Studies

The K–SADS–P, and the more recent K–SADS–P IVR, do not appear to have been used in a treatment study of suicidal youths.

Summary and Evaluation

The K–SADS–P IVR assesses both current diagnostic status and diagnostic status over the last year. The K–SADS–P IVR has a modular format that allows interviewers to administer only select portions of the interview, potentially reducing administration time compared with earlier versions of this interview. The inquiries regarding suicidal ideation and behavior on the K–SADS–P IVR are not as specific as those of the K–SADS–E. Nonetheless, the K–SADS–P has a history of extensive use in research studies, and the suicidal ideation/behavior items of the K–SADS–P have been shown to be predictive of later suicidal ideation and behavior in one study, and suicidal plans in another study.

Where to Obtain

Paul J. Ambrosini, MD, MCP Hahnemann University, EPPI, 3200 Henry Avenue, Philadelphia, PA 19129

Schedule for Affective Disorders and Schizophrenia, School-Age Present and Lifetime Version

Description

The Schedule for Affective Disorders and Schizophrenia, School-Age Present and Lifetime Version, or K–SADS–PL, assesses both lifetime and current psychiatric diagnoses (Kaufman et al., 1997; Kaufman, Birmaher, Brent, Rao, & Ryan, 1996). The K–SADS–PL was modified from an earlier version of the K–SADS–P and was influenced by several other interviews, including the K–SADS–E. The format of the K–SADS–PL differs from that of the other versions of the K–SADS. After the unstructured interview, the patient or informant is administered a Diagnostic Screening Interview. Symptoms in the screening interview are rated both according to their current severity and most severe levels in the past. Depending on the severity of key current and past symptoms reported in the screening interview, any of five diagnostic supplements (affective disorders, psychotic disorders, anxiety disorders, behavioral disorders, or substance use and other disorders) can be administered. The K–SADS–PL does not yield severity ratings for clinically significant symptoms (symptoms are rated as not present, subthreshold, or threshold). Like other versions of the K–SADS, the K–SADS–PL is appropriate for clinical research.

Populations Studied

The K–SADS–PL apparently has not been used in studies of suicidal behaviors.

Assessment and Definitions of Suicidal Behaviors

Unlike the K–SADS–P IVR and the K–SADS–L, the K–SADS–PL includes separate queries about recurrent thoughts of death and suicidal ideation. The K–SADS–PL does not include as many sample queries as the K–SADS–P IVR or the K–SADS–L, but the queries that are provided are straightforward and easy to understand.

The rating scale for suicidal ideation is similar to that of the K–SADS–P IVR and K–SADS–L; occasional thoughts of suicide without consideration of a specific method are rated as subthreshold, and thoughts that occur often and with a specific plan are rated as clinically significant. As described earlier, using the threshold of suicidal thoughts that occur often and with a specific plan is likely to yield a conservative prevalence of suicidal ideation.

This classification scheme is more conservative than both the operational definition of suicidal behavior in the *DSM–IV* criteria for major depression and the proposed operational definitions suggested by O'Carroll et al. (1996).

A second set of questions in the K–SADS–PL focuses on the presence of suicide attempts. However, the rating scale used to designate whether symptoms are clinically significant reflects a confounding of the definition of suicide attempts and the clinical characteristics of the attempts—only attempts of a certain medical lethality or intent are rated as clinically significant. Therefore, the use of this item for the detection of suicide attempts is likely to yield a conservative estimate of the behavior of interest.

Additional questions in the K–SADS–PL focus on medical lethality and intent associated with suicide attempts (and are reviewed separately). Questions also are asked about nonsuicidal physically self-damaging behavior.

Reliability

No reliability data for the suicidal items were located.

Concurrent Validity

No published data were located.

Predictive Validity

No published data were located.

Treatment Studies

The K–SADS–PL apparently has not been used in published studies of the treatment of suicidal youths.

Summary and Evaluation

The K–SADS–PL assesses both current and lifetime diagnoses. With its modular approach, the K–SADS–PL uses a more streamlined administration format than earlier versions of the K–SADS, which may serve to shorten administration time. Nonetheless, the psychometric characteristics of the suicidal ideation/behavior inquiries of the K–SADS–PL have not been published, nor has the instrument been used in studies of suicidal behavior.

Where to Obtain

Joan Kaufman, PhD, Department of Psychology, Yale University, P.O. Box 208205, New Haven, CT 06520. Also at http://www.wpic.pitt.edu/ksads

---

Pictorial Instrument for Children and Adolescents

Description

The Pictorial Instrument for Children and Adolescents (PICA–III–R) is a semistructured picture-accompanied psychiatric diagnostic interview for use with 6- to 16-year-olds (Ernst, Cookus, & Moravec, 2000). The PICA–III–R was developed for assessing symptoms of *DSM–III–R* diagnoses and has not yet been modified for use with *DSM–IV* (Ernst et al., 2000). The PICA–III–R is administered by trained clinicians. It can be used to assess both selected psychiatric disorders and severity of symptoms. Children administered the PICA–III–R are shown black-and-white drawings of a child (with ambiguous gender) evidencing various symptoms or behaviors and are asked, "How much are you like him/her?" Children respond by pointing to their answers on a 5-point visual analogue scale (illustrated by drawings of five people holding their hands different distances apart). Like the Dominic–R, the visual cues of the PICA–III–R have been chosen to be interesting and attention eliciting, and to help communicate the meaning of queries. Also similar to the Dominic–R, there is no parallel form of the PICA–III–R for eliciting information from adult informants. Unlike the structured Dominic–R, the queries of the PICA–III–R can be reworded or clarified by the clinician interviewers.

Populations Studied

The PICA–III–R was developed with inpatient youths and has not been used with other groups of youths. The PICA–III–R has not been specifically used with suicidal youths.

Assessment and Definitions of Suicidal Behaviors

There are two questions in the PICA–III–R about thoughts of death and suicidality. In the first query, youths are shown a picture of a boy thinking of images related to death (a skull, a coffin,and a graveyard) and are asked whether they have similar thoughts. In the second query, youths are shown the picture of a boy thinking about killing himself by shooting himself in the head with a gun. They are then asked whether they similarly have thought about "hurting or killing" themselves, or have ever tried to kill themselves.

The question about suicidal attempt is consistent with O'Carroll et al.'s (1996) recommended nomenclature. The wording of the question about suicidal ideation ("about hurting or killing yourself") may elicit information not only about suicidal ideation but also about nonsuicidal self-harm behavior. Nonetheless, it is of note that the picture associated with this query (the boy with the gun) clearly depicts someone considering suicide.

As noted with the Dominic–R, the effects of using visual stimuli to assess suicidality with younger children have not been well studied. It is not known whether the use of pictures portraying suicide helps children to understand queries about this symptom or whether there is any deleterious effect of showing a boy thinking of killing himself with a specific method. Although it clearly is important to assess suicidality in a high-risk population, with this particular instrument, there may be concerns about showing suggestible children a picture depicting the most lethal means of attempting suicide, that is, suicide by firearms.

Reliability

Information regarding the reliability of the PICA–III–R suicidality questions has not been published.

Concurrent Validity

No evidence regarding the concurrent validity of the PICA–III–R suicidality questions was found.

Predictive Validity

No studies evaluating the predictive validity of the PICA–III–R suicidality questions were found.

Treatment Studies

No treatment studies of suicidal youths using the PICA–III–R were found.

Summary and Evaluation

The PICA–III–R is a semi-structured psychiatric diagnostic interview for children. In the PICA–III–R, children not only are asked questions verbally but also are presented with visually engaging pictures portraying the symptoms or behaviors that are the subject of inquiry. There are two questions on the PICA–III–R for thoughts of death and suicidal behavior. However, the PICA–III–R has not been used in studies of suicidal behaviors, and the effects of assessing suicidal behavior by using visual cues have not been evaluated.

Where to Obtain

Monique Ernst, MD, PhD, NIDA, Brain Imaging Center, 5500 Nathan Shock Drive, Baltimore, MD 21224

Summary

At the time this book was written, reliability data for questions assessing suicidal behavior and data regarding the predictive utility of responses to these questions were available for only four diagnostic interviews (DICA–R, DISC–IV, ISCA, and K–SADS–E). It is not coincidental that these four instruments are also the most widely used diagnostic instruments in suicidal behavior research with youths.

The queries of four psychiatric diagnostic interviews (CAPA, ChIPS, DICA–R, and ISCA) are very consistent with O'Carroll et al.'s (1996) definitions of suicidal ideation and suicide attempts. The queries of two other interviews (DISC–IV and K–SADS–E) also are generally well worded in this respect. However, the queries of the DISC–IV may elicit conservative information about suicidal ideation, and the initial queries of the K–SADS–E may elicit information not only about suicide attempts but also about non-suicidal self-harm behavior or risk-taking behavior, requiring further clarification.

There have been precious few systematic investigations of treatment of suicidal children and adolescents. Reflecting this state of the art, none of the psychiatric diagnostic interviews have been used to assess treatment outcomes with suicidal youths. Several of the interviews (e.g., ISCA and K–SADS–E) would be well-suited for this task because of their use in repeated assessment longitudinal studies.

In Table 3.7, the characteristics of the different diagnostic interviews are summarized. The interviews are classified as to whether they are primarily structured or semistructured (although some interviews such as the CAPA

Table 3.7

Characteristics of Psychiatric Diagnostic Interviews That Can be Used in the Detection of Suicidality

Instrument	Structured or semi-structured interview	Populations in which suicidal behaviors examined[a]	Assess suicidal ideation	Assess suicide attempts	Assess total no. of attempts[b]	Assess non-suicidal self-harm	Consistent with O'Carroll et al.'s operational definitions[c]	Reliability data for suicidality items	Concurrent validity evidence	Predictive validity evidence	Used as outcome measure
CAPA	Structured	–	+	+	+	+	++	–	–	–	–
ChIPS	Structured	–	+	+	–	–	++	–	–	–	–
DICA	Structured	Abused, Bereaved, DepPar	+	+	+	–	++	+	+	+	–
DISC–IV	Structured	Clin, Sch, Incar	+	+	+	–	+	+	+	+	–
Dominic–R	Structured Pictorial	–	+	–	–	–	–	+	+	–	–
ISCA	Semi-structured	Clin, Med	+	+	+	+	++	+	+	+	–
K–LIFE/A–LIFE	Semi-structured		+	+	+	+	–	–	–	+	–
K–SADS–E	Semi-structured	Autopsy, Clin, Exposed, Incar, Sch	+	+	+	+	+	+	+	+	–
K–SADS–L	Semi-Structured	Clin	+	+	+	+	–	–	+	–	–
K–SADS–CP IVR	Semi-structured	Autopsy, Clin, Scl	+	+	+	+	–	–	+	+	–

K–SADS–PL	Semistructured	–	+	+	–	–	–	–
PICA–III–R	Semistructured (Pictorial)	–	+	+	+	–	–	–

Note. The instrument are as follows: CAPA = Child and Adolescent Psychiatric Assessment; ChIPS = Children's Interview for Psychiatric Syndromes; DICA = Diagnostic Interview for Children and Adolescents; DISC–IV = Diagnostic Interview Schedule for Children; ISCA = Interview Schedule for Children and Adolescents; K–LIFE = Kiddie—Longitudinal Interval Follow-Up Evaluation; A–LIFE = Adolescent Longitudinal Interval Follow-Up Evaluation; K–SADS–E = Schedule for Affective Disorders and Schizophrenia, School-Age Epidemiologic Version; K–SADS–L = Schedule for Affective Disorders and Schizophrenia, School-Age Lifetime Version; K–SADS–P IVR = Schedule for Affective Disorders and Schizophrenia, School-Age Present State Version; K–SADS–PL = Schedule for Affective Disorders and Schizophrenia, School-Age Present and Lifetime Version; PICA–III–R = Pictorial Instrument for Children and Adolescents.

[a]Abused = abused children or children with posttraumatic stress disorder; Bereaved = bereaved children; DepPar = children of depressed parents; Clin = inpatient and/or outpatient psychiatric clinically referred or treatment-seeking youths; Sch = school or community samples (including nonpatient controls in research studies); Incar = incarcerated youths; Med = medically ill youths; Autopsy = youths in psychological autopsy studies (studies of individuals who have completed suicide); Exposed = youths exposed to suicide.

[b]Items on the K–SADS–P IVR ask about total number of attempts in the last year or current episode of disorder.

[c]++ complete consistency with O'Carroll et al.'s (1996) operational definitions; + mostly consistent with O'Carroll et al.'s definitions, – least consistent with O'Carroll et al.'s definitions.

and DICA have elements of both structured and semistructured interviews); whether they assess suicidal ideation, suicide attempts, total number of attempts, and non-suicidal self-harm behavior; the populations with which they have been used; and the psychometric characteristics of the suicidality queries.

Interviews Specifically Focused on Suicidal Behaviors and Clinician-Rated Indices

Reviewed in this chapter are two groups of instruments: interviews developed specifically for assessing the presence of suicidal behavior and clinician-rating instruments (also typically interview based) that can be used to assess the severity of suicidal behaviors. Similar to diagnostic interviews, the suicide assessment interviews differ in terms of whether they are structured (and thereby are meant to be delivered exactly as written) or are more semistructured. For example, the Adolescent Suicide Interview (Lucas, 1997) is highly structured and can be administered by computer, whereas the Lifetime Parasuicide Count (Linehan & Comtois, 1997) and the Spectrum of Suicidal Behavior (of the Child Suicide Potential Scales; Pfeffer, 1979) depend on more semistructured inquiry.

Both the suicidal behavior interviews and the clinician-rating scales also differ in terms of the focus of their inquiries. The Lifetime Parasuicide Count focuses on the number of instances of both suicidal and nonsuicidal self-harm behavior but not suicidal ideation. The Suicidal Behaviors Interview (Reynolds, 1989), Spectrum of Suicidal Behavior, and Risk of Suicide Questionnaire (Horowitz et al., 2001) focus more specifically on severity of suicidal ideation and behavior. The Adolescent Suicide Interview, Children's Depression Rating Scale—Revised (Poznanski & Mokros, 1999), and the Hamilton Depression Rating Scale (Hamilton, 1960, 1967) provide methods of assessing severity of suicidality in the context of other depressive symptoms.

The Adolescent Suicide Interview was developed primarily as a screening instrument, as was the Suicidal Behaviors Interview and the Risk of

Suicide Questionnaire. The Risk of Suicide Questionnaire was developed specifically to screen youths in emergency departments. The Children's Depression Rating Scale—Revised and the Hamilton Depression Rating Scale are clinician-rating scales often used in treatment outcome studies that include items regarding suicidal ideation and behavior. These latter two scales, as well as the rating from the Spectrum of Suicidal Behavior, provide only a single rating regarding severity of suicidal behavior. Hence, information about internal consistency and dimensionality is not provided for these scales. In addition, C. Lucas (personal communication, November 1999) has argued that factor analysis of the Adolescent Suicide Interview would be inappropriate because many of the items in that scale are linked to a specific psychiatric diagnostic system (the criteria for diagnosis of major depressive disorder).

Adolescent Suicide Interview and Multimedia Adolescent Suicide Interview

Description

The Adolescent Suicide Interview (ASI) is a revision of a semistructured interview developed by Shaffer and colleagues. The revision is a highly structured interview that can be administered by a lay interviewer or by computer (the Multimedia Adolescent Suicide Interview, or MASI; Lucas, 1997). As such, the ASI and MASI are appropriate for screening purposes and for epidemiologic studies. The ASI has four sections for the assessment of *DSM–IV* symptoms of major depression, severity of suicidal ideation, severity of suicide attempts, and exposure to suicide.

Populations Studied

The ASI has been tested in a preliminary manner with boys admitted to Boys Town, Nebraska, and other clinical populations (Lucas et al., 1999). The ASI also has been tested in a community sample of adolescents (Lucas & Fisher, 1999).

Assessment and Definitions of Suicidal Behaviors

The ASI has separate items for thoughts of death (whether the children thought a lot about death or dying) and suicidal ideation (whether the children thought about suicide or about killing themselves). The stem question regarding suicidal ideation is followed by three questions regarding frequency of suicidal thoughts, wish to die, and suicide plans. There is a question asking whether the informant has ever had a period of recurrent suicidal ideation lasting at least a week. The ASI also has a question about lifetime suicide attempts (whether the children have ever in their whole life tried to kill themselves). If the respondent reports suicide attempts, the clinical characteristics of these are assessed separately. Questions about exposure to suicide are asked of all respondents. Consistent with O'Carroll et al.'s (1996) definitions, the stem questions regarding suicidal ideation and the question regarding lifetime attempts imply nonzero intent to die.

Reliability

Test–retest reliability (over an interval of 1 to 5 days) was assessed in a sample of 189 consecutive admissions to Boys Town (Lucas et al., 1999). Results suggested that both the interviewer-administered ASI and the computer-administered ASI yielded reliable results (intraclass correlation coefficient [ICC] = .96 and ICC = .84, respectively). Test–retest reliability in another sample of clinically referred patients was found to be moderate (ICC = .61; Lucas et al., 1999).

Internal Consistency

No data are available regarding the internal consistency of the suicidal ideation items.

Concurrent Validity

An ongoing study is investigating the relationship between the ASI and the DISC suicidality items, the Beck Depression Inventory, and clinical judgments about suicidality (C. Lucas, personal communication, November 1999).

Dimensionality

No data have been published (the author suggests that factor analysis would be inappropriate because the scale is linked to an external diagnostic system; C. Lucas, personal communication, November 1999).

Predictive Validity

No published data were located.

Treatment Studies

The ASI has not been used in treatment studies.

Summary and Evaluation

Studies with adults have indicated that patients may sometimes disclose more or prefer providing sensitive information to a computer rather than a clinician (Kobak, Greist, Jefferson, & Katzelnick, 1996; Petrie & Abell, 1994). In this context, the ASI is a structured screening interview that may have particular use in its computer-assisted administration form (the MASI). However, the ASI and MASI have not yet been used in any published studies.

Where to Obtain

Chris Lucas, MD, Department of Child and Adolescent Psychiatry, Columbia University—New York State Psychiatric Institute, 1051 Riverside Drive, New York, NY 10032

Children's Depression Rating Scale—Revised

Description

The Children's Depression Rating Scale—Revised (CDRS–R) is a semistructured clinician-rated scale that can be used as a screening instrument, diagnostic tool, and severity measure of depression in children (Poznanski & Mokros, 1999). The CDRS–R was modeled after the Hamilton Depression Rating Scale (reviewed separately) and assesses 17 groups of symptoms, including those required for *DSM–IV* diagnosis of major depression. Fourteen of these symptoms are assessed in interview; the interviewer, based on observation, rates the other three. The CDRS–R initially was developed for use with 6- to 12-year-olds, but the scale has also been used with adolescents. The manual for the CDRS–R includes suggested queries to be used in both the child and informant sections of the interview. Interestingly, given that the CDRS–R is being increasingly used as an outcome measure in treatment studies, there does not appear to be a specified time frame for the queries (i.e., the scale does not explicitly refer to last week, last 2 weeks, etc.). According to the manual, the individual administering the CDRS–R should have clinical training (especially in the assessment of suicidality) or at the very least be working under the supervision of someone with such training. The CDRS–R has been translated into Spanish and Turkish.

Populations Studied

The CDRS–R has been used to examine suicidality in an inpatient treatment setting (Brinkman-Sull, Overholser, & Silverman, 2000) in an outpatient affective disorders clinic (Poznanski & Mokros, 1999), and among non-referred students (Poznanski & Mokros, 1999). The CDRS–R also has been used to study suicidal ideation and behavior in children and adolescents of depressed and nondepressed mothers (Garber, Little, Hilsman, & Weaver, 1998).

Assessment and Definitions of Suicidal Behaviors

There are separate CDRS–R items for morbid ideation (thoughts about death) and suicidal ideation and attempts. Responses for the suicidal ideation/behavior item are rated on a continuum from 1 (*understands the word* suicide *but does not apply the term to himself/herself*) to 7 (*has made a suicide attempt within the last month or is actively suicidal*). Some of the suggested queries regarding suicidal ideation item ask about whether the children have ever thought of hurting themselves. These questions may initially evoke responses regarding ideation about nonsuicidal self-injurious behavior but eventually should allow the interviewer to discern whether youths are actually exhibiting suicidal ideation. The query about suicide attempts (whether the children ever tried to kill themselves) is consistent with O'Carroll et al.'s (1996) recommended nomenclature.

Reliability

Information regarding interrater reliability of the CDRS–R suicidal ideation item was not specifically provided in the manual. However, inter-rater reliability for the individual CDRS–R symptoms ranged from .40 to .95 (Poznanski & Mokros, 1999). Information about the test–retest reliability of the suicidal ideation item was not provided.

Internal Consistency

Not applicable because there is only a single ideation item.

Concurrent Validity

Non-referred children reporting clinically significant suicidal ideation on the CDRS–R (a rating of 3 or above) were noted to have higher scores than children without suicidal ideation on each of the other 13 depressive symptom areas assessed in interview (Poznanski & Mokros, 1999). In a sample of psychiatrically hospitalized children, the CDRS–R suicidal ideation item was moderately correlated with scores on another clinician-rated scale, the Scale for Suicidal Ideation (Allan, Kashani, Dahlmeier, Taghizadeh, & Reid, 1997).

Dimensionality

Not applicable because there is only a single suicidal ideation item. No information about the factor structure of the English version of the CDRS–R was found.

Predictive Validity

A suicide index composed of the suicide items from the CDRS–R, Children's Depression Inventory, and Youth Self-Report was predictive of suicide scores at a second assessment 1 year later (Garber et al., 1998).

Treatment Studies

The CDRS–R has been used in a number of treatment studies with children and adolescents (e.g., Bernstein, Hektner, Borchardt, & McMillan, 2001; Emslie, Rush, Weinberg, Kowatch et al., 1997; Weisz, Thurber, Sweeney, Proffitt, & LeGagnoux, 1997). However, no published treatment studies with suicidal youths were found.

Summary and Evaluation

The CDRS–R is a clinician-rated scale based on semistructured interview with children and parents. The scale was developed for use with 6- to 12-year-olds but also has been used with adolescents. There is a single item on the CDRS–R regarding both suicidal ideation and attempts. The queries provided with the CDRS–R allow for assessment of suicidal ideation and attempts in a manner that is consistent with the recommendations of O'Carroll et al. (1996).

Where to Obtain

Western Psychological Services, 12031 Wilshire Blvd., Los Angeles, CA 90025-1251

Hamilton Depression Rating Scale

Description

The Hamilton Depression Rating Scale (HAM–D, also referred to as the HDRS) is a clinician-rated scale for severity of depression (Hamilton, 1960, 1967). The HAM–D was originally intended for use with adults diagnosed with depressive disorders. The HAM–D is one of the oldest depression rating scales, and its use has become ubiquitous in depression research and treatment outcome research. In the original 17-item HAM–D, no standardized queries were provided; rather, clinicians were supposed to use the items on the rating scales as prompts for semistructured interview with patients. To facilitate consistency of inquiry about HAM–D items, a structured interview guide for use with the HAM–D has been developed (Williams, 1988). The HAM–D has been translated or published in a number of languages in addition to English, including Spanish, Italian, French, Turkish, Greek, German, Dutch, Swedish, and Chinese. Computer-assisted (Kobak, Reynolds, Rosenfeld, & Greist, 1990) and paper-and-pencil versions (Reynolds & Kobak, 1995) of the HAM–D have been developed, as well as a structured interview version for use by trained lay interviewers (Potts, Daniels, Burnam, & Wells, 1990). A revised expanded revision of the HAM–D has also been published (Warren, 1998). The HAM–D is included in this book because of its use in psychiatric treatment studies with youths (e.g., Ambrosini et al., 1999; Goodnick, Jorge, Hunter, & Kumar, 2000; Swedo et al., 1997) and because the queries of the HAM–D have been included in the K–SADS–P IVR (Ambrosini, 2000), an interview instrument explicitly meant for use with children and adolescents (see this volume, chap. 3).

Populations Studied

The HAM–D has been used with a number of child and adolescent psychiatric populations. However, no studies using the HAM–D specifically with suicidal youths were found.

Assessment and Definitions of Suicidal Behaviors

There is one item assessing suicidality in the HAM–D. Suicidal behavior is rated on a continuum from 0 (*absent*) to 1 (*feels life is not worth living*) to 2 (*wishes to be dead or has any thoughts of possible death to self*) to 3 (*suicidal ideas or gesture*) to 4 (*attempts at suicide*). This severity rating scale is problematic because it equates suicidal ideation with *gestures,* a term which is not defined but is presumed to reflect either low suicide intent or low medical lethality associated with the suicidal act, or perhaps nonsuicidal self-harm. Despite the issue of whether such equivalence in a severity rating scale is grounded in data, *suicide gesture* is not a term recommended by either O'Carroll et al. (1996) or the 1973 NIMH Task Force (Beck et al., 1973) and is a term that confounds the definitions of suicidal behavior with the clinical characteristics of the suicidal behavior.

Reliability

No information about the reliability of the suicidality items in youths has been published.

Internal Consistency

Not applicable because there is only a single suicidality rating item.

Concurrent Validity

The concurrent validity of the HAM–D suicidal behavior item has not been demonstrated with youths.

Dimensionality

A number of factor-analytic studies have been conducted with the HAM–D, but the results regarding clustering of symptoms have been inconsistent (Warren, 1998).

Predictive Validity

No studies examining the predictive validity of the HAM–D suicidal behavior item with youths were found.

Treatment Studies

The HAM–D has been used in a number of treatment studies of affective disorders among youths (e.g., Ambrosini et al., 1999; Goodnick et al., 2000; Kye et al., 1996; Swedo et al., 1997; West et al., 1994). However, the scale apparently has not been used in treatment studies of suicidal youths per se.

Summary and Evaluation

The HAM–D is one of the oldest and most widely used clinician rating scales, particularly in treatment studies. The HAM–D was developed for use with adults already diagnosed with depressive disorder. The HAM–D has one item assessing suicidal behaviors—this item is not consistent with O'Carroll et al.'s (1996) recommendations regarding nomenclature and should not be used by itself as a screen for suicidality.

Where to Obtain

Western Psychological Services, 12031 Wilshire Blvd., Los Angeles, CA 90025-1251

Lifetime Parasuicide Count

Description

The Lifetime Parasuicide Count (LPC) is a brief interview developed for use with adults meeting criteria for borderline personality disorder (Linehan & Comtois, 1997). The LPC can be used as a clinical assessment or clinical research tool to assess both suicide attempts and nonsuicidal instances of self-harm behavior (collectively referred to as *parasuicidal behavior*). The interview begins with questions about the first instance and most recent instance of self-harm behavior and whether self-harm behavior was actually suicidal in intent. The second part of the interview is intended to elicit a more detailed description of self-harm behaviors. In this part of the interview, patients are asked specifically about whether they have engaged in 12 different types of self-harm behavior; whether such behavior was associated with intent to die, ambivalence, or no intention of dying; and whether the self-harm behavior resulted in medical treatment.

Populations Studied

The LPC has been used with adolescents (primarily Latinos) attending an outpatient psychiatric clinic for the assessment of depression and suicidal behaviors (Velting & Miller, 1998).

Assessment and Definitions of Suicidal Behaviors

There are no questions for assessing suicidal ideation with the LPC. In an adolescent clinical population, Velting and Miller (1998) classified any self-harm behavior associated with *ambivalence* or *intent to die* as a suicide attempt. This classification procedure is consistent with recommendations by O'Carroll et al. (1996) that suicide attempts minimally be associated with nonzero intent to die.

Reliability

No data regarding test–retest or interrater reliability of the LPC with adolescents are available.

Internal Consistency

No published data were located.

Concurrent Validity

Adolescents in an outpatient psychiatric setting with anxiety disorder, major depression, borderline personality disorder, and/or three or more Axis I psychiatric diagnoses had more suicidal behaviors than adolescents without these disorders (Velting & Miller, 1998).

Dimensionality

No published data were located.

Predictive Validity

No published data were located.

Treatment Studies

The LPC has not been used as an outcome measure in a published treatment study with adolescents.

Summary and Evaluation

The LPC may prove useful in estimating total number of suicide attempts and nonsuicidal self-harm behaviors. In other studies, the total number of suicide attempts in particular has proved to be a strong predictor of later suicidal behavior (e.g., Goldston et al., 1999). However, little psychometric data regarding the use of the LPC with adolescents are currently available. In the assessment of actual suicide attempts, the LPC could be strengthened or complemented by asking the approximate dates of the attempts—such a procedure sometimes helps clients to differentiate and better enumerate multiple suicide attempts. The Parasuicide History Interview, developed by this same research group, potentially could be used for this purpose, but this instrument has not been used previously with adolescents.

Where to Obtain

Marsha Linehan, PhD, Department of Psychology, University of Washington, Box 351525, Seattle, WA 98195-1525

Risk of Suicide Questionnaire

Description

The Risk of Suicide Questionnaire (RSQ) is a brief screening questionnaire that was developed to assist in the assessment of "unrecognized suicidality" among children and adolescents in emergency room settings. The scale consists of four items that can be administered by non–mental health clinicians. Recorded responses for each of the four questions can be "yes," "no," or "no response." The four items chosen for this screening questionnaire were chosen because of their sensitivity and specificity as a group (out of a sample of 14 original screening questions) in identifying youths over the cutoff typically associated with clinically significant risk on the Suicidal Ideation Questionnaire (Reynolds, 1988). The pool of screening items from which the RSQ items were chosen was developed on the basis of the existing published literature regarding risk factors for suicide, interviews with clinicians, and items from the Youth Risk Behavior Survey (Kann et al., 1998). Although described as a screening instrument for suicide risk, this instrument is classified with detection instruments because three of the four questions focus on the presence or absence of suicidal behaviors.

Populations Studied

The RSQ has been used with children and adolescents in an emergency department setting (Horowitz et al., 2001).

Assessment and Definitions of Suicidal Behaviors

The four items of the RSQ focus on whether the children were in the emergency room because they tried to hurt themselves, whether they have been having thoughts about hurting themselves in the past week, whether they ever tried to hurt themselves in the past, and whether something very stressful happened to them in the past few weeks. The questions regarding both suicidal attempts and suicidal ideation (i.e., "hurting yourself") are worded in such a way as to potentially elicit information about nonsuicidal self-injurious behavior and related ideation in addition to suicidal ideation and behavior.

Reliability

No information about the reliability of the RSQ was found.

Internal Consistency

The internal consistency of the four-item screener apparently has not yet been evaluated.

Concurrent Validity

The four RSQ items were chosen on the basis of their relationship with the Suicidal Ideation Questionnaire (SIQ; Horowitz et al., 2001). The relationship of the individual screening items to the criterion SIQ was moderate to poor ($\kappa = .02$ to $\kappa = .54$; Horowitz et al., 2001). The four-item screener as a whole evidenced 98% sensitivity and 37% specificity in predicting concurrently assessed risk status on the SIQ (Horowitz et al., 2001). Beyond the initial instrument development and validation sample, no information was available regarding the concurrently assessed validity of the RSQ.

Dimensionality

No information was available.

Predictive Validity

The ability of the RSQ to predict later suicidal behavior has not been evaluated.

Treatment Studies

The RSQ is intended as a screening tool and has not been used in treatment studies.

Summary and Evaluation

The RSQ is a newly developed four-item screening instrument for identifying suicidal children and adolescents in emergency room settings. The screener can be administered by non–mental health clinicians (e.g., nurses in emergency rooms). The psychometric properties of the RSQ, including reliability and predictive validity, have not yet been evaluated.

Where to Obtain

The items of the RSQ are published in the Horowitz et al. (2001) article.

Spectrum of Suicidal Behavior Scale of the Child Suicide Potential Scales

Description

The Spectrum of Suicidal Behavior Scale (SSB) is a clinician-completed, single-item 1-to-5 rating scale included in the Child Suicide Potential Scales (CSPS; Pfeffer, Conte, Plutchik, & Jerrett, 1979). The scale is appropriate for use in clinical assessment or clinical research. The SSB is an index of the severity of suicidal behavior during the preceding 6 months and therefore is distinguished from the other scales of the CSPS, which assess constructs such as life events, assaultive behavior, and stressful life events (and should be considered "risk" scales). The SSB was developed for use with 6- to 12-year-olds but has also been used with adolescents. Final ratings on the SSB are based on information obtained in semistructured interview with both the child and parents. The SSB has been used and interpreted in various ways: as an instrument assessing presence of suicidal behavior, as an instrument assessing "dangerousness" of suicidal behaviors, and as an instrument theoretically linked to suicide potential. The CSPS (including the SSB) has been translated into Hebrew.

Populations Studied

The SSB has been used in studies of child and adolescent psychiatric inpatients (King, Franzese et al., 1995; King, Hill, Naylor, Evans, & Shain, 1993; King, Segal et al., 1995; King, Segal, Naylor, & Evans, 1993; K. Miller, King, Shain, & Naylor, 1992; Milling et al., 1992; Myers, Burke, & McCauley, 1985; Pfeffer et al., 1979, 1991, 1993; Pfeffer, Solomon, Plutchik, Mizruchi, & Weiner, 1982; Zalsman et al., 2000), in nonclinically referred children

(Pfeffer et al., 1984), and in child psychiatric outpatients (Pfeffer, Conte, Plutchik, & Jerrett, 1980). The Hebrew version of the SSB has been used in studies of Israeli adolescent psychiatric inpatients, adolescent suicide attempters presenting in an emergency room setting, and adolescent nonpatients (Apter et al., 1997; Gothelf et al., 1998; Ofek, Weizman, & Apter, 1998; Stein, Apter et al., 1998).

Assessment and Definitions of Suicidal Behaviors

The presence of suicidal behaviors is rated on a 1-to-5 continuum from nonsuicidal to completed suicide. In this rating system (Pfeffer et al., 1979, p. 683), *suicidal ideation* (a rating of 2) is defined as "thoughts or verbalization of suicidal intention." *Suicidal threat* (a rating of 3) is defined as "verbalization of impending suicidal action and/or a precursor action which, if fully carried out, could have led to harm." A *mild attempt* (a rating of 4) is defined as "actual self-destructive action which realistically would not have endangered life and did not necessitate intensive medical attention." A *serious attempt* (a rating of 5) is defined as "actual self-destructive action which realistically could have led to the child's death and may have necessitated intensive medical care."

Cutoffs on the 1-to-5 rating scale have been used to define suicidal and nonsuicidal groups in research studies and can be evaluated with regard to the recommended nomenclature for suicidal behaviors (O'Carroll et al., 1996). In this context, the SSB queries regarding suicidal ideation (a minimum rating of 2) are not so broad as to include thoughts of death or thoughts of wanting to die (without suicidal ideation). The queries regarding suicidal thoughts are distinguished from less specific thoughts of death.

The queries for suicide attempts (a rating of 4 or 5) do not necessarily imply nonzero intent to die as suggested in O'Carroll et al.'s (1996) nomenclature. Rather, the suicide attempt items refer to *self-destructive action,* a term that if taken literally could refer not only to suicidal behavior but also to a variety of other life- or health-endangering or risk-taking behaviors. The SSB ratings for suicide attempts also confound issues regarding the presence or absence of suicidal behavior with the clinical characteristics of suicidal behavior. For example, suicidal behavior that "does not necessitate intensive medical attention" is rated as less severe than suicidal behavior that "may have necessitated intensive medical care." However, in at least one study (King, Hovey, Brand, & Ghaziuddin, 1997), the two ratings designating suicide attempts have been combined, avoiding the confounding of clinical characteristics with definitions of suicidal behavior.

Reliability

In two samples of 6- to 12-year-old psychiatric inpatients (Pfeffer et al., 1979, 1989), a sample of nonclinically ascertained school children (Pfeffer, Zuckerman, Plutchik, & Mizruchi, 1984), and a sample of adolescent psychiatric inpatients (K. Miller et al., 1992), high levels of interrater agreement have been found for SSB ratings (94%, 100%, and 100% agreement, and $r = .96$, respectively). In assessing suicidal behavior over a 6- to 8-year follow-up of a mixed sample of prepubescent children who were psychiatric inpatients or normal controls, the interrater reliability of the SSB was found to be moderate ($\kappa = .55$; Pfeffer et al., 1993).

Interrater reliability for the Hebrew version of the SSB was in the range of $r = .77$ to $r = .93$ (the range is provided because reliability information for the SSB was described alongside that of two other scales; Ofek et al., 1998).

Internal Consistency

The SSB yields a single rating and is therefore not amenable to tests of internal consistency.

Concurrent Validity

In different samples, SSB-assessed suicidal children were found to evidence more preoccupation with death compared with nonsuicidal children (Gothelf et al., 1998; Pfeffer et al., 1979, 1980, 1982). A number of variables were inconsistently found to be related to SSB-assessed suicidality depending on the sample: recent depression, ego functioning, parental suicidality, parental depression, aggression, perception of death as temporary, and perception of death as pleasant (Pfeffer et al., 1979, 1980, 1982, 1984).

SSB-assessed suicidal and nonsuicidal psychiatric inpatients also were found to differ with regard to family variables not assessed with the CSPS (King, Segal, Naylor, & Evans, 1993; K. Miller et al., 1992; Myers et al., 1985). Specifically, suicidal adolescent inpatients described their families as less cohesive and less adaptable (K. Miller et al., 1992), as well as having poorer overall family functioning than nonsuicidal inpatients with mood disorders (King, Segal, et al., 1993). Suicidal adolescent inpatients with mood disorders were also found to have "more distant, unaffectionate, and uncommunicative relationships with their fathers" than nonsuicidal inpatients with mood disorders (King, Segal, et al., 1993; p. 1202).

Dimensionality

Not applicable because there is only a single rating regarding suicidal behavior.

Predictive Validity

SSB ratings of suicidal behavior among adolescent psychiatric inpatients have been found to predict SSB ratings of suicidal behavior 1 year later (Ofek et al., 1998) and SIQ–JR (Suicidal Ideation Questionnaire—Junior; Reynolds, 1988) scores 6 to 8 months later (King, Hovey et al., 1997). In addition, child psychiatric inpatients and nonclinically ascertained controls rated as having suicidal ideation and suicide attempts on the Spectrum of Suicidal Behavior were three times and six times, respectively, more likely to make suicide attempts over the 6- to 8-year follow-up (Pfeffer et al., 1993).

Treatment Studies

The SSB has not been used in treatment studies.

Summary and Evaluation

The SSB has been used extensively in studies of child suicidal behaviors. When used together with the other scales of the CSPS, the SSB offers an index of severity of suicidality complemented by assessments of various risk factors. The detection items do not strictly conform to the recommendations regarding definitions of suicidal behaviors by O'Carroll et al. (1996) but can be grouped to more closely approximate this classification scheme (King, Hovey et al., 1997). Studies regarding cross-sectional correlates of SSB-assessed suicidal behaviors have yielded inconsistencies. However, the predictive validity of suicidal behavior as assessed with the SSB has been demonstrated in two samples.

Where to Obtain

Cynthia R. Pfeffer, MD, Professor of Psychiatry, Cornell University Medical College, New York Hospital—Westchester Division, 21 Bloomingdale Road, White Plains, NY 10605

Suicidal Behaviors Interview

Description

The Suicidal Behaviors Interview (SBI; Reynolds, 1989, 1990) is a semi-structured interview for assessing current suicidal behaviors in adolescents. The most recent version of the SBI consists of 20 questions, 18 of which are scored. The SBI has two sections: The first part of the interview focuses on distress, life events, and social support; the second part of the interview focuses on suicidal ideation and attempts. Responses to the SBI can be summed to a total score that is thought to reflect level or seriousness of suicidal ideation. Reynolds (1991) described the use of the SBI as a follow-up for interviewing youths identified through other screeners as being at risk. However, the SBI can also be used by itself (not in conjunction with other instruments) as a clinical assessment and clinical research tool.

Populations Studied

The psychometric characteristics of the SBI were derived from a sample of nonclinically ascertained high school students, ages 12 to 19 (some of whom were selected because of high levels of suicidal ideation in a prior screening; Reynolds, 1990). The SBI has also been used with inner-city (primarily African American and Hispanic) children and adolescents (Reynolds & Mazza, 1999) and with psychiatrically hospitalized adolescents (Champion, Carey, & Hodges, 1994, cited in Reynolds & Mazza, 1999).

Assessment and Definitions of Suicidal Behaviors

The questions in the suicidal ideation section of the SBI are based on Reynolds's notions regarding a hierarchy of seriousness of suicidal cognitions and behavior, ranging from thoughts of death, to thoughts of wanting to be dead, to general and then specific thoughts of killing oneself, to making specific preparations for suicidal behavior, to attempting suicide (Reynolds, 1990). As such, these items parallel in part the SIQ (Reynolds, 1988).

The SBI is described as focusing on current suicidal ideation; however, only one of the suicidal behavior questions explicitly focuses on "present" feelings, and the question regarding life stresses refers to "the past several months." The suicide attempt questions refer to the most recent attempt, including those that occurred more than 1 year ago.

The SBI was designed to assess a continuum of suicidal behavior rather than discrete categories of suicidal behaviors. However, similar to the CSPS, the specific items on the SBI can be evaluated with regard to the operational definitions proposed by O'Carroll et al. (1996). On the SBI, there are separate items regarding thoughts of wishing to be dead (Item 5), thoughts of killing oneself (Item 6), suicide attempts (Item 15), and nonsuicidal self-harm (Item 14). Both the suicidal ideation and suicide attempt items implicitly refer to nonzero intent to die and are consistent with the nomenclature proposed by O'Carroll et al. (1996).

Reliability

In the initial validation sample, interrater reliability of the SBI was high, as indicated by the zero-order correlation of .97 and the intraclass coefficient of .99 between pairs of interviewers (Reynolds, 1990). In a second sample of at-risk youths, the interrater reliability of the SBI was .95 (Reynolds & Mazza, 1993).

Internal Consistency

On the basis of responses to the 18 scored items, the SBI is an internally consistent instrument (overall α = .92; for boys: α = .89, for girls: α = .93, for past suicide attempters: α = .88; Reynolds, 1990). Item–total correlations ranged from .35 to .75, with a median of .62 (Reynolds, 1990). In a second sample of adolescents (Reynolds & Mazza, 1993), the SBI also was internally consistent (α = .90). In a third sample of children and adolescents from inner-city schools (Reynolds & Mazza, 1999), the SBI suicidal ideation factor and the three-item suicide attempt factor both were internally consistent (α = .93 and .84, respectively).

Concurrent Validity

In a school-based and a clinically referred sample (Champion, Carey, & Hodges, 1994, cited in Reynolds & Mazza, 1999; Reynolds, 1990), SBI total scores and the three factor scores (suicidal ideation, distress, and suicide attempt) were moderately correlated with measure of depression. Among the factor scores, depression scores were most strongly related to the general distress factor (Reynolds, 1990). SBI total scores and factor scores also had moderate to strong correlations with a history of suicide attempts (Reynolds, 1990). Among the factor scores, the SBI suicide attempt factor scores were most strongly related to history of attempts (Reynolds, 1990). In two school-based samples (Reynolds, 1990; Reynolds & Mazza,

1999), SBI total scores and factor scores were consistently found to have moderate correlations with SIQ and SIQ–JR scores (ranging from .47 to .75).

Dimensionality

Three factors with eigenvalues greater than 1.0 were obtained in a principal-components analysis (Reynolds, 1990). The first factor included items assessing presence of suicidal thoughts, along with items assessing intent, plans, and steps toward actual suicide attempts. The second factor included items regarding general psychological distress (e.g., the questions about life events, social support, and wishing to be dead). The third factor included questions about perceived seriousness of actual suicide attempts, expected success of actual attempts, and recency of actual attempts.

Predictive Validity

No published data were located.

Treatment Studies

No published data were located.

Summary and Evaluation

The SBI is a highly reliable semistructured interview for assessing suicidal behaviors. The SBI can be used in conjunction with other screeners such as the SIQ or by itself as a clinical assessment tool. The queries of the SBI are consistent with recommendations for the definitions of suicidal behaviors by O'Carroll et al. (1996). However, other than correlations with questionnaires for assessing suicidal behavior in this same family of instruments (e.g., the SIQ), there are still few published data regarding the utility of the SBI.

Where to Obtain

William M. Reynolds, PhD, Department of Psychology, Humboldt State University, Arcata, CA 95521

Summary

All of the instruments in this chapter are interviews or based on interviews, but they differ substantially in the contexts in which they might be used and in their approaches for assessing suicidal behavior. For example, two instruments, the CDRS–R and the HAM–D, have been routinely used in clinical trials research to assess severity of depressive symptoms. These instruments offer the advantage of assessing the severity of suicidality in the context of other depressive symptoms (and changes over time in these symptoms). Of the two rating scales, the CDRS–R has queries that are more consistent with O'Carroll et al.'s (1996) recommended nomenclature. (Please refer to Table 4.1 for the complete instrument-by-instrument comparison of characteristics.)

Two additional instruments, the RSQ and the SSB, can be used as brief screeners or as brief indices of the severity of suicidality. Of these two, the RSQ was specifically developed for use in emergency department settings but has not been widely used in research. The SSB is a much more widely used measure in clinical assessment and clinical research. Although there are some inconsistencies in the cross-sectional correlates of the SSB across studies, the SSB has been shown to have predictive validity and, together with the other scales of the CSPS, may provide an index of severity of suicidality complemented by indices of presumed risk factors.

Three of the instruments reviewed provide opportunities for relatively comprehensive assessment of suicidality. The ASI assesses suicidal ideation severity, suicide attempt severity, and exposure to suicidality. The SBI also has queries regarding frequency of thoughts of death and suicidal ideation, specificity of suicide plans, communications about suicidality, and recency and intent associated with suicide attempts. The LPC provides a method for inquiring about both suicidal and nonsuicidal self-harm behavior (but not suicidal ideation) and the medical consequences of this behavior.

Table 4.1

Characteristics of Interviews Developed Specifically for Assessment of Suicidal Behaviors and Clinician-Rating Scales That Can Be Used to Assess Suicidality

Instrument	Instrument type[a]	Populations in which suicidal behaviors examined[b]	Assess suicidal ideation	Assess suicide attempts	Assess total number of attempts	Assess non-suicidal self-harm	Consistent with O'Carroll et al.'s operational definitions[c]	Reliability data[d]	Concurrent validity evidence	Predictive validity evidence	Used as outcome measure in suicidality studies
ASI/MASI	Interview	Clin, Res, Sch	+	+	+	–	++	+	–	–	–
CDRS–R	Clinician	Clin, DepPar, Sch	+	+	–	–	+	+	+	+	–
HAM–D	Clinician	–	+	+	–	–	–	–	–	–	–
LPC	Interview	Clin	–	+	+	+	++	–	+	–	–
RSQ	Clinician	ER	+	+	–	–	–	–	+	–	–
SSB	Clinician	Clin, ER, Sch	+	+	–	–	+	+	+	+	–
SBI	Interview	Clin, Sch	+	+	–	+	++	+	+	–	–

Note. The instruments are as follows: ASI = Adolescent Suicide Interview; MASI = Multimedia Adolescent Suicide Interview; CDRS–R = Children's Depression Rating Scale—Revised; HAM–D = Hamilton Depression Rating Scale; LPC = Lifetime Parasuicide Count; RSQ = Risk of Suicide Questionnaire; SSB = Spectrum of Suicidal Behavior Scale.

[a]Interview = interview designed for assessment of suicidality; Clinician = clinician rating scale.

[b]Clin = inpatient and/or outpatient psychiatric clinically referred or treatment-seeking youths; Sch = school or community samples (including nonpatient controls in research studies); DepPar = children of depressed parents; ER = youths in emergency department setting.

[c]++ complete consistency with O'Carroll et al.'s (1996) operational definitions; + mostly consistent with O'Carroll et al.'s definitions; – least consistent with O'Carroll et al.'s definitions.

[d]Reliability data for the scale if the scale was developed for the assessment of suicidality, or for specific suicidality items if the scale was developed more generally for assessment of depressive symptoms.

[e]Range of interrater reliability results given for the CDRS–R items but not specifically for the suicidality item.

Self-Report Inventories and Behavior Checklists

Many mental health professionals routinely use behavior checklists and self-report inventories in their clinical practice and in research. These behavior checklists and inventories differ in whether they are designed for assessing a broad range of behavioral problems (a *broad-band* instrument) or are more narrowly focused on a single set of problems or symptoms (a *narrow-band* instrument). With regard to the assessment of suicidality, there are two types of broad-band instruments: those that include a single or small number of items dedicated to the assessment of suicidality (e.g., Achenbach scales, including the Child Behavior Checklist [Achenbach, 1991a, 1991b], Teacher Report Form [Achenbach, 1991a, 1991c], and Youth Self-Report [Achenbach, 1991a, 1991d]) and those that include entire scales devoted to the assessment of suicidal ideation and behavior (e.g., Adolescent Psychopathology Scale; Reynolds, 1988). Paralleling the two types of broad-band instruments, there are two types of narrow-band instruments that can be used to examine suicidality. These include instruments that assess suicidality in the context of other narrowly defined problems such as depression (e.g., Beck Depression Inventory [Beck & Steer, 1987] and Children's Depression Inventory [Kovacs, 1985, 1992]) and those that are devoted specifically to the assessment of suicidality (e.g., Beck Scale for Suicidal Ideation [Beck & Steer, 1991], Suicidal Ideation Questionnaire [Reynolds, 1998], and Suicidal Behaviors Questionnaire [Linehan, 1996]).

With those instruments in which only a single item or few items are focused on assessing suicidal behaviors, clinicians and researchers can look to the specific or critical items as quick screens for the presence/absence or severity of suicidality. As is the case elsewhere in this book, when there are single or stand-alone critical items for assessing suicidal behavior (that are not meant to be combined into a single dimensional scale of suicidality), information about internal consistency and dimensionality is not provided.

Those instruments designed specifically for assessing suicidal ideation and behaviors or with scales specifically developed for this topic can be used to more thoroughly assess suicidal behaviors. Because of this more thorough assessment (and often, the greater range of responses than would be afforded with single or a small number of items), these questionnaires also have potential use as a means of monitoring the course or improvement of suicidality over time in clinical settings and in treatment outcome studies.

Achenbach Child Behavior Checklist, Teacher Report Form, and Youth Self-Report

Description

The Achenbach Child Behavior Checklist (CBCL) is a factor-analytic-derived behavior checklist completed by parents or guardians (Achenbach, 1991a, 1991b). The CBCL has extensive normative data. Assessed are total behavior problems, broad-band behavior problems (e.g., internalizing behavior problems and externalizing behavior problems), and more narrow-band behavior problems (e.g., attention problems, anxious/depressed mood, aggressive problems, and delinquent problems). The CBCL can be given to parents of 4- to 18-year-olds. A separate version of the CBCL has been developed for the assessment of 2- and 3-year-olds. Parents or informants for 18- to 30-year-olds can complete the Young Adult Behavior Checklist (YABCL; Achenbach, 1997b).

The Achenbach Teacher Report Form (TRF) is similar in form to the CBCL but is designed to be completed by teachers (Achenbach, 1991a, 1991c). A separate version, the Caregiver/Teacher Report Form, has been developed for caregivers or teachers of 2- to 5-year-olds (Achenbach, 1997a).

Youths ages 11 to 18 can complete the Youth Self-Report (YSR; Achenbach, 1991a, 1991d). Young adults ages 18 to 30 can complete the Young Adult Self-Report (YASR; Achenbach, 1997b).

The Achenbach scales are appropriate for use in clinical assessment, clinical research, epidemiologic studies, and screening surveys. These scales have been translated into nearly 60 languages. The Achenbach scales are not measures of suicidality per se, but the different versions (with the exception of the scales for assessing 2- to 5-year-olds) each contain two items assessing suicidal ideation/behavior.

Populations Studied

In studies of suicidal behaviors, the YSR has been administered to nonclinically ascertained samples of school children (Garber et al., 1998; Reinherz et al., 1995; Sourander, Helstela, Haavisto, & Bergroth, 2001; Stanger, Achenbach, & McConaughy, 1993). In one of these studies (Stanger et al., 1993), the sample was chosen to be geographically, ethnically, and socioeconomically representative of the United States. In another, the adolescents were participating in a longitudinal study of youths from ages 8 to 16 in Finland. The YSR also has been administered to adolescents clinically referred because of their suicidality (Ritter, 1990) and unselected adolescent psychiatric inpatients in Australia (Rey & Bird, 1991).

The CBCL has been administered to parents of Australian (primarily White) high school students to examine issues related to suicidality (Martin, Clarke, & Pearce, 1993; Martin & Waite, 1994). In studies of suicidal behaviors, the CBCL (and questionnaires with similar or identical items) have been used in a large nationally representative sample of American school children (Stanger et al., 1993), in a community sample in Canada (Joffe, Offord, & Boyle, 1988), and in a community sample in Finland (Sourander et al., 2001).

Assessment and Definitions of Suicidal Behaviors

On the Achenbach scales, respondents are asked to decide whether the behaviors of interest are *not true* (a score of 0), *somewhat or sometimes true* (a score of 1), or *very true or often true* (a score of 2) for the last 6 months. There are two suicidal ideation/behavior items on the CBCL, TRF, and YSR. The suicidal ideation item simply asks whether youths think about killing themselves. The suicide attempt item asks whether youths deliberately harm themselves or attempt suicide.

The suicidal ideation item is straightforward and implies nonzero intent to die. In contrast, the suicide attempt item is worded so broadly as to elicit not only responses regarding suicidal behavior but also responses about nonsuicidal self-harm behavior.

Reliability

No data are provided for the individual items regarding suicidal ideation/behavior. However, a test of 1 week test–retest reliability has been conducted for the entire scale and found to be very high (r = .95; Achenbach, 1991b).

Internal Consistency

Not applicable because there are only two items.

Concurrent Validity

In a sample of Australian students, responses to the YSR items regarding suicidal thoughts, deliberate self-harm, and the YSR depression scale (adjusted for the suicidal items for girls) were all found to be strongly interrelated as expected (Martin & Waite, 1994). In this same sample, higher scores on the suicidal thoughts and deliberate self-harm items were associated with lower perceived maternal and paternal care and higher perceived maternal and paternal protection (Martin & Waite, 1994).

In a longitudinal study of school children, suicidal ideation at age 15 as assessed with the Children's Depression Inventory and the YSR was predicted by early onset psychiatric disorders and family arguments and violence (Reinherz et al., 1995). Early health problems were related to suicidal ideation among boys, and low self-esteem was related to suicidal ideation among girls (Reinherz et al., 1995).

In a longitudinal study of youths in Finland, reports on the CBCL and YSR of suicidal ideation at age 16 were associated more with CBCL and YSR externalizing and internalizing behavioral problems and greater mental health service use at age 16 (Sourander et al., 2001). CBCL- and YSR-assessed suicidality at age 16 also was predicted by total depression scores on the Children's Depression Inventory at age 8 (Sourander et al., 2001).

Dimensionality

Depending on the age and gender group, the deliberate self-harm and suicidal thoughts items either load on factors associated with thought problems, anxiety, and depression or are associated with none of the factor-analytic-derived scales.

Predictive Validity

In a nationally representative sample, items on the ACQ (Achenbach, Conners, and Quay) Behavior Checklist regarding suicidal ideation and behavior (which are worded almost identically to those on the CBCL) were directly (in path analyses) predictive of school behavior problems and family mental health services but were not directly related to suicidality 3 years later for children and adolescents (Stanger et al., 1993). In contrast, in a sample of sixth-grade school children, Garber et al. (1998) found that a suicide index composed of the sum of responses to five measures of suicidality (including the YSR and the CBCL suicidal ideation/behavior items) was moderately predictive of suicidal ideation 1 year later.

Treatment Studies

No published treatment studies of suicidal youths with the Achenbach scales were located.

Summary and Evaluation

The Achenbach instruments are very widely used in clinical settings and in research. However, there is only minimal assessment of suicidal behaviors in these instruments, and responses to the suicidality items by themselves have not been found to be directly predictive of later suicidal behavior. Hence, the Achenbach instruments should not be used as the primary or only assessment instrument for suicidality.

Where to Obtain

University Medical Education Associations, One South Prospect Street, Room 6434, Burlington, VT 05401-3456

Adolescent Psychopathology Scale and Adolescent Psychopathology Scale—Short Form

Description

The Adolescent Psychopathology Scale (APS) is a self-report instrument designed to evaluate psychiatric disorders and other psychological problems in adolescents (Reynolds, 1998). The scale assesses symptoms of 20 clinical (*DSM–IV* Axis I; American Psychiatric Association, 1994) disorders and 5 personality disorders, 11 psychosocial problem content areas, and includes four response style indicators. The APS Suicide Scale is one of the psychosocial problem content scales and includes eight items.

An abbreviated version, the APS–Short Form (APS–SF), has also been developed and includes a six-item Suicide Scale (Reynolds, 2000). The APS and APS–SF are appropriate for clinical assessment, clinical research, and epidemiologic/screening surveys.

Populations Studied

Both the APS and APS–SF have been validated with community (school) and mixed clinical (mental health centers, psychiatric hospitals, private practices, residential treatment facilities, youth correctional facilities, etc.) samples (Reynolds, 1998, 2000). Beyond the development and validation samples, the APS also has been used to study suicidal behaviors in a high school sample (Mazza, 2000).

Assessment and Definitions of Suicidal Behaviors

In the APS, there are eight items that assess suicidal behavior and related constructs (Reynolds, 1998); in the APS–SF, there are six items assessing the same constructs (Reynolds, 2000). The Suicide Scales of the APS and APS–SF include questions about thoughts of wanting to die, suicidal ideation, suicide attempts, and whether respondents have tried to hurt themselves. With the exception of the last query regarding attempts to hurt oneself (which may elicit responses about both suicidal and nonsuicidal thoughts and behavior), the items are consistent with the nomenclature of O'Carroll et al. (1996).

Reliability

In a school-based sample, the 2-week test–retest reliability of the APS Suicide Scale was $r = .89$ (Reynolds, 1988).

Internal Consistency

In the standardization (school) sample, the internal consistency of the APS Suicide Scale was high, $\alpha = .88$ (Reynolds, 1988). Item–total Suicide Scale correlations ranged between .45 and .71 for the school sample and .57 to .76 for the clinical sample (Reynolds, 1988).

The internal consistency of the APS–SF Suicide Scale was $\alpha = .87$ (Reynolds, 2000). Item–total Suicide Scale correlations ranged from .55 to .73 for standardization sample and .60 to .80 for the clinical sample (Reynolds, 2000).

Dimensionality

The APS Suicide Scale items loaded on a single factor in the clinical and standardization samples (Reynolds, 1988). Likewise, the APS–SF Suicide

Scale items loaded on a single factor in the combined school and clinical standardization samples (Reynolds, 2000).

Concurrent Validity

In the school standardization and clinical validation samples, the APS Suicide Scale was correlated with all of the other clinical disorder, personality disorder, and psychosocial problem scales (Reynolds, 1988). Among the clinical scales, the APS Suicide Scale was most highly correlated with the Depression, Dysthymia, Schizophrenia, Posttraumatic Stress Disorder, Adjustment Disorder, and Panic scales (Reynolds, 1988). Among the personality disorder scales, the APS Suicide Scale was most highly correlated with the Borderline Personality Disorder Scale (Reynolds, 1988).

The APS–SF Suicide Scale also was correlated with all other APS–SF scales in the school standardization samples, and all other scales except the Substance Use Disorder scale in the clinical samples (Reynolds, 2000). In both samples, the APS–SF Suicide Scale was most highly correlated with the Major Depression and Post Traumatic Stress Disorder scales (Reynolds, 2000).

The APS and APS–SF Suicide Scales were significantly correlated with all of the Minnesota Multiphasic Personality Inventory (MMPI) validity and clinical scales except the Mf (Masculinity–Femininity) scale (Reynolds, 1998, 2000). The APS and APS–SF Suicide Scales were most highly correlated with the following MMPI scales: F (Infrequency or general distress), D (Depression), Pa (Paranoia or hypersensitivity), Pt (Psychasthenia or anxiety), and Sc (Schizophrenia; Reynolds, 1988, 2000).

Both the APS and APS–SF Suicide Scales were correlated in predicted manner with other depression, hopelessness, and suicidal ideation measures in school validation and clinical samples (Reynolds, 1988, 2000). In a separate study, the APS Suicide Scale suicide attempt item was found to be associated with severity of posttraumatic stress disorder symptoms, depression, and suicidal ideation (Mazza, 2000).

Predictive Validity

No published studies regarding the predictive validity of the APS Suicide Scales were found.

Treatment Studies

No published treatment studies were found.

Summary and Evaluation

The APS and APS–SF assess the severity of symptoms of several psychiatric disorders and problem areas. The items of the Suicide Scales on the APS and APS–SF are largely consistent with O'Carroll et al.'s (1996) recommended nomenclature. Both scales have been well validated, but the scales have not been used much in published studies beyond the validation samples. Furthermore, the predictive validity of the APS and APS–SF Suicide Scales has not been demonstrated.

Where to Obtain

Psychological Assessment Resources, Inc., P.O. Box 998, Odessa, FL 33556

Beck Depression Inventory Suicide Item

Description

The Beck Depression Inventory (BDI; Beck & Steer, 1987) is a 21-item self-report inventory designed to measure severity of depressive symptoms. The scale was developed for use with adults but has also been widely used with adolescents (Steer & Beck, 1988). Consistent with Beck's cognitive perspective on the etiology and treatment of depression, the BDI is weighted toward the cognitive symptoms of depression. The BDI–II (Beck, Steer, & Brown, 1996) is a 21-item revision of the BDI and is more oriented toward the symptoms of depression as described in *DSM–IV* (American Psychiatric Association, 1994) than the original BDI. The BDI and BDI–II have been translated into other languages, including Spanish, Portuguese, Chinese, French, Korean, German, Turkish, Arabic, Bulgarian, Swedish, and Danish. The scales are appropriate for clinical assessment and clinical research. The BDI and BDI–II are not measures of suicidality per se but do contain a single item assessing suicidal ideation.

Populations Studied

The BDI suicidal ideation item has been examined in studies of junior high and high school students and adolescents in the community (Ivarsson, Gillberg, Arvidsson, & Broberg, 2002; Larsson, Mein, Breitholtz, & Andersson, 1991; Lewinsohn et al., 1993, 1994; Olsson & von Knorring, 1997; Stewart, Lam, Betson, & Chung, 1999; Teri, 1982), adolescent psychiatric outpatients (Steer, Kumar, Ranieri, & Beck, 1998), and adolescent psychiatric inpatients (Ivarsson, Larsson, & Gillberg, 1998; Larsson & Ivarsson, 1998).

Assessment and Definitions of Suicidal Behaviors

The suicide items for the BDI and BDI–II are identical except for the time frames. The time frame for the BDI references the last week, and the time frame for the BDI–II references the last 2 weeks. On the BDI or BDI–II item, respondents are asked to decide whether they have had no thoughts about suicide, have had suicidal thoughts that would not be acted upon, have had a desire to kill themselves, or would kill themselves if given the chance. A rating of 2 or greater on this single item would yield a response consistent with O'Carroll et al.'s (1996) proposed nomenclature for suicidal behavior. The item does not confound thoughts of death and suicidal ideation.

There is no item on the BDI or BDI–II for assessing suicide attempts per se. However, an item has been added to the Swedish version of the BDI inquiring about previous suicide attempts (Olsson & von Knorring, 1999).

Reliability

In a community sample of adolescents, the long-term (1 year) test–retest reliability of the BDI suicidal ideation item was .27 (Lewinsohn et al., 1993). Among Swedish high school students, it was found that 40% of adolescents obtaining scores of 2 or 3 on the BDI suicidal ideation item still reported significant suicidal ideation (a score of 2 or 3) when retested 4- to 6-weeks later (Larsson et al., 1991).

Internal Consistency

Not applicable because there is only a single item.

Concurrent Validity

In a community sample of adolescents, the BDI suicidal ideation item was related to past suicide attempts (OR = 3.9; Lewinsohn et al., 1993). In a community sample of adolescents in Hong Kong, BDI-assessed suicidal ideation was moderately related to overall severity of depressive symptoms (Stewart et al., 1999). In high school students in Sweden, 27% of adolescents who received a score of 2 or 3 on the BDI suicidal ideation item had made a previous suicide attempt, in contrast to only 3% of adolescents with no or minimal suicidal thoughts (Larsson et al., 1991). Among adolescent psychiatric inpatients, 88% of adolescents reporting a prior suicide attempt (including attempts that precipitated the current hospital admissions) had moderate or severe suicidal ideation, in contrast to 16% of hospitalized adolescents without prior attempts (Larsson & Ivarsson, 1998).

Dimensionality

Factor analyses of BDI–II data from adolescent psychiatric outpatients yielded three factors that corresponded roughly to cognitive symptoms, somatic-affective symptoms, and guilt/punishment (Steer et al., 1998). The suicidal ideation BDI–II item loaded on the factor with other cognitive symptoms of depression (the largest factor). In two other samples of school children, one in the United States and one in Sweden, the BDI suicidal ideation item also loaded on the largest factor extracted in a principal-components analysis (Olsson & von Knorring, 1997; Teri, 1982).

Predictive Validity

In a community sample of adolescents, the BDI suicidal ideation item was found to be predictive of both future suicide attempts (OR = 6.9) and future depressive episodes (OR = 2.1; Lewinsohn et al., 1994). In a Swedish study, 44% of formerly psychiatrically hospitalized adolescents who at follow-up 2 to 4 years later reported moderate to severe suicidal ideation also had such thoughts during their index hospitalization (Ivarsson et al., 1998).

D. Shaffer (personal communication, October 1999) screened a large number of high school students with instruments including the BDI. Students were considered to be at risk on the basis of their responses to another instrument, the Columbia Teen Screen (see chap. 8, this volume). A large sampling of students, approximately half of whom were thought to be at risk, were followed up approximately 3 to 4 years later. A response of >0 (0 to 4 rated) on the BDI suicidal ideation item was found to have 57% sensitivity and 64% specificity in predicting suicidal ideation over 1 year according to the DISC administered at the second assessment. A response of >1 on the suicidal ideation had only 7% sensitivity and 94% specificity in predicting DISC-assessed suicidal ideation. In this same study, scores of >0 on the BDI suicidal ideation item had 74% sensitivity and 64% specificity in predicting suicide attempts since the initial screen (D. Shaffer, personal communication, October 1999). Scores of >1 had 20% sensitivity but 95% specificity in predicting later attempts.

Treatment Studies

The BDI has been used in multiple treatment studies with adults, but the BDI suicidal ideation item has not specifically been used in treatment studies with youths.

Summary and Evaluation

The BDI is a widely used measure of depression severity in adolescents and adults but is not appropriate for preadolescents. The BDI suicidal ideation item has been used in studies of suicidal behavior but does not yield any information about suicide attempts. An additional suicide attempt item has been added by researchers to the Swedish version of the BDI. The BDI suicidal ideation item has been shown to have predictive use; however, scores of >0 (0 to 4 rated) on this item have generally been found to be much more sensitive in predicting later suicidal ideation and attempts than scores of >1.

Where to Obtain

The Psychological Corporation, 555 Academic Court, San Antonio, TX 78204

Beck Scale for Suicidal Ideation

Description

The Beck Scale for Suicidal Ideation (BSI, also referred to as the BSS; Beck & Steer, 1991) is a self-report measure based on the semistructured interview, the Scale for Suicidal Ideation, or SSI (Beck, Kovacs, & Weissman, 1979). The SSI was developed for use with adult psychiatric patients and assesses suicidal ideation over the last week. Steer and Beck (1988) suggested that the SSI is appropriate for research with adolescents as well, and one study has even used the SSI with preadolescents (e.g., Kashani, Soltys, Dandoy, Vaidya, & Reid, 1991). A French self-report adaptation of the SSI was developed (De Man, Balkou, & Iglesias, 1987), validated in French-speaking adolescents (De Man, Leduc, & Lebreche-Gauthier, 1993), and then translated back into English and used with English-speaking adolescents (De Man & Leduc, 1994). A modified (self-report) version of the Scale for Suicidal Ideation (the MSSI) has also been developed (I. Miller, Norman,

Bishop, & Dow, 1986) but has rarely been used with adolescents (Esposito & Clum, 1999).

The BSI is an easy-to-administer 21-item self-report questionnaire (only 19 of the items are scored) that has promise for greater use with adolescents than the SSI (Beck & Steer, 1991). The authors of the BSI suggested that the instrument is best used to detect and measure severity of suicidal ideation, which is considered to be an indication for suicide risk (Beck & Steer, 1991). As such, the BSI is appropriate for both clinical assessment and clinical research. However, the authors cautioned that the BSI should not be the only instrument used for assessing suicidality and suggested that "any positive response to any BSI item may reflect the presence of suicide intention and should be investigated by the clinician" (Beck & Steer, 1991, p. 8).

Populations Studied

The BSI has been used with adolescent psychiatric inpatients (Kumar & Steer, 1995; Steer, Kumar, & Beck, 1993b) and outpatients (Rathus & Miller, 2002) but apparently has not yet been used in published studies of nonclinically ascertained participants.

Assessment and Definitions of Suicidal Behaviors

The BSI begins with five items assessing wish to live, wish to die, reasons to live versus reasons to die, active suicidal ideation (e.g., the respondents have a moderate to strong desire to kill themselves), and passive suicidal ideation (e.g., the respondents would not take the steps necessary to avoid death if they found themselves in a life-threatening situation). If the respondents totally deny active or passive suicidal ideation, they are directed to the last two items (Items 20 and 21) of the questionnaire assessing past suicide attempts and wish to die during the last attempt. If respondents do admit to at least some active or passive suicidal ideation, they complete Items 6 through 19, assessing duration and frequency of suicidal ideation, ambivalence regarding the suicidal ideation, specific deterrents to suicide and reasons for living, suicide plan and opportunity, expectations about following through with an attempt, and preparations in anticipation of suicide.

The BSI is one of the more thorough instruments for assessing severity of suicidal ideation and one of the only assessment devices for assessing passive suicidal ideation. The total score yields a severity score, but individual items can be used as screens for active suicidal ideation, passive ideation, and past attempts. The items assessing thoughts of death are separate from items assessing suicidal ideation per se. The active suicidal ideation screening item (Item 4) is consistent with the O'Carroll et al. (1996) recommended nomenclature.

Reliability

No published data were located.

Internal Consistency

In two samples of adolescent psychiatric inpatients, the BSI was found to be internally consistent as indicated by αs of .95 and .96 (Kumar & Steer, 1995; Steer et al., 1993b).

Concurrent Validity

Among adolescent psychiatric inpatients, BSI scores have been found to be positively correlated with the total number of presenting problems (Kumar & Steer, 1995), severity of depression (Kumar & Steer, 1995; Reinecke, DuBois, & Schultz, 2001; Steer et al., 1993b), severity of anxiety (Kumar & Steer, 1995; Reinecke et al., 2001; Steer et al., 1993b), the diagnosis of mood disorder (Steer et al., 1993b), negative problem-solving orientation (Reinecke et al., 2001), avoidant problem-solving style (Reinecke et al., 2001), hopelessness (Reinecke et al., 2001; Steer et al., 1993b), the BDI suicidal ideation item (Steer et al., 1993b), and another measure of suicidal ideation (Reinecke et al., 2001). Findings regarding the relationship between BSI scores and past suicidal behavior have been inconsistent (Kumar & Steer, 1995; Steer et al., 1993b).

Dimensionality

In data from adult inpatients, five factors were extracted from the BSI. These were interpreted as reflecting intensity of suicidal ideation, active suicidal desire, suicide planning, passive suicide desire, and concealment (Beck & Steer, 1991). No factor-analytic studies have been conducted with adolescents.

Predictive Validity

In recent studies with adult psychiatric outpatients, suicidal ideation "at its worst point" and current suicidal ideation assessed with the SSI were found to predict later suicide (Beck, Brown, Steer, Dahlsgaard, & Grisham, 1999; G. Brown, Beck, Steer, & Grisham, 2000). However, no studies have examined the predictive use of the BSI with adolescent populations.

Treatment Studies

In a pilot study of dialectical behavior therapy (biweekly individual and family sessions) with 10 suicidal adolescents who exhibited symptoms of borderline personality disorder, suicidal ideation as assessed with the self-report version of the SSI decreased from mean scores of 9.8 (SD = 5.3) at pretreatment to 3.8 (SD = 4.6) at posttreatment 12 weeks later (Rathus & Miller, 2002).

Summary and Evaluation

The BSI is one of the more thorough instruments for assessing suicidal ideation and one of the only scales to assess passive suicidal ideation in addition to active suicidal ideation. The BSI is appropriate for use with adolescents and has been used in a small pilot study of dialectical behavioral therapy with suicidal adolescents who exhibited symptoms of borderline personality disorder. Nonetheless, test–retest reliability data are not available for the BSI with adolescents, nor has the BSI been used in nonclinically ascertained samples. In adult samples, current suicidal ideation and suicidal ideation at its worst point have been found to be predictive of later suicide; however, the predictive validity of the BSI (and the interview form, the SSI) has not been demonstrated with adolescents.

Where to Obtain

The Psychological Corporation, 555 Academic Court, San Antonio, TX 78204

Children's Depression Inventory Suicide Item

Description

The Children's Depression Inventory (CDI) is a self-report inventory designed for the assessment of depression with children and adolescents ages 7 to 17 (Kovacs, 1985, 1992). The CDI was initially developed because of concerns regarding the use of the BDI with younger populations. The

CDI is appropriate for clinical assessment and research and has 27 sets of items; respondents are asked to choose which of three sentences (in each set) best describes his or her thoughts and feelings over the last 2 weeks. The CDI yields a total score (ranging from 0 to 54) as well as five subscores: Mood, Interpersonal Problems, Ineffectiveness, Anhedonia, and Negative Self-Esteem. Scores of 19 and above are thought to be associated with clinically significant depression. The CDI is not a measure of suicidality per se, but it does include a single item assessing suicidal ideation. A parent-report version of the CDI, the P–CDI, has also been developed (Garber, 1984).

Populations Studied

The CDI suicidal ideation item has been examined in samples of school children and adolescents (Chartier & Lassen, 1994; Kovacs, 1992; Larsson & Melin, 1992; Overholser, Adams, Lehnert, & Brinkman, 1995), bereaved children and adolescents (Cerel et al., 1999; Pfeffer, Karus, Siegel, & Jiang, 2000), adolescents referred to outpatient psychiatry settings (Kovacs, 1992), inpatient psychiatry children and adolescents (Joiner et al., 2000; Overholser et al., 1995), and sexually abused children and adolescents (Wozencraft, Wagner, & Pellegrin, 1991).

Assessment and Definitions of Suicidal Behaviors

Suicidal ideation is measured with one item with the following response choices: respondents do not think about killing themselves (rated 0), they think about killing themselves but would not do it (rated 1), or they want to kill themselves (rated 2). Scores of 1 or 2 on this item obviously indicate suicidal thoughts. This item refers to thoughts about suicidal actions with nonzero intent to die and is therefore consistent with O'Carroll et al.'s (1996) suggested definitions.

There is not an item on the CDI assessing suicide attempts. Therefore, the CDI in its copyrighted form is not well suited to screening for individuals with suicide attempts. However, Overholser et al. (1995) has developed several additional questions that can be appended to the CDI assessing previous suicidal behavior.

Reliability

In a sample of second- to sixth-grade school children, researchers found that 50% of the youths who endorsed the CDI suicidal ideation item at an initial screening continued to endorse the suicidal ideation item at a second testing 6 to 9 weeks later (Larsson & Melin, 1992).

Internal Consistency

Not applicable because there is only a single item.

Concurrent Validity

In the normative sample of youths, the CDI suicidal ideation was correlated with the total scores from the remaining CDI items, $r = .45$ (Kovacs, 1992). In an outpatient psychiatric sample, a sample of youths newly diagnosed with diabetes, and a second sample of school children, the CDI suicidal ideation item was correlated with CDI total scores, $rs = .52, .22$, and .49, respectively (Kovacs, 1992). In a sample of sexually abused youths, the CDI item regarding suicidal ideation was correlated with the rest of the CDI, $r = .27$ (Wozencraft et al., 1991). In a sample of second- to sixth-grade school children, endorsement of the CDI ideation item was significantly related to scoring above the cutoff for clinically significant depression scores on the CDI (Larsson & Melin, 1992).

In a sample of clinically referred sexually abused youths (ages 5 to 17), endorsement of the CDI suicidal ideation item was related to several characteristics of abuse, such as the perpetrator being a family member, having a mother who was rated as less compliant with the evaluation, and remaining in the family home following the investigation of abuse (Wozencraft et al., 1991). In a longitudinal study of school children, suicidal ideation at age 15 as assessed with the CDI and the Achenbach YSR was predicted by early onset psychiatric disorders and parental arguments and violence (Reinherz et al., 1995). Early health problems were related to suicidal ideation among boys, and low self-esteem was related to suicidal ideation among girls (Reinherz et al., 1995). A relationship between low self-esteem and CDI suicidal ideation also was found in a sample of adolescent psychiatric inpatients and a high school comparison group (Overholser et al., 1995).

Dimensionality

In addition to a single higher order factor (depression), five primary factors have been identified in factor-analytic studies of the CDI: Negative Mood, Interpersonal Problems, Ineffectiveness, Anhedonia, and Negative Self-Esteem (Kovacs, 1992). In the normative sample, the suicidal ideation most strongly loads on the Negative Self-Esteem factor (Kovacs, 1992). In a clinical sample, the suicidal ideation item most strongly loads on the Negative Mood factor (Kovacs, 1992). In a sample of incarcerated adolescents (Esposito & Clum, 1999), the suicidal ideation item was one of two items that did not load on any of the seven factors identified.

Predictive Validity

In a sample of sixth-grade school children, Garber et al. (1998) found that a suicide index composed of the sum of responses to five measures of suicidality (including the CDI suicidal ideation item) was moderately predictive of suicidal ideation 1 year later.

Treatment Studies

No published studies of the treatment of suicidal youths were located that used the CDI suicidal ideation item.

Summary and Evaluation

The CDI is a widely used self-report questionnaire for assessing severity of depressive symptoms. For younger children (for whom "older" depression inventories such as the BDI are not appropriate), the CDI may be particularly useful. The CDI assesses only suicidal ideation and not suicide attempts, but a suicide attempt item has been developed by researchers for use with the CDI. However, the predictive validity of the CDI suicidal ideation item, by itself, has not been evaluated.

Where to Obtain

Multi-Health Systems, Inc., 908 Niagara Falls Boulevard, North Tonawanda, NY 14120-3003

Dimensions of Depression Profile for Children and Adolescents

Description

The Dimension of Depression Profile for Children and Adolescents (DDPCA) is a self-report inventory that assesses five dimensions of depressive symptomatology: mood, global self-worth, energy and age-appropriate interest in activities, self-blame, and suicidal ideation. This scale was developed based on the premise that low self-esteem or low self-worth is one of the central features of depression but is often treated as a secondary symptom in diagnostic systems and depression screening instruments. The DDPCA was developed as a screening instrument for depression. The DDPCA also has potential use in clinical assessment and clinical research studies; validation with a (psychiatric) clinically referred sample is being undertaken.

The DDPCA has 30 items. For each item, respondents are given two statements (e.g., some children feel depressed a lot of the time versus other children feel happy most of the time). They are asked to decide which of the statements best describes them, and they are then asked to choose whether that statement is "sort of true for me" or "really true for me." The DDPCA yields a total score and five scale scores (corresponding to the dimensions described above).

Populations Studied

The DDPCA Suicide Ideation Scale has been administered to samples of children in the school and to youths with spina bifida (Appleton et al., 1997; Harter & Nowakowski, 1987). The manual for the DDPCA notes that studies with clinically referred youths are planned.

Assessment and Definitions of Suicidal Behaviors

The DDPCA Suicidal Ideation Scale has six items assessing whether the respondents see themselves as (a) caring if they live or die, (b) thinking about committing suicide, (c) having thoughts about killing themselves, (d) wanting to commit suicide, (e) spending long periods of time thinking about killing themselves, and (f) having reasons to live. The dimensional scale therefore does not just assess suicidal ideation but rather is a composite of responses about suicidal ideation, thoughts of wanting to die, and having deterrents to suicide. Four of the six items explicitly refer to suicide or killing oneself (implying nonzero intent to die), but these items are not separated out from the scale score for screening purposes. There is no item on the DDPCA regarding suicide attempts.

Reliability

In a sample of school children, the DDPCA Suicidal Ideation Scale had moderate test–retest stability ($r = .48$) over 1 year (Harter & Nowakowski, 1987).

Internal Consistency

The Suicidal Ideation Scale of the DDPCA was found to be internally consistent (αs = .88 and .90) in two samples of sixth- to eighth-grade school children (Harter & Nowakowski, 1987).

Concurrent Validity

The Suicidal Ideation Scale of the DDPCA was moderately correlated with the Mood (rs = .62 and .64), Self-Worth (rs = .59 and .62), Energy/Interest (rs = .46 and .41), and Self-Blame (rs = .42 and .33) DDPCA Scales in two samples of school children (Harter & Nowakowski, 1987). Scores on the DDPCA Suicidal Ideation Scale were lower (lower scores indicate more problems/distress) for 12- to 18-year-olds with spina bifida than for youths without the disease (Appleton et al., 1997). Perceived social support from parents, classmates, and teachers was negatively related to suicidal ideation scores in this same sample (Appleton et al., 1997).

Dimensionality

A factor analysis of the DDPCA yielded four factors. In two different samples, the six suicidal ideation items on the DDPCA all had moderate to high loadings on a factor of the DDPCA that was primarily related to suicidal ideation (Harter & Nowakowski, 1987). These items did not load highly on any other factors.

Predictive Validity

No published data regarding the predictive validity of the Suicidal Ideation Scale items were located.

Treatment Studies

No published treatment studies with the DDPCA Suicidal Ideation Scale were located.

Summary and Evaluation

The DDPCA is a potentially useful scale of depressive symptomatology that reflects its authors' theoretical notions regarding the centrality of low self-esteem in the experience of depression. The DDPCA Suicide Ideation Scale has not been well studied beyond the original validation samples. Data regarding the use of the DDPCA in clinically ascertained samples have not been published, and the predictive validity of the DDPCA Suicidality Scale has not yet been established.

Where to Obtain

Dr. Susan Harter, University of Denver, Department of Psychology, 2155 S. Race Street, Denver, CO 80208-0204

Harkavy Asnis Suicide Scale

Description

The Harkavy Asnis Suicide Scale (HASS) was designed as an information-gathering tool to directly assess current and past suicidal behavior (Harkavy Friedman & Asnis, 1989a, 1989b). The self-report scale has three sections. The first section (HASS–Demo) is used for assessing demographic information (including factors found in the past to be related to suicidal behavior) and current (last week) and lifetime suicidal ideation and plans, suicide attempts, and exposure to suicidal behavior. The second section (HASS–I) has 21 questions for assessing the frequency of suicide-related and substance abuse behaviors in the last 2 weeks. The third section (HASS–II) has essentially the same questions as the second section but references lifetime suicide-related and substance abuse behaviors (except for the last 2 weeks). The HASS is appropriate for clinical assessment and clinical research.

Populations Studied

The HASS has been used both with nonclinical high school samples (Harkavy Friedman& Asnis, 1989a), with referrals to an outpatient psychiatry clinic for depression and suicidal behaviors serving primarily African American and Hispanic adolescents (Velting, Rathus, & Asnis, 1998; Velting, Rathus, & Miller, 2000; Wetzler et al., 1996), and in a treatment trial evaluating dialectical behavior therapy with adolescents who were suicidal and had at least three symptoms of borderline personality disorder (Rathus & Miller, 2002).

Assessment and Definitions of Suicidal Behaviors

The queries in the HASS–Demo regarding suicidal ideation and attempts (e.g., whether the children ever thought about killing themselves but did not actually try, whether they ever tried to kill themselves) are straightforward screening questions and are consistent with recommended definitions by O'Carroll et al. (1996).

The questions in the HASS–I and HASS–II are used to assess a continuum of nonsuicidal and suicidal ideation and behavior from feelings of worthlessness, to thoughts of death and wanting to die, to specific suicidal plans, to initiation of suicide attempts, to actually attempting suicide. Responses are summed to yield total scores reflective of frequency of suicidal thoughts and behavior; however, questions of substance abuse have also been included in the HASS–I and HASS–II because "substance abuse has been found to be associated with suicidal behavior" (Harkavy, Friedman, & Asnis, 1989a, p. 384). Hence, the total scores of the HASS–I and HASS–II confound assessment of suicidal ideation and behavior with a risk factor for suicidal ideation/behavior and substance abuse.

Reliability

No published data were located.

Internal Consistency

In nonclinical and unspecified clinical samples of adolescents, both the HASS–I and the HASS–II were found to be internally consistent (αs = .90 to .92, and .91 to .92, respectively; Harkavy Friedman & Asnis, 1989a).

Concurrent Validity

In high school students, HASS–I and HASS–II total scores correlated moderately with depression, impulsiveness, aggression, and negative life stress (Harkavy Friedman & Asnis, 1989a). These scores did not correlate with life stress or social desirability (Harkavy Friedman & Asnis, 1989a).

In a primarily African American and Hispanic outpatient psychiatric sample, adolescents with histories of suicide attempts or suicidal ideation (defined on the basis of the HASS screening questions) scored higher than nonsuicidal youths on the Recent Passive Suicidal Ideation, Lifetime Suicidal Plans and Action, Lifetime Suicidal Ideation, and Lifetime Thoughts of Death factors of the HASS (Wetzler et al., 1996). Adolescents with suicide attempts also had higher scores on the Recent Suicidal Plans and Action and Lifetime Suicidal Plans and Actions factors of the HASS than youths with suicidal ideation only (Wetzler et al., 1996). All three suicide attempt and ideation groups reported more severe depression symptoms than non-suicidal youths (Wetzler et al., 1996).

Velting et al. (1998) reported that 50% of adolescents in a primarily African American and Hispanic outpatient psychiatric setting provided discrepant information about past suicide attempts on the screening items of the HASS and a structured diagnostic interview, the Structured Clinical Interview for DSM–IV (SCID). However, the largest number of discrepant reports in this study were attributable to confusion between suicide attempts and suicide gestures (the latter defined as not being associated with *intent*); suicide intent is not an all-or-nothing categorization, and suicide gesture is not a recommended term by O'Carroll et al. (1996), clouding the interpretation of these results.

Dimensionality

In a sample of high school students who completed the HASS anonymously, the HASS–I was found to have three factors: thoughts of death and suicide, active suicidal behavior including suicide plans and suicide attempts, and substance abuse (Harkavy Friedman & Asnis, 1989a). The HASS–II was found to have four factors: thoughts of suicide, substance abuse, thoughts of death, and suicide plans and actions (Harkavy Friedman & Asnis, 1989a).

Predictive Validity

No published data were located.

Treatment Studies

The HASS has been used to assess current suicidal ideation, part of the inclusion criteria for a study of dialectical behavioral therapy with suicidal adolescents (Rathus & Miller, 2002). However, the HASS has not been used as an outcome measure in published treatment studies with adolescents.

Summary and Evaluation

The HASS assesses both suicidality and substance abuse and has been used with nonreferred patients and African American and Latino clinically referred adolescents. The screening questions of the HASS are consistent with recommended definitions of suicidal ideation and attempts by O'Carroll et al. (1996). However, the test–retest reliability of the HASS has not been demonstrated. Moreover, HASS–I and HASS–II total scores are derived in part from responses about frequency of substance use, in addition to questions about suicidal ideation and behavior.

Where to Obtain

The HASS is in Harkavy Friedman and Asnis (1989a, 1989b).

Suicidal Ideation Questionnaire

Description

The Suicidal Ideation Questionnaire (SIQ) is a screening measure for severity or seriousness of suicidal ideation (Reynolds, 1988). There are two self-report forms of the SIQ: a 30-item version originally designed for 10th, 11th, and 12th graders (named simply the SIQ), and the 15-item version originally designed for adolescents in Grades 7, 8, and 9 (named the SIQ–JR). Although the SIQ–JR was developed for use with younger adolescents, it also has been used in studies with older adolescents (Hovey & King, 1996; King, Hill, et al., 1993; King, Hovey, et al., 1997; King, Segal, et al., 1995; Sieman, Warrington, & Mangano, 1994). According to the publisher, the SIQ and SIQ–JR are not currently available in languages other than English (although investigators in Puerto Rico are currently translating the SIQ–JR into Spanish).

Respondents are asked to consider the time period of the last month when completing the SIQ. Adolescents completing the SIQ and SIQ–JR rank each of the items on a 7-point scale, ranging from 0 (*I never had this thought*) to 6 (*almost every day*). The scores of each item are summed to yield a total score, reflecting severity of suicidal ideation. Normative data (stratified by gender and junior versus high school) are provided for the SIQ and SIQ–JR. On the basis of data in a nonclinically referred sample, Reynolds (1988) suggested that adolescents who have a raw score of >41 on the SIQ or >31 on the SIQ–JR be evaluated further for "potentially significant psychopathology and suicide risk" (p. 11). In an inpatient psychiatric sample, Pinto, Whisman, and McCoy (1997) found that a cutoff score of 41 on the SIQ was highly specific but missed a significant number of suicide attempters. Hence, it was argued that a cutoff score of 20 on the SIQ in a clinical setting might prove more useful than the higher cutoff in identifying youths in need of further evaluation for suicide risk.

The SIQ and SIQ–JR can be used for clinical assessment, clinical research, and epidemiologic/screening surveys. Reynolds (1991) described the use of the combined use of the SIQ and the SBI in a multiple-stage screening procedure for identifying youths at risk for suicidal behaviors (see this volume, chap, 8).

Populations Studied

The standardization samples for the SIQ were normal high school populations (Reynolds, 1988). The SIQ also has been used with junior high school samples (Lamb & Pusker, 1991), high school samples (Carlton & Deane, 2000; Chang, 2002; Mazza & Reynolds, 1988), suicide attempters (L. Brown, Overholser, Spirito, & Fritz, 1991; Harrington et al., 1998; Shaunesey, Cohen, Plummer, & Berman, 1993; Spirito, Stark, Fristad, Hart, & Owens-Stively, 1987), adolescents in inpatient psychiatric settings (Hewitt, Newton, Flett, & Callander, 1997; Pinto & Whisman, 1996; Pinto, Whisman, & Conwell, 1998; Pinto et al., 1997; Reinecke et al., 2001; Shaunesey et al., 1993), physically abused adolescents (Shaunesey et al., 1993), nonsuicidal patients on a pediatric floor (Spirito et al., 1987), and adolescent suicide attempters presenting in an emergency room setting (Horowitz et al., 2001).

The standardization samples for the SIQ–JR were nonclinically ascertained 7th, 8th, and 9th graders (Reynolds, 1988). The SIQ–JR also has been used with high school (Grades 9–12) students (Mazza, 2000), immigrant and second-generation Latino American adolescents (Hovey and King, 1996), American Indian adolescents (Dick, Beals, Manson, & Bechtold, 1994; Keane, Dick, Bechtold, & Manson, 1996; Novins, Beals, Roberts, & Manson, 1999), primarily African American and Hispanic children and adolescents from the inner city (Reynolds & Mazza, 1999), adolescents in inpatient psychiatric settings (King, Franzese, et al., 1995; King, Hill, et al, 1993; King, Segal, et al., 1995; Sieman et al., 1994), parentally bereaved adolescents (Gutierrez, 1999), and adolescent suicide attempters in an emergency room setting (Horowitz et al., 2001).

Assessment and Definitions of Suicidal Behaviors

The questions in the SIQ and SIQ–JR are based on Reynolds's (1988) theoretical notions regarding a hierarchy of seriousness of suicidal cognitions and behavior. In this scheme, suicidal thoughts and behavior form a continuum ranging from thoughts of death, to thoughts of wanting to be dead, to general and then specific thoughts of killing oneself, to making specific preparations for suicidal behavior, to attempting suicide (Reynolds, 1988).

However, similar to Reynolds's Suicide Behavior Interview, the specific items of the SIQ and SIQ–JR can be evaluated with regard to the operational definitions proposed by O'Carroll et al. (1996). On the SIQ and the SIQ–JR, there are separate items for thoughts of death and dying (Items 5 and 6 on both the SIQ and SIQ–JR), thoughts of wishing to be dead (Item 12 on the SIQ, Item 11 on the SIQ–JR), and thoughts of killing oneself (Item 2 on both the SIQ and SIQ–JR). The wording of the suicidal ideation question refers implicitly to nonzero intent to die, consistent with the nomenclature proposed by O'Carroll et al., (1996). There is no item regarding past or current suicide attempts, so the SIQ and SIQ–JR cannot be used as an instrument to identify attempters.

Reliability

In a large sample of high school students, the SIQ had a test–retest reliability, over an interval of approximately 4 weeks, of .72 (Reynolds, 1988). In a sample of inner-city children and young adolescents, the SIQ–JR had test–retest reliability of .89 over approximately 3 weeks (Reynolds & Mazza, 1999).

Internal Consistency

In the standardization samples of 7th, 8th, and 9th graders, the SIQ–JR was found to be internally consistent (α = .94; Reynolds, 1988). Most of the item–total correlations of the SIQ–JR ranged from .62 to .86 (Reynolds, 1988). The SIQ–JR also was found to be internally consistent (αs = .96 and .91, respectively) in a sample of American Indian boarding school high school students (Dick et al., 1994) and in a sample of primarily African American and Hispanic inner-city adolescents (Reynolds & Mazza, 1999).

In the standardization samples of 10th, 11th, and 12th graders, the SIQ was found to be internally consistent (α = .97; Reynolds, 1988). Most of the item–total correlations for the SIQ range from .70 to .84 (Reynolds, 1988). In addition, the SIQ was found to be internally consistent (α = .97 and .98, respectively) among adolescents in two inpatient psychiatry samples (Hewitt et al., 1997; Pinto et al., 1997).

Concurrent Validity

In various samples of clinically and nonclinically ascertained adolescents, higher SIQ scores have been found to be related to severity of depression (Mazza, 2000; Pinto & Whisman, 1996; Reinecke et al., 2001; Reynolds, 1988), greater likelihood of mood disorder (Pinto et al., 1997), hopelessness

(Hewitt et al., 1997; Pinto & Whisman, 1996; Reinecke et al., 2001; Reynolds, 1988), anxiety (Pinto & Whisman, 1996; Reinecke et al., 2001; Reynolds, 1988), low self-esteem (Pinto & Whisman, 1996; Reynolds, 1988), more negative problem-solving orientation (Reinecke et al., 2001), more impulsive-careless and avoidance problem-solving styles (Reinecke et al., 2001), lower Reasons for Living Inventory (RFL) total scores (Pinto et al., 1998), suicide attempts (King, Raskin, Gdowski, Butkus, & Opipari, 1990), nonimpulsive (as opposed to impulsive) suicide attempts (L. Brown et al., 1991), higher scores on another suicidality measure (Reinecke et al., 2001; Reynolds & Mazza, 1994), greater severity of physical abuse (Shaunesey et al., 1993), posttraumatic stress disorders symptoms (Mazza, 2000), life stress (Chang, 2002), socially prescribed perfectionism (Hewitt et al., 1997), and anger (Pinto & Whisman, 1996).

In inpatient psychiatric samples, adolescent suicide attempters and adolescent suicide ideators did not differ with regard to scores on the SIQ. However, both groups had higher scores on the SIQ than nonsuicidal adolescent inpatients (Pinto et al., 1997; Shaunesey et al., 1993). In addition, among adolescent pediatric inpatients, suicide attempters rated as having chronic psychiatric problems had higher scores on the SIQ than did suicide attempters with acute problems (Spirito et al., 1987).

In various samples of clinically and nonclinically ascertained adolescents, higher SIQ–JR scores have been found to be associated with increased severity of depression (Dick et al., 1994; Gutierrez, 1999; Hovey & King, 1996; King , Hill et al., 1993; Mazza, 2000; Reynolds, 1988), higher levels of anxiety (Dick et al., 1994; Reynolds, 1988), posttraumatic stress disorder symptoms (Mazza, 2000), decreased self-esteem (Reynolds, 1988), higher scores on other measures of suicidality (Dick et al., 1994; King, Hill et al., 1993; King, Katz, Ghaziuddin, Brand, & McGovern, 1997; Reynolds & Mazza, 1999), suicide attempts (Mazza, 2000; Reynolds & Mazza, 1999), greater "repulsion by life" on the Multi-Attitude Suicide Tendency Scale (Gutierrez, 1999), greater acculturative stress (Hovey & King, 1996), and alcohol use (King, Hill et al., 1993). Findings regarding whether SIQ–JR scores are related to family functioning have been inconsistent (Hovey & King, 1996; King, Hill et al., 1993).

In an adolescent psychiatric inpatient sample, there was a moderate agreement (κ=.49) between adolescent reports of suicidal ideation in response to the DISC and "caseness" as defined by scoring above the 70th percentile on either the SIQ or SIQ–JR (Prinstein et al., 2001). There was fair agreement (κ=.38) between clinican ratings of suicidality and scoring above the 70th percentile on either the SIQ or SIQ–JR (Prinstein et al., 2001).

When data from the Suicidal Behaviors Interview were used as the criterion for determining clinical level of suicidal risk, cutoffs of 41 or above on the SIQ and 31 and above on the SIQ–JR were found to have use as screens for suicidal behavior (sensitivity of 79% and specificity of 69%; and sensitivity of 92% and specificity of 76%, respectively; Reynolds, 1992).

Dimensionality

A principal-components analysis of SIQ from the standardization sample of high school students yielded three factors with eigenvalues greater than 1.0 (Reynolds, 1988). The first factor (on which the majority of items loaded) included items assessing suicidal ideation, thoughts about not wanting to be alive, and thoughts regarding preparations for suicide. The second factor primarily consisted of items assessing the responses of others to suicide. The third factor included items assessing general thoughts of death and an item regarding the writing of a will.

In an inpatient psychiatric sample, a principal-components analysis of the SIQ yielded four factors; however, similar to the results in the standardization sample, the first factor accounted for a much greater proportion of variance than the other factors, suggesting the possibility that the SIQ may be assessing one primary dimension of suicidal thoughts (Pinto et al., 1997).

A principal-components analysis of the SIQ–JR from the standardization sample of seventh, eighth, and ninth graders also yielded three factors with eigenvalues greater than 1.0 (Reynolds, 1988). The first factor consisted primarily of items assessing thoughts about death or dying. The second factor included items more specifically assessing suicidal thoughts and suicidal plans. Similar to the third factor for the SIQ, the third factor of the SIQ–JR included two items assessing general thoughts of death.

Predictive Validity

The manual for the SIQ explicitly says that the "SIQ is *not* an instrument for the prediction of suicide per se" (Reynolds, 1988, p. 35). Nonetheless, in a sample of American Indian adolescents, the SIQ–JR was found to be more predictive of subsequent suicide attempts in a suicide attempt cluster 2 months later than anxiety, depression, and alcohol use (Keane et al., 1996). Moreover, among adolescent psychiatric inpatients, SIQ–JR scores have been found to be predictive of later suicide attempts (King, Segal, et al., 1995) and SIQ–JR scores half a year later (King, Hovey, et al., 1997).

Treatment Studies

When evaluating the use of the SIQ as an outcome measure, one should remember that the time frame for the SIQ is the last month. If assessments of suicidal ideation are desired more frequently than once a month, successive administrations of the SIQ will have overlapping time frames. The SIQ was used as an outcome measure in a controlled intervention trial (routine follow-up care vs. routine care in addition to home visits and family problem-solving assistance) with suicide attempters ages 16 and younger. However, no differences were found between the two interventions (Harrington et al., 1998).

The SIQ was also used as an outcome measure in an open-label trial of fluoxetine for adolescents with major depression (Colle, Belair, DiFeo, Weiss, & LaRoche, 1994). In that study, seven of the eight patients who remained on fluoxetine at least 24 weeks had significant (>50%) reductions in suicidal ideation as assessed with the SIQ. The gradual reduction in suicidal ideation was noted throughout the period of active treatment, and the lower levels of suicidal ideation were largely maintained at 1-year follow-up.

The SIQ also is being used as a measure of suicidality in the ongoing multisite NIMH-funded Treatment of Depression Study, or TADS. The TADS is a study of the relative efficacy of cognitive behavior therapy, pharmacotherapy (fluoxetine), combined pharmacotherapy and cognitive behavior therapy, and pill placebo in the treatment of major depression in adolescents.

No published treatment studies with the SIQ–JR were located.

Summary and Evaluation

The SIQ is one of the most widely used screening measures for suicidal ideation in adolescents. Both a shorter junior high and longer high school version of the SIQ are available. The junior high version of the SIQ–JR may be used with older adolescents (as well as younger youths), particularly when the sample includes youths who may have difficulty with reading or when the study requirements necessitate a brief instrument. The SIQ and SIQ–JR have been used both with clinically ascertained samples and with nonclinically ascertained adolescents including American Indians and immigrant Latino Americans. Considerable data regarding the concurrent validity of both the SIQ and SIQ–JR have been published, as well as evidence pertaining to the predictive validity of the SIQ–JR.

There are no items on the SIQ and SIQ–JR regarding attempted suicide, which is unfortunate given that history of attempted suicide is one of the strongest predictors of future suicidal behavior. The SIQ is one of the few measures of suicidality in youths that has been used as a primary outcome measure in treatment studies. In one trial, no differences were found between two interventions, but in another open-label study, suicidal ideation decreased during the period of active treatment with pharmacotherapy.

Where to Obtain

Psychological Assessment Resources, Inc., P.O. Box 998, Odessa, FL 33556

Suicidal Behaviors Questionnaire and Suicidal Behaviors Questionnaire for Children

Description

The Suicidal Behaviors Questionnaire (SBQ–14) is a self-report questionnaire designed to assess suicidal ideation and suicidal behavior (Linehan, 1996). Intake and repeated assessments versions of the SBQ–14 are available. The SBQ–14 is an expanded version of an earlier 4-item questionnaire (Linehan & Nielsen, 1981). Although responses to the items on the SBQ–14 can be summed to give an overall score reflecting seriousness of suicidal behavior for clinical assessment or research, the individual items on the SBQ also have been extracted and used as screening items for suicidal behavior and suicide risk.

The SBQ–14 is one of the few instruments to assess expectations about suicidal behavior: expectations about the likelihood of considering suicide, expectations about the likelihood of attempting suicide, expectations that death will occur if the respondent makes an attempt, expectations about problems being solved with suicide, and expectation about the availability of a means for attempting suicide.

A four-item children's version of the SBQ simplified to the third-grade level (the SBQ–C) has been developed (Cotton & Range, 1993).

Populations Studied

SBQ questions have been used in nonclinically ascertained samples (Cole, 1989a, 1989b; Osman et al., 1998), with adolescent psychiatric inpatients (Kashden, Fremouw, Callahan, & Franzen, 1993; Osman et al., 1996), and with incarcerated adolescents (Cole, 1989b).

Assessment and Definitions of Suicidal Behaviors

The most common items from the SBQ–14 for screening are those assessing suicidal ideation and behavior, suicidal communications, and expectations about future suicidal behavior. SBQ items can be used to assess frequency of suicidal thoughts, as well as frequency, methods, and intent of self-harm and suicidal behavior

The first screening item on the SBQ–14 asks about suicidal ideation and attempt together. A rating on the item of 1, 2, or 3 denotes suicidal ideation, a rating of 4 denotes suicidal ideation with a plan, and a rating of 5 or 6 denotes actual self-injurious behavior. The wording of the question ("thought about or attempted to kill yourself") implies nonzero intent to kill oneself. However, one of the rating choices (5 = "I attempted to kill myself, but I do not think I really meant to die") may elicit ambiguous information. Specifically, this rating choice may elicit responses about suicidal behavior associated with nonzero intent to die but considerable ambivalence. However, it also may elicit responses about nonsuicidal self-injurious behavior.

The four questions on the SBQ–C are very similar (and one is identical) to questions on the adult SBQ–14. These include whether the children have ever thought about or tried to kill themselves, how many times they have thought about killing themselves, whether they ever told someone that they were going to kill themselves, and whether they think that they might kill themselves someday.

Similar to the adult SBQ–14, the first question on the SBQ–C asks about both suicidal thoughts and attempts. The wording of the 6-point rating scale for this question is slightly different from that of the adult SBQ; however, ratings of 1, 2, or 3 still denote suicidal ideation, a rating of 4 corresponds to suicidal ideation with a plan, and a rating of 5 or 6 refers to suicide attempts. The wording of this first question does imply nonzero intent to kill oneself, consistent with O'Carroll et al.'s (1996) definition of suicide attempts. Nonetheless, similar to the SBQ–14, the fifth rating of the SBQ–C (on the 0-to-6 rating scale; "Yes, I tried to kill myself, but I didn't really want to die") may elicit difficult-to-interpret responses. Specifically, this rating may be used by youths who actually made suicide attempts (e.g., nonzero intent) but experience ambivalence. Youths who engage in nonsuicidal self-injurious behavior may also accurately choose this rating as best describing their behaviors.

Reliability

There are no data regarding the test–retest reliability of items on the SBQ among adolescents (although such data have been published for samples of adults; Cotton, Peters, & Range, 1995). The SBQ–C had high test–retest reliability over 2 to 4 weeks ($r = .92$; Payne & Billie, 1996).

Internal Consistency

There are no published data regarding the internal consistency of the SBQ–14 among adolescents (although such data have been published for samples of adults; Cotton et al., 1995). However, in a mixed sample of children from an inpatient psychiatric facility and from the community, Cronbach's α for the SBQ–C was .83 for a first administration and .79 for the retest (Payne & Billie, 1996).

Concurrent Validity

In a sample of high school students, the sum of three SBQ items was found to be positively related to severity of depression (as assessed with three different questionnaires), severity of hopelessness (as assessed with three different questionnaires), and a rating of potential suicide (Cole, 1989a). In high school students (Grades 10–12), the SBQ items regarding suicidal ideation, suicide threats, likelihood of future suicide attempts, and seeing suicide as a solution to problems were all negatively correlated with the Survival and Coping Beliefs and the Responsibility to Family scales of the RFL (Cole, 1989b). In a sample of juvenile delinquents, a version of each of the above SBQ questions (and three others) were all negatively related to Survival and Coping Beliefs. Response to the question regarding attempts was negatively associated with the Responsibility to Family scale of the RFL as well (Cole, 1989b). In a different sample of adolescents in high school, responses to the SBQ questions regarding suicidal ideation, suicidal threats, and likelihood of future suicide attempts were all negatively related to each of the scales as well as the total score from the RFL—Adolescent Version scale (Osman et al., 1998).

Among adolescent psychiatric inpatients, responses to the SBQ items regarding suicidal ideation and likelihood of future suicidal behavior were negatively associated with the scores on the Survival and Coping Beliefs and the Responsibility to Family scales of the Brief Reasons for Living— Adolescent Version scale (Osman et al., 1996). The suicide likelihood question was also negatively related to having moral objections to suicide (Osman et al., 1996). Suicidal adolescents (assessed in part with the SBQ) on an adolescent psychiatry unit were found to be more impulsive, depressed, and hopeless than nonsuicidal inpatients and a control group of high school students (Kashden et al., 1993).

The children's version of the SBQ (the SBQ–C) was found to have moderate correlations with severity of depression and hopelessness ($rs =$ .58 and .68, respectively; Payne & Billie, 1996).

Dimensionality

No published data were located regarding the factor structure of the SBQ when used with children or adolescents.

Predictive Validity

No published data regarding the predictive use of the SBQ items with youths were located.

Treatment Studies

No published treatment studies with suicidal youths were located.

Summary and Evaluation

Little psychometric data are available for SBQ–14 (used as an intact measure) in an adolescent population. Somewhat more psychometric data are available for the children's version of the SBQ, the SBQ–C. Several researchers have extracted questions from the SBQ and found these to be correlated with constructs theoretically related to suicidality (e.g., reasons for living), but responses to these have not been demonstrated to have predictive use.

Where to Obtain

The SBQ–14 can be obtained from Marsha M. Linehan, PhD, Behavioral Research and Therapy Clinic, Department of Psychology, University of Washington, Seattle, WA 98195-1525. The SBQ–C can be obtained from Lillian Range, PhD, Department of Psychology, Box 5025, University of Southern Mississippi, Hattiesburg, MS 39406-5025.

Summary

At the beginning of this chapter, four types of self-report questionnaires and behavior checklists were described: broad-band instruments that include relatively few items assessing suicidality, broad-band instruments that include a more substantial "suicide scale," narrow-band instruments focused on depression but including suicide items, and narrow-band instruments specifically focused on suicidality. Among the broad-band instruments, the Achenbach scales assess suicidality with only a few critical items but offer the advantage of having versions of the instruments that can be completed by youths, parents, and teachers. The Adolescent Psychopathology Scale, in contrast, is strictly a self-report instrument but does contain a more substantial Suicide Scale. Although this scale has demonstrated test–retest reliability and concurrent validity, it has not been used much in clinical research at this juncture beyond the initial validation samples. (Please refer to Table 5.1 for a complete instrument by-instrument comparison.)

Among the narrow-band instruments, three instruments were reviewed that focus on depressive symptoms. Both the Beck Depression Inventory (appropriate for adolescents) and the Children's Depression Inventory (appropriate for children or adolescents) include a single item assessing severity of suicidal ideation. However, for both of these scales, other researchers have developed "add-on" items assessing suicide attempts. The Dimensions of Depression Profile for Children and Adolescents is considerably less well studied beyond initial validation samples but does include an entire subscale of items assessing suicidal ideation.

Four narrow-band instruments focus specifically on suicidality: the BSI, the SIQ, the SBQ, and the HASS. The HASS is distinguished from the other scales because of the assessment of substance abuse along with the assessment of suicidal ideation and behavior. Items from the SBQ have been used to validate other suicidality scales, but total scores from the questionnaire have not been well studied in adolescents. Of particular interest, the SBQ is one of the few scales to assess expectations about suicidal behavior, and a version of this scale has been developed for use with younger children. By far the two most well-studied self-report instruments focused on the assessment of suicidality are the BSI and the SIQ. Both of these scales have demonstrated test–retest reliability and have been used as outcome measures in treatment research. The BSI has been used with clinically referred populations, but not with nonreferred groups, and focuses on the time frame of the last 1 week. In contrast, the SIQ has been used with both clinically referred and nonreferred adolescents and focuses on the time frame of the last 1 month. Neither instrument has items specifically inquiring about recent suicide attempts. However, the BSI does have an item asking respondents whether they have made a single or more than one suicide attempt in the past. Particularly when used as a screening instrument, the SIQ can be used in conjunction with the Suicidal Behaviors Interview, which does include questions about suicide attempts.

Table 5.1

Characteristics of Self-Report Questionnaires and Behavior Checklists as Instruments for the Detection of Suicidality

Instrument	Instrument type[a]	Populations in which suicidal behaviors examined[b]	Assess suicidal ideation	Assess suicide attempts	Assess total number of attempts	Assess non-suicidal self-harm	Consistent with O'Carroll et al.'s operational definitions[c]	Reliability data	Concurrent validity evidence	Predictive validity evidence	Used as outcome measure in suicidality studies
Achenbach CBCL, YSR, TRF	Cklist, Self	Sch, Clin	+	+	–	–	+	+[d]	+	+	–
APS, APS–SF	Self	Clin, Incar, Res, Sch	+	+	–	–	++	+	+	–	–
BDI	Self	Clin, Sch	+	–	–	–	++	+	+	+	–
BSI	Self	Clin	+	+	+[e]	–	++	–	+	+[g]	+
CDI	Self	Abuse, Bereave, Clin, Sch	+	–	–	–	++	+	+	+	–
DDPCA	Self	Med, Sch	+	–	–	–	+	+	+	–	–
HASS	Self	Clin, (mostly minority), Sch	+	+	+	–	++	–	+	–	–
SIQ, SIQ–JR	Self	Abuse, Bereave, Clin, ER, Sch, Med	+	–	–	–	++	+	+	+	+
SBQ	Self	Clin, Incar, Sch	+	+	+	+	+	+[f]	+	–	–

Note. The instruments are as follows: CBCL = Child Behavior Checklist; YSR = Youth Self-Report; TRF = Teacher Report Form; APS = Adolescent Psychopathology Scale; APS–SF = Adolescent Psychopathology Scale—Short Form; BDI = Beck Depression Inventory; BSI = Beck Scale for Suicidal Ideation; CDI = Children's Depression Inventory; DDPCA = Dimension of Depression Profile for Children and Adolescents; HASS = Harkavy Asnis Suicide Scale; SIQ = Suicidal Ideation Questionnaire; SIQ—JR = Suicidal Ideation Questionnaire for Grades 7, 8, and 9.

[a]Cklist = Behavior checklist; Self = Self-report questionnaire.

[b]Sch = School or community samples (including nonpatient controls in research studies); Clin = inpatient and/or outpatient psychiatric clinically referred or treatment-seeking youths; Incar = incarcerated youths; Res = youths in residential treatment; Abuse = abused children or children with posttraumatic stress disorder; Bereaved = bereaved children; Med = medically ill youths; ER = youths in emergency department setting.

[c]++ complete consistency with O'Carroll et al. (1996) operational definitions; + mostly consistent with O'Carroll et al. (1996) definitions; – least consistent with O'Carroll et al. (1996) definitions.

[d]Test–retest reliability data for all items analyzed together is provided, but the test–retest reliability of the suicidality items is not.

[e]Provides information about whether respondents are nonattempters, single attempters, or repeat attempters.

[f]For SBQ–C but not SBQ.

[g]With adults.

Survey Screening Items for Suicidal Behaviors

In this chapter, instruments are reviewed that have been developed specifically for screening and epidemiologic studies. The surveys reviewed tend to have a small number of items assessing history of suicidal ideation or attempts. The instruments include depression screeners such as the DSM Scale for Depression (DSD; Roberts, Chen, & Roberts, 1998; Roberts, Roberts, & Chen, 1998) and the Center for Epidemiologic Studies Depression Scale (CES–D; Radloff, 1977) with its added suicide screening items (Garrison, Addy, Jackson, McKeown, & Waller, 1991; Garrison, Jackson, Addy, McKeown, & Waller, 1991; Lewisohn et al., 1996), the survey instrument used for surveillance of risk-taking behaviors by the Centers for Disease Control and Prevention (the Youth Risk Behavior Survey; Kann et al., 1998), and instruments that have been used in surveys of suicidal behavior and correlates in special populations such as gay, lesbian, and bisexual youths, American Indian youths, and homeless and runaway youths.

When items on these surveys can be or are meant to be combined to form a *screener* regarding suicidal behaviors (as is the case for the added suicide screening items for use with the CES–D and the DSD suicide screening items), information on internal consistency and dimensionality is provided. Otherwise, items on surveys are assumed to be stand-alone items, and this information is not described. Because the questionnaires in this chapter are specifically developed as epidemiologic or survey instruments, they typically are not well suited for use as outcome measures in treatment studies, and indeed, none of these instruments have been used in this manner (hence, there is no "Treatment" heading in the reviews in this chapter).

Center for Epidemiologic Studies Depression Scale Suicidal Ideation Items (Added to the Original Measure)

Description

The Center for Epidemiologic Studies Depression Scale (CES–D; Radloff, 1977) is a 20-item screening self-report measure of depressive symptoms. As the name implies, this measure is appropriate for epidemiologic and screening surveys. The scale was developed for use with adults but has also been used with adolescents (Radloff, 1991). Responses are ranked on a 4-point Likert scale, ranging from *rarely or none* to *most or all of the time.* The CES–D has been translated into a number of different languages, including Spanish, French, Chinese, Dutch, Korean, German, and Russian. The CES–D is not a measure of suicidal ideation/behaviors and does not have suicidal ideation/behavior items. However, two different sets of screening items have been developed for use with the CES–D (Garrison, Addy et al., 1991; Garrison, Jackson, Addy, et al., 1991; Lewinsohn et al., 1996).

Populations Studied

The CES–D screeners have been used primarily in general community samples (e.g., Garrison, Addy, et al., 1991; Garrison, Jackson, et al., 1991; Lewinsohn et al., 1996; Roberts & Chen, 1995). However, Lewinsohn et al.'s (1996) screener has also been used with incarcerated adolescents (Rohde, Seeley, & Mace, 1997) and with homeless adolescents (Rohde, Noell, Ochs, & Seeley, 2001).

Assessment and Definitions of Suicidal Behaviors

The first suicidality screener developed in the format of the CES–D (Garrison, Addy, et al, 1991; Garrison, Jackson, et al., 1991) includes items asking whether respondents considered life to not be worth living, felt like hurting themselves, and felt like killing themselves. The reference period for these questions is the 1 week prior to the assessment. A total suicidal ideation score is computed from the 0-to-3 responses for each of these questions (ranging from 0 to 9). A dichotomous score also can be used, with scores greater than 5 considered to represent a high suicidality score.

The single item, that the respondents felt like killing themselves, is consistent with O'Carroll et al.'s (1996) definitions of suicidal behavior because of the implication of the nonzero intent to die. However, the three items taken as a whole are problematic for two reasons. First, one of the items (felt life was not worth living) does not focus on suicidal behavior per se, and in a narrow but literal sense, does not even assess thoughts of death or wanting to die. Second, another of the screening items (felt like hurting themselves) is worded so broadly as to elicit not only responses about ideation regarding suicidal behavior but also thoughts about nonsuicidal self-harm behavior. In addition, this set of screening items focuses only on suicidal ideation and therefore cannot be used as a screen for suicide attempts.

The second set of suicidality screening items developed in the format of the CES–D (Lewinsohn et al., 1996) includes items assessing whether respondents had thoughts about death, felt their friends and family would be better off if they were dead, had thought about killing themselves, and would kill themselves if they knew how. The reference period for these questions is the 1 week prior to the assessment. These questions can be summed or focused on individually.

The item in which the respondents thought about killing themselves is a very straightforward item for assessing suicidal ideation. Moreover, this item is clearly differentiated from another item assessing thoughts about death. The summation of the four items, however, yields a sum of questions about both thoughts of death and thoughts about suicide. As with the Garrison, Addy, et al. (1991) and Garrison, Jackson, et al. (1991) screening items, there is no separate screener for suicide attempts.

Reliability

No published data regarding the reliability of the two sets of added CES–D suicidality screening items were located.

Internal Consistency

Garrison et al.'s (Garrison, Addy, et al., 1991; Garrison, Jackson, et al., 1991) screener is internally consistent, with αs ranging from .87 to .90 for each year of baseline screening in an epidemiologic study of adolescents (R. McKeown, personal communication, November 1999). Lewinsohn et al.'s (1996) CES–D suicide screener was found to be internally consistent, with αs ranging from .86 to .92 among different ethnic and gender groups (Roberts & Chen, 1995; Tortolero & Roberts, 2001).

Concurrent Validity

In a large community sample of 12- to 14-year-olds, responses to the Garrison, Addy, et al. (1991) screening questions were significantly related to the classification of "moderate" to "very extreme" suicidal ideation and suicide attempts with "serious" or greater intent on the K–SADS–P (Garrison,

Jackson, et al., 1991). Across 3 years of a longitudinal study of young adolescents in the community, the most consistent cross-sectional (same year) correlate of Garrison, Addy, et al.'s (1991) CES–D screener for suicidal ideation was severity of depression as assessed with the CES–D.

In a large sample of sixth- to eighth-grade students, responses to Lewinsohn et al.'s (1996) screener were strongly correlated ($r = .70$) with CES–D total scores (Roberts & Chen, 1995). In addition, suicidal ideation as assessed with the CES–D screener was found to be related to loneliness, living in other than a two-parent family, living in a family in which English is not the primary language, and being of Mexican American as opposed to Anglo heritage (Roberts & Chen, 1995; Tortolero & Roberts, 2001).

Two additional studies focused on incarcerated and homeless youths. In the sample of incarcerated adolescents, several variables were found to be correlated with Lewinsohn et al.'s (1996) CES–D suicidal ideation screener (for both genders): current depression, features of borderline personality disorder, major life events, loneliness, lower self-esteem, and greater impulsivity (Rohde, Seeley, & Mace, 1997). Among homeless adolescents, suicidal ideation assessed with the CES–D screener was related to lifetime history of suicide attempts, use of intravenous drugs, nonheterosexual orientation, and lifetime (any) homosexual experience (Rohde et al., 2001).

Dimensionality

A principal-components analysis indicated that responses to the Lewinsohn et al. (1996) screener and to K–SADS questions regarding suicidality loaded on a single principal factor. No published data were located for the Garrison, Addy, et al. (1991) and Garrison, Jackson, et al. (1991) screener.

Predictive Validity

In an epidemiologic survey of adolescents, responses to Garrison et al.'s (Garrison, Addy, et al., 1991; Garrison, Jackson, et al., 1991) screener at baseline had low to moderate correlations with scores on the screener 1 year hence ($r = .22$ for Caucasian males, $r = .36$ for Caucasian females, $r = .44$ for both African American males and females; R. McKeown, personal communication, November 1999).

Responses to Lewinsohn et al.'s (1996) CES–D screening items were related to later suicidal behavior. Specifically, 16.7% of adolescents defined as having high ideation at an initial screening (because they had two or more items occurring "all the time" during the last week) made a suicide attempt within the following year. In addition, 6.7% of adolescents reporting moderate ideation at an initial screening (by virtue of reporting two more items occurring "occasionally" or one item occurring "all the time") made suicide attempts within a year. Of youths with mild ideation at the initial screening (one or more items occurring "some of the time"), 2.8% made suicide attempts within the year. Last, of youths reporting no suicidal ideation at the initial screening, only 0.3% made suicide attempts within the year. In the prediction of future suicide attempts within the next year, a cutoff score of 5 on the four-item screener was found to have sensitivity of 81%, specificity of 81%, positive predictive value of 7%, and negative predictive value of 100%.

Summary and Evaluation

Both the Garrison et al. (Garrison, Addy, et al., 1991; Garrison, Jackson, et al., 1991) and the Lewinsohn et al. (1996) suicidal ideation screeners were meant to be appended to, or written in the format of, the CES–D (which contains no suicidal ideation items). Both sets of screeners have been useful in their own respective research programs. However, more psychometric data have been collected for Lewinsohn et al.'s screener than for the Garrison et al. screener.

Where to Obtain

The Garrison et al. CES–D screening items are described in Garrison, Addy, et al. (1991) and Garrison, Jackson, et al. (1991). The items on the Lewinsohn et al. CES–D screener are in Table 1 of Lewinsohn et al. (1996, p. 28).

Challenges and Coping Survey for Lesbian, Gay, and Bisexual Youth

Description

The Challenges and Coping Survey for Lesbian, Gay, and Bisexual Youth (D'Augelli & Hershberger, 1993; Hershberger & D'Augelli, 1995; Hershberger, Pilkington, & D'Augelli, 1997) is the only instrument reviewed that focuses specifically on youths with same-sex or both-sex sexual orientation. The epidemiologic/screening survey includes questions about sexual orientation and behavior, social aspects of sexual orientation (including openness about gay/lesbian/bisexual identity), victimization (including discrimination and violence), disclosure of sexual orientation within the family, self-acceptance (degree of comfort with sexual orientation), suicidal thoughts and behavior, and mental health problems.

Populations Studied

This survey was developed for and has been used in samples of lesbian, gay, and bisexual youths.

Assessment and Definitions of Suicidal Behaviors

There are several items in this survey that assess suicidal behaviors and constructs. The questions regarding suicidal ideation ask whether respondents ever seriously thought about taking their own lives or considered this within the last year and whether such thoughts were related to sexual orientation. Additional questions assess whether respondents considered hurting or killing themselves or made any plans to hurt or kill themselves in the last week. The stem question regarding suicide attempts is straightforward and asks whether respondents have ever tried to kill themselves. The follow-up questions assess age and method of each attempt (up to six attempts), whether each attempt was related to sexual orientation, and whether the attempt(s) occurred within the last 12 months. Additional questions assess exposure to completed or attempted suicide within the family and among peers (and whether these peers were gay/lesbian/bisexual).

The questions regarding lifetime suicidal ideation and suicidal ideation within the last year are likely to elicit a conservative estimate of suicidal ideation because of the word *seriously* used in the query. The word *seriously* can be interpreted in various ways by respondents and is not consistent with O'Carroll et al.'s (1996) recommended definition of suicidal ideation, which requires only thoughts associated with nonzero intent to kill oneself. In addition, the questions regarding thoughts and plans of hurting or killing oneself within the last week are likely to elicit information not only about suicidal ideation but also about nonsuicidal self-harm behaviors. Lastly, the question regarding lifetime suicide attempts is consistent with O'Carroll et al.'s proposed nomenclature.

Reliability

No published data regarding test–retest reliability of the suicidal behavior items were located.

Internal Consistency

No data regarding the internal consistency of the suicidal ideation/behavior items were located.

Concurrent Validity

In samples of adolescents attending lesbian and gay community centers and organized youth groups, past suicide attempts were related to lower self-esteem, increased suicidal ideation, depression, anxiety, feelings of being overwhelmed, increased problems in relationships, and increased drug use (D'Augelli & Hershberger, 1993; Hershberger & D'Augelli, 1995; Hershberger et al., 1997). Past suicide attempts were also found to be related to number of friends lost due to sexual orientation, age of first awareness of sexual orientation, number of same-gender sexual partners, years between first disclosure of sexual orientation and telling a parent, keeping parents unaware of their sexual orientation, and victimization, particularly sexual victimization (D'Augelli & Hershberger, 1993; Hershberger & D'Augelli, 1995).

Dimensionality

No published data were located.

Predictive Validity

No published data regarding the predictive validity of the suicidal ideation/behavior questions were located.

Summary and Evaluation

This is the only instrument reviewed that has been developed specifically for use with lesbian, gay, and bisexual youths. The questions regarding the relationship between sexual orientation issues and suicidality are particularly useful. However, because of their wording, some of the questions regarding suicidal ideation might yield prevalence rates that are too low, whereas others might elicit responses about nonsuicidal behaviors in addition to suicidal behaviors.

Where to Obtain

Anthony R. D'Augelli, PhD, Department of Human Development and Family Studies, College of Health and Human Development, The Pennsylvania State University, 110 Henderson Building South, University Park, PA 16802-6504

DSM Scale for Depression

Description

A self-report screening inventory, the DSM Scale for Depression (DSD), was developed from the major depression items of the DISC–2.3 (Roberts, Chen, & Roberts, 1997; Roberts et al., 1998). The DSD has 31 items, and the respondent is asked to report whether these symptoms have been present in the last 2 weeks. The scores of the DSD can be summed to yield a severity score for depression, or the responses to the individual items can be used to determine whether the respondent would likely meet criteria for major depression. The DSD is not a questionnaire for assessing suicidality per se. However, there are eight suicidal ideation/behavior questions on the DSD that can be used separately as a screener. The DSD was developed as an instrument for use in epidemiologic studies and screening surveys.

Populations Studied

The DSD has been used in large school-based screenings with several different ethnic groups (Olvera, 2001; Roberts et al., 1997, 1998). In the Roberts et al. samples, the largest ethnic groups included Anglo American, African American, Central American, Mexican American, Native American, Indian American, Chinese American, Pakistani American, Vietnamese American, and mixed-ancestry youths. The DSD has not been used with clinically referred samples.

Assessment and Definitions of Suicidal Behaviors

The DSD has eight questions assessing suicidal behaviors and related constructs in a self-report format. There are separate questions regarding hopelessness, thoughts of death and dying, thoughts of wishing to be dead, suicidal ideation, suicide plans, and suicide attempts. The individual questions are straightforward and are totally consistent with the suggested nomenclature of O'Carroll et al. (1996) for definitions of suicidal ideation and suicide attempts. The total score from the eight questions (a suicide severity score) combines the responses to the individual items, but the individual items (e.g., the suicidal ideation item) can and have been used as screens in and of themselves (Roberts et al., 1997).

Reliability

No published data were located.

Internal Consistency

The DSD has been found to be internally consistent (α = .85, Olvera, 2001; α > .93, Roberts et al., 1998), as have the DSD suicide screening items (α = .84 overall, and .78 to .91 for the different ethnic groups in Roberts et al., 1997; αs = .81 to .87 for the different ethnic and gender groups in Tortolero & Roberts, 2001).

Concurrent Validity

Adolescents with higher scores on the DSD suicide items have been found to be more depressed, lonely, pessimistic, and fatalistic and to have more life stress, family problems, and lower self-esteem (Olvera, 2001; Roberts et al., 1998). In addition, several studies have documented higher rates of suicidal ideation among Latino and mixed-ancestry youths compared with Anglo American youths (Olvera, 2001; Roberts et al., 1997; Tortolero & Roberts, 2001). There have been inconsistent findings regarding the possible relationship between suicidality as assessed with the DSD suicide items and gender, age, and socioeconomic status of youths (Olvera, 2001; Roberts et al., 1997, 1998).

Adolescents with a history of suicide attempts as assessed with the DSD suicide items were more likely to report any ideation regarding death or suicide, were 7 times more likely to report suicidal ideation, and were 11 times more likely to report a suicide plan (Roberts et al., 1998). The combination of depression and past history of attempt multiplied the risk; for example, adolescents with a history of attempt but no depression were 10 times more likely to have a recent suicide plan, but youths with both depression and a past attempt were 27 times more likely to have a current suicide plan (Roberts et al., 1998).

Dimensionality

No published data were located.

Predictive Validity

No published data were located.

Summary and Evaluation

The DSD is a new self-report screening measure of depression developed from the DISC queries for major depression. The DSD can be used to estimate severity of depressive symptomatology or to determine if a respondent likely meets criteria for major depression. The DSD has been used with several different ethnocultural groups. The queries regarding suicidal behaviors are consistent with recommendations by O'Carroll et al. (1996) regarding the definitions of suicidal behaviors. However, the predictive validity of the suicide items has not been demonstrated.

Where to Obtain

Robert E. Roberts, PhD, Behavioral Sciences, School of Public Health, University of Texas—Houston Health Science Center, P.O. Box 20186, Houston, TX 77225

Indian Health Service Adolescent Health Survey

Description

The Indian Health Service Adolescent Health Survey is a survey instrument that has been administered to American Indian and Alaskan Native youths in the 6th to the 12th grades in reservation communities serviced by the Indian Health Service. The survey includes items assessing health risk behaviors (including suicidal behaviors), resiliency or protective factors, and health outcomes. This survey is included here because of its extensive use with Native Americans and because of the strong focus of the survey on the assessment of protective factors.

Populations Studied

The Indian Health Service Adolescent Health Survey has been administered to 6th- through 12th-grade American Indian and Alaskan Native youths (Blum, Harmon, Harris, Bergeisen, & Resnick, 1992; Borowsky, Resnick, Ireland, & Blum, 1999; Grossman, Milligan, & Deyo, 1991; Pharris, Resnick, & Blum, 1997). By 1997, it had been administered to over 75,000 youths (Pharris et al., 1997).

Assessment and Definitions of Suicidal Behaviors

Items regarding suicidal behaviors include questions about exposure to suicide attempts and completion (whether any of the respondents' friends attempted suicide and whether any of their friends actually completed suicide), suicide attempts (whether the respondents ever tried to kill themselves), recency of last suicide attempt, treatment following suicide attempt, and suicidal ideation (the respondents would like to kill themselves, the respondents have thoughts about killing themselves but would not act on these thoughts). The question about suicide attempts obviously refers to nonzero intent to kill oneself. The questions regarding suicidal ideation also implicitly refer to nonzero intent to kill oneself (O'Carroll et al., 1996). However, it is possible to have thoughts about killing oneself, without strongly desiring to do so or being on the verge of doing so. Therefore, this item may yield a conservative estimate of suicidal ideation.

Reliability

No published data were located.

Internal Consistency

No published data were located.

Concurrent Validity

For American Indian youths, individuals considered at high risk for suicide (because they reported a suicide attempt within the last year and current suicidal ideation or a history of multiple attempts) differed from youths at low risk in several respects (Blum et al., 1992). The high-risk youths more often had a family member who tried suicide or a friend who completed suicide, more often had been physically or sexually abused, more often were involved with heavy drinking and at least weekly marijuana use, and were more likely to have been pregnant or to have caused a pregnancy (Blum et al., 1992). American Indian youths who had a history of attempts more often knew where to get a gun, more often knew a friend or family member who had attempted or completed suicide, were less connected with their community and families, more often had a parent with a substance abuse problem, and were more likely to be physically or sexually abused (Borowsky et al., 1999).

For sexually abused American Indian youths, the absence of suicidal ideation (assessed with the Indian Health Service Adolescent Health Survey) was found to be associated with family attention and the perceived caring of school officials, among other factors (Pharris et al., 1997). The strongest factor associated with absence of suicide attempts was family attention (Pharris et al., 1997).

Dimensionality

No published data were located.

Predictive Validity

No published data were located.

Summary and Evaluation

The Indian Health Service Adolescent Health Survey has already yielded important information about suicidal ideation and behavior among Native American youths. It should be considered to be primarily a screening or epidemiologic survey instrument. A strength of the survey as a whole is that it focuses not only on problem behaviors or risk factors but also on various potential protective factors. Because of its wording, the Indian Health Service Adolescent Health Survey may yield a conservative estimate of suicidal ideation. Moreover, the suicidal ideation/attempt items on this instrument have not been examined as possible predictors of future behavior.

Where to Obtain

Center for Adolescent Nursing, 6-101 Weaver-Densford Hall, 308 Harvard Street S.E., Minneapolis, MN 55455-0342

Middle Adolescent Vulnerability Study Survey

Description

The Middle Adolescent Vulnerability Study Survey (Windle & Windle, 1997) is a survey instrument that has been used in a longitudinal study of the interrelationship among alcohol and drug use, depression, and suicidal behaviors. The survey assesses suicidal behaviors, frequency and amount of alcohol use, other substance use, percentage of friends who drink or use drugs, drinking disinhibitions, motives for drinking, stressful life events, family support, and severity of depressive symptoms. This is the only survey instrument in the book to specifically focus on the interrelationship between alcohol/substance use and suicidal behaviors among youths.

Populations Studied

The Middle Adolescent Vulnerability Study Survey has been used with high school students.

Assessment and Definitions of Suicidal Behaviors

Depending on the assessment, respondents are asked about either lifetime suicidal behaviors or suicidal behaviors during the last 6 months. With reference to those time frames, respondents are asked to rate the frequency (*not at all, once, twice,* or *three or more times*) with which they thought about killing themselves, told someone that they were going to kill themselves, or attempted to kill themselves. If respondents say that they had attempted suicide in the last half year, they are then asked to describe the methods of the attempts. The questions both about suicidal ideation and suicide attempts are straightforward and consistent with the recommendations regarding definitions of suicidal behavior by O'Carroll et al. (1996).

Reliability

No published data on the test–retest reliability of the suicide items were located.

Internal Consistency

The three-item screener has been found to be internally consistent (α = .74; M. Windle, personal communication, December 1999).

Concurrent Validity

In a longitudinal sample of high school sophomores and juniors, the cumulative or lifetime suicidal thoughts (from baseline and subsequent semiannual assessments over 2 years) were related primarily to depressive thoughts, whereas cumulative suicide attempts were highest among youths with both problem drinking and depression (Windle & Windle, 1997). For both genders, suicide attempters reported more frequent illicit drug use, more depression, and more cigarette smoking than suicide ideators (Windle & Windle, 1997).

Dimensionality

No published data were located.

Predictive Validity

In a sample of high school students, suicidal thoughts and attempts were found to be predictive of subsequent suicidal ideation and communications, even after controlling for depression, hopelessness, and alcohol consumption (Reifman & Windle, 1995).

Summary and Evaluation

This is a survey that likely yields very useful information regarding the interrelationship among substance abuse, depression, and suicidal behaviors in youths. The questions regarding suicidal behavior are well worded and straightforward, but data regarding their reliability have not been collected.

Where to Obtain

Michael Windle, PhD, Department of Psychology, The University of Alabama at Birmingham, 415 Campbell Hall, 1300 University Boulevard, Birmingham, AL 35294-1170

Midwest Homeless and Runaway Adolescent Project Survey

Description

The Midwest Homeless and Runaway Adolescent Project Survey (MHRAP) is an instrument that has been used in a study of 602 homeless and runaway adolescents. These adolescents have been interviewed on the streets, in shelters, and so on. The MHRAP has sections assessing the following: (a) sociodemographic variables (including sexual orientation); (b) family factors (including questions about alcohol/drug problems in the home, psychiatric/emotional problems of caregiver, physical abuse, and sexual abuse); (c) street factors (including physical and sexual victimization); (d) peer factors (including questions related to peers attempting and completing suicide); (e) externalizing behavior (including questions regarding alcohol and drug abuse); and (f) internalizing behavior (including items regarding depression, self-esteem, and suicidal behaviors). The MHRAP screening survey is included in this book because of the unique population with which this survey has been used.

Populations Studied

The MHRAP has been used in samples of runaway and homeless youths (Yoder, 1999; Yoder, Hoyt, & Whitbeck, 1998).

Assessment and Definitions of Suicidal Behaviors

On the MHRAP, there are four questions regarding suicidal ideation and four items regarding suicide attempts. The suicidal ideation items include questions about hurting oneself, feeling that one would be better off dead, thinking about killing oneself, and suicidal plans. The third question of this series (thinking about killing oneself) is totally consistent with the operational definition of suicidal ideation proposed by O'Carroll et al. (1996).

The MHRAP suicide attempt items begin with a stem question of whether the respondents have ever tried to kill themselves. If respondents answer positively, they are asked about the number of total suicide attempts, the time of their last suicide attempt, and the method of their last attempt. The stem question is straightforward and explicitly is consistent with O'Carroll et al.'s (1996) suggestion that suicide attempts be associated with non-zero intent to kill oneself.

Reliability

No published data were located regarding test–retest reliability of these items.

Internal Consistency

In the sample of homeless and runaway youths, the suicidal ideation section of the MHRAP was found to be internally consistent ($\alpha = .89$; Yoder et al., 1998).

Concurrent Validity

On the basis of responses to the survey items, homeless and runaway adolescents were classified as nonsuicidal, suicidal ideators, and suicide attempters (Yoder, 1999). Suicide ideators and suicide attempters were both more likely to have low self-esteem and be depressed than the nonsuicidal youths. Suicide attempters were more likely to report psychiatric/emotional problems among caretakers and a friend who completed suicide than other adolescents. The suicide attempters also reported more physical abuse, more sexual abuse, and more sexual victimization on the streets than suicide ideators, who, in turn, reported more abuse and victimization than nonsuicidal youths.

Dimensionality

No published data were located.

Predictive Validity

No data are available, although an ongoing longitudinal study should allow assessment of this issue.

Summary and Evaluation

This is a potentially very useful survey that can be used to assess suicidal behaviors and associated risk factors in the difficult-to-track but high-risk population of homeless and runaway youths. The suicidal ideation/behavior items are straightforward, consistent with O'Carroll et al.'s (1996) recommended nomenclature for suicidal behavior, and elicit responses that are correlated with variables that would be expected to be associated with suicidality. However, the test–retest reliability of the items has not been ascertained.

Where to Obtain

Les B. Whitbeck, PhD, Department of Sociology, University of Nebraska-Lincoln, 711 Oldfather Hall, P.O. Box 880324, Lincoln, NE 68588-0324

Youth Risk Behavior Survey

Description

The Youth Risk Behavior Survey (YRBS) is a school-based epidemiologic survey developed and administered by the Centers for Disease Control and Prevention in conjunction with state and local agencies (Kann et al., 1998). The YRBS was designed for the monitoring of six categories of health-risk behaviors: behaviors associated with unintentional and intentional injuries, tobacco use, alcohol and drug use, sexual behaviors, unhealthy dietary behaviors, and physical inactivity.

Populations Studied

The YRBS has been used in large-scale epidemiologic school-based surveys across the United States.

Assessment and Definitions of Suicidal Behaviors

There are four items on the YRBS assessing suicidal behaviors. Respondents were asked if, during the past 12 months, they ever seriously considered attempting suicide, made a plan about how they would attempt suicide, how many times they actually attempted suicide, and, if they attempted suicide during the past 12 months, whether any attempt resulted in a serious condition that required medical treatment. The first item regarding the presence of suicidal ideation implies at least nonzero intent to die. However, the item also uses the word *seriously* to describe the act of considering suicide; the word *seriously* might be interpreted in different ways by respondents. In O'Carroll et al.'s (1996) proposed nomenclature, there is no requirement that individuals with suicidal ideation consider suicide *seriously,* and therefore, this question is likely to yield a conservative estimate of suicidal ideation.

Using the item (asking how may times the respondent actually attempted suicide) will yield an estimate of suicide attempts that is consistent with the definitions of suicide attempts proposed by O'Carroll et al. (1996). Using the next item (requiring the presence of medical attention for suicide attempts) as some researchers have done will yield a conservative estimate of suicide attempts. In O'Carroll et al.'s nomenclature, it is specifically noted that suicide attempts may or may not be associated with injury, as long as they are potentially associated with harm.

The suicide attempt item, like the suicidal ideation item, refers to the last year. Although useful in estimating the 1-year prevalence of this and other risk behaviors (the purpose of the survey), the 1-year requirement does not yield important information about total lifetime suicide attempts (often considered to be the best predictor of later attempts).

Reliability

In a sample of high school students (7th to 12th grades) sampled 14 days apart, the suicidal ideation/behavior questions of the YRBS (with reference to the last year) were found to have the following test–retest reliability—suicidal ideation: $\kappa = .84$; suicide plan: $\kappa = .77$; suicide attempt: $\kappa = .76$; and suicide attempt with injury: $\kappa = .60$ (Brener, Collins, Kann, Warren, & Williams, 1995).

Internal Consistency

No published data were located.

Concurrent Validity

R. McKeown (personal communication, September 1999) found that of 9 older adolescents who attempted suicide in the past (as assessed with the K–SADS), 5 (55.6%) reported seriously thinking about suicide in the last year on the YRBS. Of 14 adolescents reporting current suicidal ideation on the semistructured K–SADS interview, 11 (78.6%) also reported seriously thinking about suicide on the YRBS. In contrast, of the 440 adolescents who reported no suicidal ideation or attempts on the K–SADS, 30 (6.8%) reported seriously thinking about suicide on the YRBS. R. McKeown (personal communication, December 1999) noted that these results should be interpreted cautiously because of the low number of suicide ideators and attempters.

There also is a wealth of information about the relationship between the YRBS suicidal behaviors questions and other potentially health-endangering behaviors, which can be interpreted as providing some evidence of convergent validity. Other health-endangering behaviors that are related to YRBS-assessed suicidal ideation and attempts include use of cigarettes (Garrison et al., 1993; Woods et al., 1997); use of alcohol and recreational drugs, particularly potentially dangerous drugs (Burge et al., 1995; Felts et al., 1992; Garofalo et al., 1999; Woods et al., 1997); use of anabolic steroids (Middleman, Faulkner, Woods, Emans, & Durant, 1995); carrying a weapon (Durant et al., 1999; Orpinas et al., 1995; Woods et al., 1997); being in physical fights (Garofalo et al., 1999; Garrison et al., 1993; Woods et al., 1997); sexual behavior (Burge et al., 1995; Nelson et al., 1994); and extreme weight control methods (Neumark-Sztainer, Story, Dixon, & Murray, 1998). In addition, consistent with other literature, YRBS suicidal behaviors have been found to be associated with sexual victimization and same-sex orientation or behaviors (Durant, Krowchuk, & Sinal, 1998; Garofalo et al., 1999).

Dimensionality

No published data were located.

Predictive Validity

No published data regarding the predictive utility of YRBS suicidality items were located.

Summary and Evaluation

In terms of evaluating the prevalence of suicidal ideation/behavior among youths in the United States, or the relationship between suicidal behaviors and other health-endangering behaviors, perhaps no other instrument has prompted as much research as the YRBS. Nonetheless, because of its wording, the suicidal ideation query of the YRBS is likely to generate a conservative estimate of suicidal ideation; use of the item regarding suicide attempts requiring medical attention can likewise yield conservative estimates of suicide attempts. The predictive utility of the YRBS items has not been evaluated.

Where to Obtain

The YRBS can be downloaded at http://www.cdc.gov/nccdphp/dash/yrbs/

Summary

Most of the surveys reviewed in this chapter have been administered to school and community samples of youths (the CES–D screeners, the DSD, the Indian Health Service Adolescent Health Survey, the Middle Adolescent Vulnerability Study Survey, and the YRBS). Surveys also have been specifically developed for use with samples of Native Americans (the Indian Health Service Adolescent Health Survey), youths with substance abuse problems (the Middle Adolescent Vulnerability Study Survey), homeless and runaway youths (the MHRAP), and gay, lesbian, and bisexual youths (the Challenges and Coping Survey for Lesbian, Gay, and Bisexual Youth). All of the instruments reviewed here have queries for assessing suicidal ideation, all of the instruments except the CES–D screeners assess suicide attempts, and two (the Challenges and Coping Survey for Lesbian, Gay, and Bisexual Youth and the MHRAP) assess total number of events. Of the surveys, the YRBS is the only one for which test–retest reliability data are available. Items assessing suicidality in each of the surveys have shown evidence of concurrent validity, and items in five surveys (DSD, Middle Adolescent Vulnerability Study Survey, MHRAP, and the two CES–D screeners) have been shown to have predictive validity. (Please refer to Table 6.1 for an instrument-by-instrument comparison.)

Table 6.1

Characteristics of Surveys With Items Regarding Assessment of Suicidal Ideation and Behavior

Instrument	Populations in which suicidal behaviors examined[a]	Asses suicidal ideation	Assess suicidal attempts	Assess total number of attempts	Assess non-suicidal self-harm	Consistent with O'Carroll et al.'s operational definitions[b]	Reliability data	Concurrent validity evidence	Predictive validity evidence
CES-D added items (Garrison)	Sch	+	–	–	–	–	–	+	+
CES-D added items (Lewinsohn)	Sch, Incar, Homeless	+	–	–	–	+	–	+	+
Challenges and Coping Survey for Gay, Lesbian, and Bisexual Youth	LGB	+	+	+	–	+	–	+	–
DSM Scale for Depression	Sch (multiethnic)	+	+	–	–	++	–	+	+
Indian Health Service Adolescent Health Survey	Sch (Native American)	+	+	–	–	+	–	+	–
Middle Adolescent Vulnerability Study Survey	Sch	+	+	–	–	++	–	+	+
Midwest Homeless and Runaway Adolescent Project Survey	Homeless	+	+	+	–	++	–	+	+

Youth Risk Behavior Survey	Sch	+	+	−	+	−	+	+	+	−

Note. Abbreviations in the "Instrument" column are as follows: CES–D = Center for Epidemiologic Studies Depression Scale; DSM = Diagnostic and Statistical Manual of Mental Disorders.

ªSch = school or community samples; Incar = incarcerated youths; Homeless = runaway and homeless youths; LGB = lesbian, gay and bisexual youths.

ᵇ++ complete consistency with O'Carroll et al. (1996) operational definitions; + mostly consistent with O'Carroll et al. (1996) definitions; − least consistent with O'Carroll et al. (1996) definitions.

Part III

Risk Assessment and Other Instruments

Assessing Risk of Suicidal Behaviors: Self-Report Questionnaires and Clinician Rating Scales

This chapter is dedicated to instruments that have promise in the prediction of future suicidal behaviors and therefore can truly be conceptualized as indices of future "risk." In this section, a primary (but often ignored) consideration is the predictive use of the measure of interest. A clinician is typically not interested in predicting something that has already happened (e.g., a past suicide attempt); it is usually easier to just ask whether it (e.g., a suicide attempt) has happened. Therefore, the most important challenge for a measure of risk or propensity for suicidal behaviors is whether the measure actually has use in predicting the future occurrence of that behavior.

Clinicians often do not use objective rating scales in judging risk for suicidal behavior (Jobes, Eyman, & Yufit, 1995). This is unfortunate because traditional clinical assessments can be unreliable as sources of important decision-making information and are sometimes less accurate as predictors of future behaviors than information obtained in more objective formats (Dawes et al., 1989). Objective measures of risk with demonstrated predictive validity therefore should be considered and are particularly needed as *supplements* to the clinical armamentarium for evaluating risk for suicidal behavior.

The instruments in this section include both self-report questionnaires and clinician rating scales. These instruments can be used in clinical settings, individual screenings, or research. These scales assess a variety of constructs: Some focus on single constructs such as hopelessness, reasons for living, or attitudes toward life, whereas others assess multiple areas thought to be relevant to risk of suicidal behavior.

Four of the instruments in this section (the Beck Hopelessness Scale [Beck & Steer, 1988; Beck, Weissman, Lester, & Trexler, 1974], the Hopelessness Scale for Children [Kazdin, Rodgers, & Colbus, 1986], the Inventory for Suicide Orientation–30 [King & Kowalchuk, 1994], and the Israeli Index of Potential Suicide [Orbach & Bar-Joseph, 1993]) have been used as outcome measures in intervention (treatment or prevention) studies. However, two of the four intervention studies were not controlled, and no significant differences were found in a third.

Adapted SAD PERSONS Scale

Description

The Adapted SAD PERSONS scale (Juhnke, 1996) is a school-age version of the SAD PERSONS scale used with adults. The Adapted SAD PERSONS Scale is a clinician-rated instrument used to identify risk factors for suicide. SAD PERSONS is an acronym for 10 different risk factors for suicidal behavior: *S*ex, *A*ge, *D*epression or affective disorder, *P*revious attempts, *E*thanol-drug abuse, *R*ational thinking loss, *S*ocial supports lacking, *O*rganized plan, *N*egligent parenting, family stresses, or modeling of suicide by family members, and *S*chool problems.

In estimating risk, each of these factors, with the exception of gender, is rated from 0 (*complete absence*) to 10 (*significant manifestation*). For the gender item, males receive 10 points and females 0. Interventions are suggested depending on total risk severity scores. School counseling visits, provision of crisis telephone numbers, and a no-suicide contract are recommended for youths considered at risk but receiving risk severity scores of less than 30. For youths considered at risk and with scores from 30 to 49, guidance counselors are encouraged to speak with parents or guardians. For youths thought to be at risk and with scores of 50 to 69, counselors are encouraged to proceed with an evaluation for hospitalization. Youths with scores of 70 or above are considered to be at greatest risk and potentially in need of immediate hospitalization.

Populations Studied

The Adapted SAD PERSONS was developed for screening, particularly in school settings. However, its use with suicidal youths has not been systematically evaluated.

Reliability

No data were found regarding the interrater or test–retest reliability of the Adapted SAD PERSONS scale.

Internal Consistency

The internal consistency of the Adapted SAD PERSONS scale has not been evaluated.

Concurrent Validity

No data pertaining to the concurrently assessed validity of the Adapted SAD PERSONS scale were found.

Dimensionality

No data were found.

Predictive Validity

The predictive validity of the Adapted SAD PERSONS scale has not been evaluated.

Treatment Studies

The Adapted SAD PERSONS scale is primarily a screening instrument and has not been used in treatment studies.

Summary and Evaluation

The Adapted SAD PERSONS scale is a screening instrument for identifying risk factors for suicide among youths, particularly in school settings. The Adapted SAD PERSONS has been used as a teaching tool, but its psychometric characteristics have not been evaluated.

Where to Obtain

Gerard A. Juhnke, PhD, Department of Counseling and Educational Development, University of North Carolina at Greensboro, 223 Curry Building, 1000 Spring Garden Street, Greensboro, NC 27412

Beck Hopelessness Scale

Description

Hopelessness is the experience of despair or extreme pessimism about the future and, as such, is part of the "cognitive triad" (along with a negative view of oneself and one's world) described in Beck's cognitive model of depression (Beck, Rush, Shaw, & Emery, 1979). According to Shneidman (1996), hopelessness–helplessness is the most common emotion experienced among suicidal persons. The Beck Hopelessness Scale (BHS; Beck & Steer, 1988; Beck, Weissman, et al., 1974; Steer & Beck, 1988) is a 20-item assessment device designed to measure negative expectations about the future. Individuals completing the BHS are asked to answer the questionnaire on the basis of their attitudes during the preceding week. The self-report instrument may be administered in written or oral form, and each item is scored with a true/false response. Total scores range from 0 to 20, with higher scores indicating a greater degree of hopelessness. The BHS has been translated into Dutch (DeWilde, Kienhorst, Diekstra, & Wolters, 1993) and Hebrew (Pershakovsky, 1985, cited in Orbach & Bar-Joseph, 1993) and is appropriate for clinical research and assessment.

Populations Studied

The BHS has been used with high school students and other nonclinically ascertained populations (DeWilde et al., 1993; Osman et al., 1998), homeless youths (Rohde et al., 2001), adolescent psychiatric outpatients (Brent et al., 1997, 1998) and inpatients (Enns, Inayatulla, Cox, & Cheyne, 1997; Goldston et al., 2001; Kashden et al., 1993; Kumar & Steer, 1995; Morano, Cisler, & Lemerond, 1993; Reinecke et al., 2001; Rotheram-Borus & Trautman, 1988; Steer, Kumar, & Beck, 1993a, 1993b; Topol & Reznikoff, 1982), adolescent suicide attempters in a pediatrics unit (Swedo et al., 1991), and adolescent suicide attempters in an emergency room setting (Rotheram-Borus & Trautman, 1988; Swahn & Potter, 2001).

Reliability

Among adolescents who have been psychiatrically hospitalized, hopelessness as assessed with the BHS seems to be a relatively stable construct (correlation between serial administrations 6 months apart = .63; Goldston, 2000). These data dovetail with data from adult samples, suggesting that hopelessness as assessed with the BHS has some "trait characteristics" (Young et al., 1996).

Internal Consistency

In adolescent psychiatric inpatients (Steer et al., 1993a), the BHS has been found to be internally consistent (KR–20 coefficient = .86). Both the Dutch translation of the scale (in three samples of adolescents; DeWilde et al., 1993) and the Israeli version of the BHS (Orbach & Bar-Joseph, 1993) have been found to be internally consistent (αs from .68 to .75, and α = .89, respectively).

Concurrent Validity

In two United States adolescent psychiatric inpatient samples (Goldston et al., 2001; Reinecke et al., 2001), in Canadian samples of Aboriginal psychiatric inpatient suicide attempters and non-Aboriginal psychiatric inpatient suicide attempters (Enns et al., 1997), and in a United States emergency department setting (Rotheram-Borus & Trautman, 1988), BHS scores have been found to have moderate to high correlations (rs = .69 to .82) with severity of depression as measured with the BDI. In an adolescent inpatient sample (Goldston et al., 2001), BHS scores have also been found to be positively related to dysfunctional attitudes and, to a lesser extent, expectations about future suicidal behavior. BHS scores have been found to be negatively correlated with positive problem-solving orientation and positively correlated with negative, impulsive-careless, and avoidant problem-solving orientations (Reinecke et al., 2001). BHS scores also were found to be negatively related to the Reasons for Living Inventory (RFL) Survival and Coping Beliefs, Responsibility to Family, Fear of Social Disapproval, and Moral Objection scales but not the RFL Fear of Suicide scale (Goldston et al., 2001). In nonreferred adolescents, BHS scores were negatively related with RFL–Adolescent Version total scores (Osman et al., 1998). In adolescent psychiatric inpatients, severity of hopelessness was positively related to suicidal ideation (Reinecke et al., 2001; Steer et al., 1993b). Likewise, changes in hopelessness over 1 year among high school students were related to changes in suicidal ideation over the same period of time, after controlling for changes in depression (Mazza & Reynolds, 1998).

In both Caucasian and Aboriginal adolescent psychiatric inpatient suicide attempters, BHS scores were related to suicide intent; the relationship between BHS scores and suicide intent remained significant for Caucasian but not Aboriginal youths after controlling for concurrent depression (Enns et al., 1997). BHS scores were not found to be related to suicidal intent among primarily Hispanic and African American adolescent psychiatry inpatient suicide attempters (Rotheram-Borus & Trautman, 1988).

In one study, adolescent suicide attempters reported more hopelessness at psychiatric hospitalization than did adolescents without a history of suicide attempts (Goldston et al., 2001). In another study, suicidal adolescents as well as depressed nonsuicidal adolescents reported more hopelessness than nondepressed, nonsuicidal adolescents (DeWilde et al., 1993). In this study, depressed adolescents also reported more hopelessness than suicidal youths, although it is worth noting that some of the suicide attempters made their suicide attempts as long ago as 1 year before the study.

Psychiatrically hospitalized adolescent suicidal youths had higher hopelessness scores than nonattempters, both in samples matched for severity of depression (Morano et al., 1993) and in samples not matched for depression scores (Kashden et al., 1993; Topol & Reznikoff, 1982). Hopelessness was one of two variables that were used to discriminate between (or correctly classify) 76% of suicide attempters hospitalized on a pediatrics unit, other at-risk youths, and normal controls (Swedo et al., 1991). By contrast, in a paradoxical finding, lower rates of clinically significant hopelessness were found among suicide attempters (a mixed sample of adolescents and adults) classified as being "nearly lethal" in level of medical lethality, compared with "less lethal suicide attempters" (Swahn & Potter, 2001).

Dimensionality

A principal-components analysis of BHS responses for adolescent inpatients revealed three components or factors (Steer et al., 1993a). These factors were described as reflecting rejection (of "the possibility of the future being hopeful"), acceptance (of the "inevitability of a hopeless future"), and resignation ("loss of motivation or resignation to the futility of changing the future for the better;" Steer et al., 1993a, pp. 562–563). These factors correspond roughly to the factors identified previously in adult samples by Beck, Weissman, et al. (1974), although it should be mentioned that other studies in adults have found that one- or two-factor models better characterize adult BHS data (Aish & Wasserman, 2001; Steer, Beck, & Brown, 1997).

Predictive Validity

Among adults, hopelessness has repeatedly been found to be associated with eventual suicide (Beck, Brown, Berchick, Stewart, & Steer, 1990; Beck,

Steer, Kovacs, & Garrison, 1985; Fawcett et al., 1990) and repeat self-harm behaviors (Brittlebank et al., 1990; Scott, House, Yates, & Harrington, 1997) in clinically referred samples. Among adolescent psychiatric inpatients with a history of suicide attempts, BHS scores have been found to be predictive of repeat suicide attempts following discharge from the hospital (Goldston et al., 2001). These predictive effects were not apparent among adolescents without a history of attempts and were no longer statistically significant after controlling for depression (Goldston et al., 2001).

In a second study (Hawton, Kingsbury, Steinhardt, James, & Fagg, 1999), the BHS failed to differentiate between adolescents who made repeat attempts and adolescents who did not make repeat attempts in a 1-year follow-up after hospitalization for self-poisoning. However, this study was limited in power because of the small number of youths attempting suicide in the follow-up. When Hawton et al. (1999) combined for statistical analyses the adolescents who presented at hospitalization with repeat suicide attempts and the adolescents who made repeat suicide attempts over the follow-up, the repeaters did on average have higher BHS scores than the youths with single overdoses.

In a controlled treatment study, Brent et al. (1997) found that adolescents who dropped out of therapy had higher hopelessness scores than adolescents who remained in therapy. Brent et al. (1998) also found higher BHS scores to be associated with failure to achieve clinical remission of major depression.

Treatment Studies

A suicide prevention program in Israel was found to reduce BHS scores among targeted students in some but not all high schools (Orbach & Bar-Joseph, 1993). However, BHS scores were generally low in this population even before the intervention.

In a South African study (Pillay & Wassenaar, 1995), adolescents with suicidal behavior selected from among consecutive admissions to a general hospital showed significant declines in BHS scores from their initial assessments to 6-month follow-ups after treatment with individual and family psychotherapy. Adolescents with suicidal behaviors who declined treatment did not show the same decline over time in hopelessness. Two control groups of nonsuicidal (and nonpsychiatrically treated) youths also did not evidence significant declines in hopelessness over time (although these adolescents had very low BHS scores at their initial assessments, limiting their room for change; i.e., there was a *floor effect* in this analysis). The BHS has been used in multiple treatment studies with adults (e.g., Rush, Beck, Kovacs, Weissenburger, & Hollon, 1982). However, it has not been used as a primary outcome measure in a randomized controlled treatment trial with suicidal youths.

Summary and Evaluation

The BHS is an excellent scale based on the cognitive theory of depression that has been widely used with adults but is less used in studies with adolescents. Among adults, the BHS repeatedly has been found to be associated with repeat suicide attempts and completed suicide in clinically ascertained samples. Hopelessness has been found to predict later suicide attempts (over 5 years) among psychiatrically hospitalized adolescents with a history of prior attempts (but not among youths without prior attempts). An important consideration in treatment studies is that BHS scores have been found to be associated with treatment dropout.

Where to Obtain

The Psychological Corporation, 555 Academic Court, San Antonio, TX 78204

Child–Adolescent Suicidal Potential Index

Description

The Child–Adolescent Suicidal Potential Index (CASPI; Pfeffer, Jiang, & Kakuma, 2000) is a 30-item self-report instrument based in part on the clinician-rated Child Suicide Potential Scales (CSPS, reviewed later; see Pfeffer et al., 1979). The CASPI was developed for use with children and adolescents ages 6 through 17 (although it is recommended that 6- and 7-year-olds have the questionnaire read to them). Children answer "yes" or "no" to each of the items on the CASPI. The time frame of reference for the CASPI is the last 6 months. The scale was developed for use in screening children and adolescents for risk of suicidality.

Populations Studied

The CASPI was validated with a group of children and adolescents referred for psychiatric services and a group of control children from the local schools (Pfeffer, Jiang, & Kakuma, 2000).

Reliability

In a subset of the children in the validation sample, 2-week test–retest reliability (ICC) of the total CASPI was .76 (Pfeffer, Jiang, & Kakuma, 2000). Test–retest reliabilities for the three CASPI factors ranged from ICC = .59 to ICC = .76 (Pfeffer, Jiang, & Kakuma, 2000).

Internal Consistency

The internal consistency of the total CASPI was reported as α = .90. Depending on the age of the children, the internal consistency of three factors of the CASPI ranged from α = .74 to α = .89 (Pfeffer et al., 1989).

Concurrent Validity

The construct validity of the CASPI was evidenced by its moderate correlations with a depression inventory, an anxiety inventory, and the Hopelessness Scale for Children (Pfeffer, Jiang, & Kakuma, 2000). Total CASPI scores and scores for each of the three CASPI factors were higher among suicidal than among nonsuicidal youths (Pfeffer, Jiang, & Kakuma, 2000). A cutoff of 11 on the CASPI identified 70% of the children and adolescents in the validation sample who made suicide attempts (sensitivity) and identified 65% of those who did not make attempts (specificity; Pfeffer, Jiang, & Kakuma, 2000).

Dimensionality

In the validation sample, a three-factor solution was extracted, which accounted for 37% of the variance in CASPI responses. The first factor was accounted for by items regarding anxiety, depression, anger, and impulsivity. The second factor included items regarding the assessment of suicide attempts and suicidal ideation. The third factor included items regarding family problems (parental arguments, parental depression, parental alcohol use, domestic violence, etc.).

Predictive Validity

The predictive validity of the CASPI has not yet been demonstrated (Pfeffer, Jiang, & Kakuma, 2000).

Treatment Studies

The CASPI has not been used in treatment studies.

Summary and Evaluation

The CASPI is a self-report instrument for estimating the risk of suicidal behavior in children and adolescents. It is based in part on the CSPS, which is reviewed below. The use of the CASPI has not been evaluated beyond the original validation samples, and the predictive validity of the CASPI has not been determined.

Where to Obtain

Cynthia R. Pfeffer, MD, New York-Presbyterian Hospital—Westchester Division, 21 Bloomingdale Road, White Plains, NY 10605

Child Suicide Potential Scales

Description

The clinician-rated Child Suicide Potential Scales (CSPS), with the exception of the Spectrum of Suicidal Behavior (SSB; see this volume, chap. 4), is designed to assist in the assessment of risk or potential for suicidal behavior (Pfeffer et al., 1979). The CSPS includes sections assessing the Spectrum of Assaultive Behavior, Precipitating Events, Affects and Behavior (recent), Affects and Behavior (past), Family Background, Concept of Death, Assessment of Current Ego Functions, and Ego Defenses (Pfeffer et al., 1979). Some of the CSPS scales (e.g., the scales assessing ego functioning and ego defense mechanisms) are grounded in developmental and psychodynamic theory. The CSPS was developed for use with 5- to 12-year-olds but also has been used with adolescents. Clinicians rate items on the basis of semistructured interviews with children and parents. The CSPS has been translated into Hebrew and has been used in clinical research.

Populations Studied

The CSPS has been used in studies of child and adolescent psychiatric inpatients (Pfeffer et al., 1979, 1982; Zalsman et al., 2000), in nonclinically referred children (Pfeffer et al., 1984), and in child psychiatric outpatients (Pfeffer et al., 1980). The Hebrew version of the CSPS has been used in studies of Israeli adolescent psychiatric inpatients, adolescent suicide attempters presenting in an emergency room setting, and adolescent nonpatients (Apter et al., 1997; Gothelf et al., 1998; Ofek et al., 1998; Stein, Apter, et al., 1998).

Reliability

In a sample of school children, estimates of interrater reliability for the CSPS were as follows—Spectrum of Assaultive Behavior: $r = .97$; Precipitating Events: $r = .95$; Recent Affects and Behavior: $r = .93$; Past Affects and Behavior: $r = .94$; Concepts of Death: $r = .92$; Family Background: $r = .96$; Ego Mechanisms: $r = .54$ to .80; and Ego Defenses: $r = .52$ to .96 (Pfeffer et al., 1984).

Interrater reliability for the Spectrum of Assaultive Behavior scale of the Hebrew version of the CSPS was .91 (Ofek et al., 1998). Interrater reliabilities ranged from .89 to .90 for the Concept of Death scales (Ofek et al., 1998), from .65 to 1.0 for the Ego Mechanism Scales (Ofek et al., 1998), and from .83 to 1.0 in one study (Ofek et al., 1998) and from .57 to .93 in another study (Apter et al., 1997) for the Ego Defense Scales.

In a 6- to 12-month follow-up, estimates of the long-term test–retest stability of the CSPS items and scales were as follows—Preoccupation With Death: $r = .78$; Perception of Death as Final and Perception of Death as Pleasant: $r = -.04$ to $r = +.23$, ns; Total Defense Mechanisms: $r = .25$, ns; Violence (Assaultiveness): $r = .52$; Destructiveness: $r = .11$, ns; Recent Affects and Behavior: $r = .28$ to $r = .41$, ns; and Past Affects and Behavior: $r = .45$ to $r = .62$.

Internal Consistency

In psychiatrically hospitalized 6- to 12-year-old children, the internal consistency for the CSPS was reported as follows—Affects and Behavior (recent): $\alpha = .82$; Affects and Behavior (past): $\alpha = .98$; Concept of Death: $\alpha = .86$; Family Background: $\alpha = .71$; and Precipitating Events: $\alpha = .57$ (Pfeffer et al., 1979). In a sample of adolescent inpatients, the internal consistency of selected sections of the Hebrew version of the CSPS was generally in the moderate range ($\alpha = .39$ to .79; Ofek et al., 1998).

Concurrent Validity

Because each scale of the CSPS is scored separately (rather than contributing to an overall index of risk or suicidal propensity), the concurrent construct-related validity of each scale is summarized in the following sections.

Spectrum of Assaultive Behavior

In a sample of psychiatrically hospitalized children, assaultiveness was positively correlated with suicidal behavior (Pfeffer et al., 1989). Also among adolescent inpatients, CSPS assaultiveness was related to another measure of aggression but not to anger (Ofek et al., 1998).

Precipitating Events

Environmental stresses on the CSPS almost uniformly did not differenti-ate between suicidal and nonsuicidal children in the same setting (Pfeffer et al., 1979, 1980, 1982, 1984).

Affects and Behavior (Recent)

Recent general psychopathology distinguished between suicidal and nonsuicidal children (Pfeffer et al., 1982, 1984). There have been mixed findings regarding whether CSPS-assessed recent depression is related to suicidality (Pfeffer et al., 1979, 1980, 1982, 1984). Recent CSPS-assessed anxiety and aggression were found to be related to other indices measuring state and trait anxiety and aggression, respectively (Ofek et al., 1998).

Affects and Behavior (Past)

Past general psychopathology distinguished between suicidal and non-suicidal children (Pfeffer et al., 1982, 1984). However, there have been inconsistent findings regarding the relationship between CSPS-assessed past depression and suicidality (Pfeffer et al., 1979, 1980, 1982, 1984).

Family Background Scale

Most variables on the family background scale have not been found to be related to suicidality among children (Pfeffer et al., 1979, 1980, 1982). There have been inconsistent findings regarding the relationship between parental psychopathology and child suicidal behavior (Pfeffer et al., 1979, 1980, 1982).

Concept of Death

Preoccupation with death was related to suicidality in several samples of children (Pfeffer et al., 1979, 1980, 1982, 1984). Using the Hebrew version of the CSPS, Gothelf et al. (1998) found that suicidal inpatients had significant preoccupations with death, but suicidal inpatients in an emergency room setting did not. There have been inconsistent findings regarding whether suicidality is related to the perception among children of death as pleasant or as temporary (Gothelf et al., 1998; Pfeffer et al., 1979, 1980, 1982, 1984).

Ego Functioning

There have been inconsistent findings regarding the relationship be-tween CSPS-assessed impulse control and suicidality (Pfeffer et al., 1979,

1980, 1982, 1984). Most other aspects of ego functioning have not been found to be related to suicidality. The CSPS assessment of impulse control was modestly but statistically significantly related to another scale assessing impulse control (Ofek et al., 1998).

Ego Defenses

There have been inconsistent findings regarding the relationship between defense mechanisms, especially introjection, and suicidality among youths (Apter et al., 1997; Pfeffer et al., 1979, 1980, 1982, 1984). Using the Hebrew version of the CSPS, Apter et al. (1997) found modest but statistically significant relationships between 7 of 11 defense mechanisms and suicidality rated on an ordinal scale with the SSB. CSPS-assessed repression was related to another measure of repression, but three other CSPS-assessed defense mechanisms (regression, reaction formation, and displacement) were not related to external measures (Ofek et al., 1998).

Dimensionality

No published data were located.

Predictive Validity

No data were found regarding the predictive validity of indices from the CSPS other than the SSB.

Treatment Studies

The scales of the CSPS apparently have not been used as outcome measures in treatment studies.

Summary and Evaluation

The scales of the CSPS together form a clinician-rated instrument for use in evaluating both the risk or potential of suicidal behaviors among children, and the presence or severity of suicidal behaviors among children (the latter is assessed with the SSB Scale reviewed earlier; see this volume, chap. 4). The CSPS has been very well studied. However, the evidence regarding the concurrent construct-related validity of some of the indices of the CSPS has been inconsistent, and none of the CSPS scales (other than the SSB) have demonstrated predictive validity.

Where to Obtain

Cynthia R. Pfeffer, MD, New York-Presbyterian Hospital—Westchester Division, 21 Bloomingdale Road, White Plains, NY 10605

Child Suicide Risk Assessment

Description

The Child Suicide Risk Assessment (CSRA) is an instrument developed for identifying youths at risk for suicide or in need of suicide precautions, particularly youths under the age of 12 for whom most other suicide risk instruments are not appropriate (Anderson & Larzelere, 1997; Larzelere, Jorgensen, & Anderson, 2001). The CSRA has four main sections. The first section focuses on "Worsening Depression" (e.g., worry, sadness, crying, sleep problems, guilt). The second section focuses on "Lack of Support" (e.g., feeling loved by family, availability of someone to talk to). The third section focuses on "Death as Escape" (e.g., whether people are happier when they die, whether people can come back to live on earth after they die). The answers to the queries to the first three sections are summed to yield an overall *risk score*. There also is a fourth section with four questions assessing current and past suicidal ideation and attempts (this section was not reviewed separately with the other detection instruments as it is meant to be used with other risk items as an additional indicant of risk). Different levels of risk (with minimum recommended actions) are described based on the total scores to the first three sections and positive responses to the critical items regarding suicidal ideation and behavior. The authors of this scale are careful to point out its limitations and to suggest that the CSRA should be used in conjunction with other available information in estimating suicide risk.

Populations Studied

The CSRA has been developed and pilot tested with children receiving services at Boys Town sites (Anderson & Larzelere, 1997; Larzelere et al., 2001).

Reliability

No published data were located.

Internal Consistency

In a sample of 140 youths evaluated subsequent to their statements of self-harm or at the time of their admission to out-of-home placement, α for the total scale (first three sections) was .72 (Lazelere et al., 2001). Item–total correlations ranged from .07 to .42 (Larzelere et al., 2001).

Concurrent Validity

Seven of eighteen items on the CSRA were modestly but statistically significantly related to whether children reported current suicidal ideation (Lazelere et al., 2001). Six items were related to whether children reported ever making a suicide attempt. Eight items were related to lifetime history of suicidal ideation.

Receiver operating characteristic (ROC) curve analysis was used to help determine cutoff scores. This method indicated that a score of 8 was the best cutoff score on the risk scale, identifying 82% of children who reported a history of attempts on the CSRA critical items, with a false positive rate of 14% (Lazelere et al., 2001). No data regarding the relationship between CSRA and external scales or indices were found.

Dimensionality

A principal-components analysis with varimax rotation yielded a three-factor solution for the CSRA risk items. These factors (which now make up the three scales) accounted for 38% of the variance in scores.

Predictive Validity

No published data were located.

Treatment Studies

No published data were located, but the CSRA is being developed primarily as a screening instrument.

Summary and Evaluation

This CSRA is an interview-based screening instrument developed for assessing suicide risk. The authors developed this instrument because of a lack of suitable screening instruments for suicide risk assessment in children between the ages of 6 and 12. Data regarding the test–retest reliability, predictive validity, and convergent validity of the scale using measures in addition to the CSRA have not yet been published.

Where to Obtain

Robert E. Larzelere, PhD, Director of Behavioral Healthcare Research, Youth Care Building, Father Flanagan's Boys Home, 13603 Flanagan Blvd., Boys Town, NE 68010

Expendable Child Measure

Description

The Expendable Child Measure is a 12-item clinician-rated scale predicated on the assumption that suicidal youths may perceive the parents' (conscious or unconscious) wish to be rid of them or for them to die (Woznica & Shapiro, 1990, 1998). Items on the scale assess whether respondents feel like they are a burden on the family, or feel like they are an unwanted or unnecessary part of the family. The scale may be used to help determine which adolescents may be at particularly high risk for suicide, and therefore warrant additional evaluation by clinicians, or may be used to complement other measures of depression and suicidality.

Populations Studied

This scale has been used with adolescents being seen in therapy in a hospital setting or outpatient clinic (Woznica & Shapiro, 1998).

Reliability

No published data were located.

Internal Consistency

In a sample of both suicidal and nonsuicidal adolescent psychiatric outpatients, the Expendable Child Measure was found to be internally consistent ($\alpha = .92$; Woznica & Shapiro, 1990).

Concurrent Validity

Suicidal adolescents in psychiatric outpatient settings (with attempts or ideation) were rated by psychology interns as higher on the Expendable

Child Measure than nonsuicidal adolescents (Woznica & Shapiro, 1998). Subsequent analyses revealed no differences between youths who attempted suicide and youths with high suicidal ideation.

Dimensionality

No published data were located.

Predictive Validity

No published data were located.

Treatment Studies

No published data were located.

Summary and Evaluation

This measure is predicated on the interesting notion that youths who perceive themselves to be expendable by their families will be at higher risk for suicidal behavior. However, relatively little data on the psychometric characteristics of this clinician-rated scale have been published.

Where to Obtain

The scale is reproduced in Woznica and Shapiro (1998).

Firestone Assessment of Self-Destructive Thoughts

Description

The Firestone Assessment of Self-Destructive Thoughts (FAST) is a self-report instrument based in part on the theory associated with voice therapy, a variation of psychodynamic therapy (Firestone & Firestone, 1998). *Voices* are conceptualized as internalized self-destructive negative thoughts that are in part introjected from one's parents. The developers of the FAST posit that suicide potential can be predicted on the basis of the types and intensity of self-destructive thoughts. Within the FAST, self-destructive thoughts are organized into 11 levels along a continuum. The first 5 levels are considered to be thoughts associated with low self-esteem and self-defeating tendencies. Level 6 is considered to be a class of thoughts that is associated with and supports addictions. The last 5 levels are thoughts that are assumed to be associated with increasing suicide risk. These range from "thoughts contributing to a sense of hopelessness" (Level 7) to "injunctions to carry out suicide plans" (Level 11). A *suicide intent composite* is constructed from items on Levels 7 to 11 which were found to best differentiate individuals with and without suicidal ideation. The authors of this scale suggest that it is useful in clinical assessment and treatment planning.

Populations Studied

The FAST was developed and has been used with clinically ascertained inpatient and outpatient samples (Firestone & Firestone, 1998).

Reliability

In a sample of adolescent and (primarily) adult psychiatric inpatients, the test–retest reliability of the 11 levels of the FAST (over 1 to 31 days) ranged from $r = .63$ to $r = .88$; test–retest reliability for the entire scale was .88 and for the suicide intent composite was .93 (Firestone & Firestone, 1998). In outpatients, the test–retest reliability (over 28 to 266 days) of the 11 levels ranged from .69 to .90. Test–retest reliability for the entire FAST was .92, and for the suicide intent composite was .85.

Internal Consistency

In a sample with both adolescents (age 16 and older) and adults, the internal consistency of the 11 levels of the FAST range from $\alpha = .76$ to .91, with the total FAST score having Cronbach α of .97 and the suicide intent composite having α of .95 (Firestone & Firestone, 1998).

Concurrent Validity

The FAST was found to correlate with the Suicide Probability Scale total score ($r = .76$) and the Beck Depression Inventory ($r = .73$) and Hopelessness Scale ($r = .63$; Firestone & Firestone, 1998). The FAST total score and suicide intent composite were found to correlate with a criterion measure reflecting past and current suicidal behavior.

Dimensionality

Factor analysis revealed three factors corresponding to items on Levels 1 through 5 (the Self-Defeating Composite), Level 6 (the Addictions Composite), and Levels 7 through 11 (the Self-Annihilating Composite).

Predictive Validity

No published data were located.

Treatment Studies

No published data were located.

Summary and Evaluation

The FAST is based on theory related to voice therapy. The FAST was developed with patients ranging in age from 16 to 80. The scale has not yet been used in published studies beyond that describing the development and validation of the measure. The FAST was developed in part to measure patients' suicide potential, but the predictive validity of the scale has not been examined.

Where to Obtain

The Psychological Corporation, 555 Academic Court, San Antonio, TX 78204

Hopelessness Scale for Children

Description

The Hopelessness Scale for Children (HPLS; Kazdin et al., 1986) is a 17-item modification of the Beck Hopelessness Scale (BHS). Items are rated either true or false, and total scores range from 0 to 17. As with the BHS, higher scores in the HPLS indicate a greater degree of hopelessness. Readability of the HPLS is at first- to second-grade level. The HPLS has been used in clinical assessment and clinical research.

Populations Studied

The standardization sample for the HPLS was 6- to 13-year-old psychiatric inpatients (Kazdin, Rodgers, & Colbus, 1986). The HPLS also has been used with other nonclinically ascertained samples of high school students (Cole, 1989a; Reifman & Windle, 1995; Spirito, Williams, Stark, & Hart, 1988), suicide attempters in pediatric and emergency room settings (Boergers, Spirito, & Donaldson, 1998; Donaldson, Spirito, & Fawcett, 2000; Fritsch, Donaldson, Spirito, & Plummer, 2000; Spirito et al., 1987, 1988), child and adolescent psychiatric inpatients (Asarnow & Guthrie, 1989; Dori & Overholser, 1999; Fritsch et al., 2000; Hewitt et al., 1997; Kashani et al., 1991; Kashani, Suarez, Allan, & Reid, 1997; Nock & Kazdin, 2002; Pinto & Whisman, 1996; Pinto et al., 1998; Sadowski & Kelley, 1993; Whisman & Pinto, 1997), child and adolescent psychiatric outpatients (Spirito et al., 1988), and incarcerated youths (Cole, 1989a).

Reliability

There was moderate stability in HPLS scores over a 6-week period of time among child psychiatric inpatients (r = .52; Kazdin et al., 1986). Among nonclinically referred young adolescents (ninth graders), there again was moderate stability over a 10-week test–retest interval (r = .49; Spirito et al., 1988).

Internal Consistency

In a sample of 6- to 13-year-old (Kazdin et al., 1986) psychiatric inpatients, the HPLS was internally consistent (α = .97; Spearman–Brown split-half reliability = .96). The HPLS was also internally consistent among adolescent psychiatric inpatients (α = .89; Hewitt et al., 1997; and α = .84, Spearman–Brown split-half reliability = .91; Spirito et al., 1988). In a large sample of nonclinically referred ninth graders (Spirito et al., 1988), the coefficient α for the HPLS was .69, and Spearman–Brown split-half reliability coefficient was .75.

Concurrent Validity

Among high school students, HPLS scores were positively correlated with a five-item questionnaire used by Beck, Weissman, et al. (1974) to validate the BHS (r = .71; Cole, 1989a). Hospitalized suicide attempters have been found to have higher HPLS scores than adolescents in a nonclinically referred sample (Sadowski & Kelley, 1993; Spirito et al., 1988). Evidence is mixed as to whether suicide attempters have higher HPLS scores than nonsuicidal psychiatric controls (Sadowski & Kelley, 1993; Spirito et al.,

1988). Psychiatrically hospitalized adolescents with histories of multiple suicide attempts reported more hopelessness than nonsuicidal youths (Dori
& Overholser, 1999). HPLS scores did not differentiate between adolescents
hospitalized on a pediatric unit following overdoses and adolescents on the
same unit receiving psychiatric consultations for other reasons (Spirito et
al., 1987).

In different samples of child and adolescent pediatric and psychiatric
inpatients, higher HPLS scores have been found to be associated with greater
severity of depressive symptoms (Asarnow & Guthrie, 1989; Cole, 1989a;
Dori & Overholser, 1999; Kazdin et al., 1986; Marciano & Kazdin, 1994;
Nock & Kazdin, 2002; Overholser, Freiheit, & DiFilippo, 1997; Spirito et
al., 1988), severity of anhedonia (Nock & Kazdin, 2002), a higher prevalence
of depressive diagnoses (Kashani et al., 1991), more automatic negative
thoughts (Nock & Kazdin, 2002), a greater number of total diagnoses
(Kashani et al., 1991), poorer self-esteem or self-image (Fritsch et al., 2000;
Kashani et al., 1991; Kazdin et al., 1986; Marciano & Kazdin, 1994; Overholser
et al., 1995), self-criticism (Donaldson et al., 2000), poorer self-rated social
skills (Kazdin et al., 1986), more anxiety (Kashani et al., 1991), greater
socially prescribed perfectionism (Donaldson et al., 2000; Hewitt et al.,
1997—girls only), more difficult temperament (Kashani et al., 1991), inhibi-
tion (Fritsch et al., 2000), sensitivity (Fritsch et al., 2000; Kashani, Nair, Rao,
Nair, & Reid, 1996), family and academic problems (Fritsch et al., 2000),
child abuse (Grilo, Sanislow, Fehon, Martino, & McGlashan, 1999), lower
estimated intellectual functioning (Kashani et al., 1991), suicidal ideation
(Hewitt et al., 1997; Kashani et al., 1991; Nock & Kazdin, 2002; Whisman
& Pinto, 1997), suicidal tendencies (suicidal ideation and attempts rated
on a continuous scale; Asarnow & Guthrie, 1989; Cole, 1989a), suicide
attempts (McLaughlin, Miller, & Warwick, 1996), suicide intent associated
with suicide attempts (Nock & Kazdin, 2002), and presumed risk for suicide
as assessed with a suicide risk instrument (Pfeffer, Jiang, & Kakuma, 2000).
Results regarding the relationship between hopelessness and decreased impulse control have been mixed (Fritsch et al., 2000; Kashani et al., 1996).

There also have been mixed results regarding whether HPLS scores
are related to suicidality after controlling for depression. In one study, the
correlation between hopelessness and suicidal tendencies did not remain
statistically significant after controlling for severity of depression (Asarnow
& Guthrie, 1989). In another study, hopelessness continued to be correlated
with an index of suicidal behavior after controlling for depression for high
school girls but not for high school boys (Cole, 1989a). Nock and Kazdin
(2002) found that the relationship between hopelessness and severity of

suicidal ideation and suicide intent (among suicide attempters) remained statistically significant after controlling for severity of depressed mood, but the relationship between hopelessness and presence or absence of a suicide attempt prior to psychiatric hospitalization did not. In a mixed sample of child psychiatric outpatients and inpatients, HPLS scores were related to a continuous index of suicidality, even after controlling for severity of symptoms of depression and self-esteem (Myers, McCauley, Calderon, Mitchell, et al., 1991). However, HLPS scores were not related to the suicidality index among youths with major depression after controlling for severity of depression (Myers, McCauley, Calderon, Mitchell, et al., 1991).

In two studies of child psychiatric inpatients, HPLS scores have contributed to discriminant function analyses in classifying children with suicidal ideation or attempts and nonsuicidal youths (Asarnow & Guthrie, 1989; Marciano & Kazdin, 1994). In both studies, approximately 40% of cases were incorrectly classified even after consideration of HPLS scores.

In samples of both adolescents recruited from high schools and incarcerated juvenile delinquents, higher HPLS scores have been found to be associated with fewer or less strong reasons for living, particularly survival and coping beliefs (Cole, 1989b; Pinto et al., 1998). HPLS scores have been found to be associated with a "wish to die" as a primary motivation for adolescent suicide attempts (Boergers et al., 1998). HPLS scores have been found to be related to expectations of poorer outcome associated with suicide attempts (Spirito, Sterling, Donaldson, & Arrigan, 1996) and less impulsive suicide attempts (L. Brown et al., 1991; Spirito et al., 1996). In one study, the relationship between HPLS scores and overall suicide intent scores was stronger among female than among male adolescent psychiatric inpatients (Overholser et al., 1997). HPLS scores were not found to be associated with medical lethality of suicide attempts among adolescent psychiatric inpatients (Nasser & Overholser, 1999).

Dimensionality

A principal-components analysis with data from child psychiatric inpatients yielded one primary and one secondary factor, both assessing negative expectancies for the future, and overlapping in content (Kazdin et al., 1986).

Predictive Validity

In an 18-month follow-up of psychiatrically hospitalized adolescents, HPLS scores were the strongest predictor of subsequent suicide attempts

(Brinkman-Sull et al., 2000). In another study of both children and adolescents recruited from inpatient and outpatient psychiatric settings (100 with diagnoses of major depression and 38 without major depression diagnoses), HPLS scores were not related to suicidality over a 3-year follow-up (Myers, McCauley, Calderon, & Treder, 1991).

Treatment Studies

The HPLS was used as one of the outcome measures in a comparison of two interventions—routine care versus a combination of routine care, home visits, and family problem-solving sessions—for adolescents who had taken overdoses (Harrington et al., 1998). At 2- and 6-month follow-ups, the two groups did not differ with regard to hopelessness (the intervention did result in a reduction in suicidal ideation, but only for youths with major depression).

The HPLS also was examined as a potential moderator variable in a clinical trial examining the use of a problem-solving intervention to improve aftercare following suicide attempts. However, HPLS scores were found to be unrelated to number of therapy sessions attended (Spirito, Boergers, Donaldson, Bishop, & Lewander, 2002).

Summary and Evaluation

The HPLS has been widely used in research studies of suicidality among youths. The scale may be particularly useful for preadolescents (an age group for whom the BHS is not appropriate). The great majority of studies using the HPLS have been cross-sectional in design and have demonstrated the correlation between HPLS scores and other constructs related to depression, distress, or suicidal ideation/behavior. Two follow-up studies examining the predictive use of HPLS scores have been conducted; one found hopelessness scores to be predictive of later suicidal behavior, and the other did not.

Where to Obtain

The items on the HPLS are reproduced in Kazdin et al. (1986).

Inventory of Suicide Orientation—30

Description

The Inventory of Suicide Orientation—30 (ISO–30; King & Kowalchuk, 1994) is a 30-item self-report instrument designed for assessing suicidality in 13- to 18-year-old adolescents. The test's content is heavily influenced by theoretical notions that stress the individual's belief systems and "life-affirming orientation" as central to understanding the process that results in suicide. Nonetheless, statements of the purpose of the test are contradictory. In the "Cautions Regarding Test Interpretation" part of the manual, it is stated that the objective of the ISO–30 is to assess "two key indicators of suicide risk (orientation and ideation), not to *predict* suicidal behavior per se" (p. 34). However, elsewhere in the manual, it is stated that "the primary objective of the ISO–30 is to identify adolescents who are at high risk for suicide" (p. 2) and that "the aim of the ISO–30 is to assess suicide risk" (p. 15); in that vein, a framework is provided for forming "an overall index of suicide risk" (p. 15).

The ISO–30 is a revised version of what formerly was known as the Life Orientation Inventory. There are five scales on the ISO–30: Hopelessness, Suicidal Ideation, Perceived Inadequacy, Inability to Cope With Emotions, and Social Isolation and Withdrawal. Respondents are asked to decide whether they feel 30 statements on the inventory describe the way they have been thinking over the last 6 months. For each item, they are asked to choose one of four options: 1 (*I am sure I disagree*), 2 (*I mostly disagree*), 3 (*I mostly agree*), or 4 (*I am sure I agree*). The 8 items assessing suicidal ideation are considered to be critical items. Risk classifications (low, moderate, high) are based on a combination of the total scores and the scores on the critical items. The ISO–30 has been translated into Spanish. It is appropriate for clinical research, clinical assessment, and screening in clinical settings

Populations Studied

The ISO–30 has been tested in clinically referred (King & Kowalchuk, 1994; Piersma & Boes, 1997) and student samples (King & Kowalchuk, 1994).

Reliability

Over a period of 3 to 4 days, the test–retest reliability of the ISO–30 was .80 for the total score and .70 for the critical items (King & Kowalchuk, 1994).

Internal Consistency

The ISO–30 was found to be internally consistent (α = .92 and .90) in clinical and student samples of adolescents, respectively (King & Kowalchuk, 1994). Cronbach α was .79 for the critical item score in the clinical sample, and .78 in the student sample (King & Kowalchuk, 1994).

Concurrent Validity

In clinical and student samples, ISO–30 total scores correlated .64 and .52, respectively, with the SIQ and .55 and .78, respectively, with the SIQ–JR (King & Kowalchuk, 1994). In the clinical and student samples, the ISO–30 critical item scores correlated .72 and .43, respectively, with the SIQ and .64 and .66, respectively, with the SIQ–JR (King & Kowalchuk, 1994). Scores on the ISO–30 in youths with and without suicidal attempts apparently have not been evaluated.

Dimensionality

No published data were located.

Predictive Validity

No published data were located.

Treatment Studies

The ISO–30 was used to evaluate adolescents who were psychiatrically hospitalized both at admission and approximately 6 days later (Piersma & Boes, 1997). As expected (because the second administration was part of the process of determining whether patients were ready for discharge), the proportion of patients classified as high risk fell substantially during the hospitalization from 61% to 26% (Piersma & Boes, 1997).

Summary and Evaluation

The ISO–30 is a theory-based instrument that is described as both a measure of life orientation and a measure of suicide risk. The test's validation procedures have focused only on suicidal ideation, the risk of which is obviously far different than the risk of completed suicide (which is implied when the phrase *suicide risk* is used). Differences in the test scores have not been demonstrated for suicide attempters and nonattempters, and the predictive validity of the ISO–30 has not been demonstrated.

Where to Obtain

National Computer Systems, Inc., P.O. Box 1416, Minneapolis, MN 55440

Life Attitudes Schedule

Description

The Life Attitudes Schedule (LAS) is a self-report instrument that is predicated on theoretical notions that "there is a single domain of behaviors to which all life-enhancing and life-threatening behaviors belong" (Lewinsohn et al., 1995, p. 458). This domain can be viewed as a continuum from positive to negative, and can be conceptualized as including four content areas: death-related, health-related, injury-related, and self-related. A primary goal is to assess behaviors in these four domains. A related goal for the LAS is the assessment of "a person's propensity at a point in time to engage in suicidal behavior," broadly conceptualized to include "subtle/nonobvious self-destructive behaviors . . . and risk-taking behaviors, as well as behaviors that are obviously and overtly suicidal" (pp. 459–460). On the LAS, half of the items assess life-enhancing behaviors, and half assess life-threatening behaviors. In addition, the LAS is constructed so that there are equal numbers of items assessing three categories of behavior: thoughts, actions, and feelings. Three alternative forms of the LAS have been developed (Lewinsohn et al., 1995), in addition to a short form (Rohde, Lewinsohn, Seeley, & Langhinrichsen, 1996). The LAS is scored so that higher scores are thought to represent greater suicidal or self-destructive behavior. The LAS has been used in clinical research and has potential use as a clinical assessment tool.

Populations Studied

The LAS has been used both with nonclinically ascertained samples of high school students and with adolescents participating in a treatment study for depression (Lewinsohn et al., 1995).

Reliability

In high school students, the 30-day test–retest reliability for the LAS ranged from .75 to .88 (Lewinsohn et al., 1995). Test–retest reliability ranged from .76 to .82 for the death-related items, from .68 to .82 for health-related items, from .68 to .88 for injury-related items, and from .72 to .79 for self-related items. Moreover, test–retest reliability ranged from .59 to .88 for items assessing actions, from .69 to .90 for items assessing thoughts, and from .71 to .81 for items assessing feelings.

The short form of the LAS has not been administered on two separate occasions to assess test–retest reliability. However, because items from the short form were selected from the longer form, estimates of the test–retest reliability of the shorter form have been published (Rohde et al., 1996). Test–retest reliability for the entire LAS–Short Form is comparable with that of the longer version of the LAS. Test–retest reliability for the content areas and behavior categories is comparable, or in some cases, somewhat less than that reported for the longer version of the LAS.

Internal Consistency

In high school students, the internal consistency of the alternative forms of the LAS (as measured by α) ranged from .92 to .94 (Lewinsohn et al., 1995). Internal consistency for the scales assessing different content areas are as follows—Death-Related: $\alpha = .77$ to .85; Health-Related: $\alpha = .71$ to .77; Injury-Related: $\alpha = .82$ to .86; Self-Related: $\alpha = .87$ for all forms. The internal consistency of items assessing the different behavioral categories are as follows—Actions: $\alpha = .71$ to .82; Thoughts: $\alpha = .82$ to .87; and Feelings: $\alpha = .81$ to .88.

The LAS–Short Form has not been administered in a separate sample from the longer version of the LAS to assess internal consistency. However, because items from the short form were selected from the longer form, estimates of the internal consistency have been published (Rohde et al., 1996). The internal consistency of the LAS–Short Form total scores and scales scores is somewhat less than the comparable internal consistency of the longer version of the LAS.

Concurrent Validity

The LAS is one of the only instruments for which attention has been paid not only to issues of convergent validity but also to issues of discriminant validity. To reduce redundancy, the researchers selected items with the goal of limiting the degree of correlation with depression, hopelessness, and social desirability. In a sample of high school students, the correlation between the LAS total scores and depression scores (assessed with the CES–D) ranged from .43 to .59 across forms (Lewinsohn et al., 1995). The correlation between the LAS and BHS scores ranged from .55 to .65 across forms. The correlation between the LAS and the Marlow–Crowne Social Desirability Scale ranged from .38 to .39 across forms (comparable with the correlations with past accidental and intentional injury, as described below).

The correlation between the LAS scales and an interview developed to assess the same constructs (the Life Attitude Interview Schedule or LAIS) was also assessed. In general, the correlations between the LAS scales and the scales on the LAIS assessing the same constructs were higher than correlations between different constructs (Lewinsohn et al., 1995).

Correlations between reporting "accidentally hurt or injured self" during the "worst past time" (assessed with the LAIS, described earlier) and the six scales of the LAS were low to moderate and ranged from .18 (ns) to .32 (Lewinsohn et al., 1995). Correlations between reports of "intentionally hurting or injuring self" during "worst past time" ranged from .21 to .30 for the scales of the LAS. Correlations with lifetime history of suicide attempts were higher, but still moderate, ranging from .30 to .46.

Dimensionality

A confirmatory factor analysis (with LAS items constrained to load on their respective content areas and behavior types) provided a good fit (Lewinsohn et al., 1995). A second-order factor analysis revealed a single dimension for LAS items, which was interpreted as suicide proneness.

Predictive Validity

No published data were located.

Treatment Studies

No published data were located.

Summary and Evaluation

The LAS is a carefully developed measure based on the notion of a "single domain of behaviors to which all life-enhancing and life-threatening behaviors belong" (Lewinsohn et al., 1995, p. 458). However, information about the predictive validity of the measure (and the degree to which it actually assesses "suicide proneness" in a predictive sense) has yet to be published. Assessment of the predictive validity of the scale is acknowledged to be a priority area of research by the authors of the scale (Rohde et al., 1996).

Where to Obtain

The long forms of the LAS may be obtained from Peter M. Lewinsohn, PhD, Oregon Research Institute, 1715 Franklin Boulevard, Eugene, OR 97403-1983. The short form of the LAS is reproduced in Rohde et al. (1996).

Millon Adolescent Clinical Inventory Suicidal Tendency Scale

Description

The Millon Adolescent Clinical Inventory (MACI) is a 160-item true/false self-report inventory designed to assess a variety of personality constructs and psychological symptoms in adolescents (Millon, 1993). The inventory is written at a sixth-grade reading level. The MACI is designed to be a replacement for the Millon Adolescent Personality Inventory (MAPI) that "was developed specifically for use in clinical, residential, and correctional settings" (Hiatt & Cornell, 1999, p. 64). Results from the MACI can be computer-generated, with detailed summaries of the respondent's assessment. Of interest in this chapter is a scale on the MACI titled "Suicidal Tendency."

Populations Studied

The MACI Suicidal Tendency Scale has been used with clinically referred populations of adolescents (Hiatt & Cornell, 1999; Millon, 1993).

Reliability

The MACI Suicidal Tendency Scale was found to have good test–retest reliability ($r = .91$) in a sample of 13- to 19-year-old clinically referred youths (Millon, 1993).

Internal Consistency

The MACI Suicidal Tendency Scale has been found to be internally consistent in the development ($\alpha = .87$) and the cross-validation ($\alpha = .87$) samples of 13- to 19-year-old clinically referred youths (Millon, 1993).

Concurrent Validity

The MACI Suicidal Tendency Scale has moderate to strong correlations with scales (not on the MACI) assessing constructs such as severity of depression, hopelessness, anxiety, social insecurity, problems with impulse regulation, and sense of ineffectiveness, with which it might be expected to be correlated (Millon, 1993). It essentially has no or low correlations with several constructs that are not typically thought to be associated with suicidal tendencies, such as vocational status, problems with leisure/recreation activities, and asceticism (Millon, 1993).

In an adolescent inpatient psychiatric sample (on a unit in which patients were automatically retained on suicide precautions for the first 24 hours of their hospitalization, and then retained on suicide precautions if thought to be at risk), scores on the MACI Suicidal Tendency Scale were moderately predictive (classification accuracy of 64% and $\kappa = .18$, or accuracy of 69% and $\kappa = .12$, depending on the cutoff used) of whether patients were retained on precautions (Hiatt & Cornell, 1999).

Dimensionality

No published data were located.

Predictive Validity

No published data were located.

Treatment Studies

No published treatment studies using the MACI Suicidal Tendency Scale were located.

Summary and Evaluation

The psychometric properties of the MACI Suicidal Tendency Scale have not been evaluated well outside of the initial validation studies. The predictive validity of the scale is unknown.

Where to Obtain

National Computer Systems, Inc., P.O. Box 1416, Minneapolis, MN 55440

Multi-Attitude Suicide Tendency Scale for Adolescents

Description

The Multi-Attitude Suicide Tendency Scale for Adolescents (MAST) is a 30-item measure assessing risk for suicidal behavior (Orbach et al., 1991). The MAST is predicated "on the premise that suicidal behavior evolves around a basic conflict among attitudes toward life and death" (Orbach et al., 1991, p. 398). The four sets of attitudes include those related to (a) attraction toward life (arising from one's sense of security and the fulfillment of needs), (b) repulsion by life (arising from pain, suffering, and unresolvable problems), (c) attraction to death (arising from the notion that aspects of death might be preferable to life), and (d) repulsion by death (arising from fear of death and permanent cessation). The newer version of this scale was developed for adolescents (Orbach et al., 1991). An earlier version (the Fairy Tales Test) was developed for children (Orbach, Feshbach, Carlson, & Ellensberger, 1984; Orbach, Feshbach, Carlson, Glaubman, & Gross, 1983) but is not reviewed here because few published studies (e.g., Cotton & Range, 1993) have used the instrument since 1989.

Populations Studied

The MAST has been used with samples of nonclinically ascertained high school students (Orbach, Lotem-Peleg, & Kedem, 1995; Orbach, Mikulincer, Blumenson, Mester, & Stein, 1999; Orbach et al., 1991), psychiatric outpatients (Orbach et al., 1991, 1999), psychiatric inpatients (Orbach et al., 1991, 1995, 1999), and parentally bereaved adolescents (Orbach et al., 1999).

Reliability

No published data were located.

Internal Consistency

In a mixed sample of nonclinically ascertained high school students, adolescents with suicide attempts (from outpatient and inpatient settings), and nonsuicidal psychiatric inpatients, the internal consistency of the four factor-derived scales was as follows—Attraction to Life: α = .83; Repulsion by Life: α = .76; Attraction to Death: α = .76; and Repulsion by Death: α = .83 (Orbach et al., 1991). Cronbach α for the entire scale was .92. In a different mixed sample of Israeli youths, Cronbach α ranged from .69 to .88 for the four MAST scales (Orbach et al., 1999). In a mixed clinical and nonclinical sample of American adolescents, Cronbach α ranged from .70 to .91 (Osman et al., 1994)

Concurrent Validity

In psychiatrically referred, bereaved, and nonclinical samples of adolescents, the MAST Repulsion to Life scale has been found to be positively correlated with indices of current suicidal ideation and behavior (Gutierrez, 1999; Osman et al., 1994), indices purporting to measure suicide potential (Orbach et al., 1991; Osman et al., 1994), and estimates of future suicidality (Osman et al., 1994). Similarly, the Attraction to Life scale has been found to be negatively correlated, and the Attraction to Death scale positively correlated, with indices of estimated suicide potential (Orbach et al., 1991; Osman et al., 1994), current suicidal behaviors (Osman et al., 1994), and self-rated likelihood of future suicidal behavior (Osman et al., 1994). In none of these studies was the Repulsion by Death scale associated with predicted correlates.

In Osman et al.'s (1994) sample, it was found that social desirability was positively correlated ($r = .24$) with the Attraction to Life scale, and was negatively associated ($r = -.31$) with the Attraction to Death scale. In the latter case, the reported correlation with social desirability was stronger than the correlations reported with the criterion measures used to demonstrate convergent validity.

In two studies, suicidal adolescents were found to have lower Attraction to Life and higher Repulsion by Life and Attraction to Death scores than nonreferred adolescents (Orbach et al., 1991; Osman et al., 1994). In both of these studies, suicidal patients also were found to have higher scores on the Attraction to Death and Repulsion by Life scales than nonsuicidal psychiatric patients (Orbach et al., 1991; Osman et al., 1994). Findings regarding differences between suicidal patients and nonsuicidal patients on the Attraction to Life scale were mixed (Orbach et al., 1991; Osman et al., 1994). In neither of these studies were there any differences found between suicidal and nonsuicidal youths on the Repulsion by Death scale (Orbach et al., 1991; Osman et al., 1994).

In a different mixed clinical and nonclinical sample of adolescents, the four Subjective Experience of Problem Irresolvability (SEPI) scales were all negatively related to the Attraction to Life scale, and positively related to the Attraction to Death and Repulsion by Life scales (Orbach et al., 1999). The SEPI was not related to the Repulsion by Death scale.

Lastly, in an Israeli adolescent inpatient sample, the Attraction to Life and Repulsion by Death MAST scales were positively related, and the Repulsion by Life scale was negatively related to more positive or adaptive sense of body self-preservation as evidenced by three of four factors (body image attitudes, body care, body protection) of the Body Investment Scale (BIS; Orbach & Mikulincer, 1998). All of the MAST scales except the Repulsion by Death scale were also related in a predicted manner to the comfort in physical contact BIS factor, and all of the MAST scales except the Attraction to Death scale were related in a predicted manner to the body care BIS factor (Orbach & Mikulincer, 1998).

Dimensionality

In a mixed clinically and nonclinically ascertained sample of Israeli adolescents, the four-factor structure of the MAST that was apparent in the item selection process (corresponding to attraction and repulsion by life and attraction and repulsion by death) was replicated with the final 30-item version of the scale (Orbach et al., 1991). This same factor structure was replicated in a mixed clinical and nonclinical sample of American youths (Osman et al., 1994).

Predictive Validity

No published data were located.

Treatment Studies

No published data were located.

Summary and Evaluation

The MAST is a theoretically based attitudinal scale that has been shown to differentiate between nonsuicidal and suicidal youths. It is one of the few instruments reviewed that assesses deterrents to suicide in addition to other constructs. The test–retest reliability and the predictive validity of the scale have not been demonstrated. Responses to the Attraction to Death scales are negatively related to social desirability. In addition, the Repulsion by Death scale of the MAST does not appear to be as useful as the other scales in differentiating among suicidal and nonsuicidal youths.

Where to Obtain

Items on the MAST are listed in Orbach et al. (1991).

Positive and Negative Suicide Ideation Inventory

Description

The Positive and Negative Suicide Ideation (PANSI) Inventory is a self-report questionnaire for assessing both risk factors and protective factors for suicidal behavior. The instrument was developed because the authors felt the need for an instrument that examined both factors that increase the risk and decrease the risk of suicidal behaviors. The 14-item instrument consists of six items assessing "positive suicide ideation" and eight "negative suicide ideation" items. Negative risk factors assessed include depression and hopelessness. Protective factors include family connectedness and friendships. Each item in the scale is rated on a 1- to 5-point scale, with reference to how the respondent has been feeling over the last two weeks.

Populations Studied

The PANSI has been administered to samples of high school students (Gutierrez et al., 2002; Osman et al., in press) and psychiatrically hospitalized adolescents (Osman et al., 2002, in press).

Reliability

Among adolescent inpatients, the PANSI Negative Ideation Scale had two-week test–retest reliability of .79 and the PANSI Positive Ideation Scale had two-week test–retest reliability of .69 (Osman et al., 2002).

Internal Consistency

Among adolescent inpatients, the internal consistency of the PANSI Positive Ideation scale was $\alpha = .89$, with item-total correlations ranging from .65 to .78 (Osman et al., 2002). In this same sample, the internal consistency of the PANSI Negative Ideation scale also was high, $\alpha = .96$, with item-total correlations ranging from .75 to .90 (Osman et al., 2002). Similar results have been found in two samples of high school students: $\alpha = .95$ and .94 for the PANSI Negative Ideation Scale and $\alpha = .86$ and .81, respectively, for the PANSI Positive Ideation Scale (Gutierrez et al., 2002; Osman et al., in press).

Concurrent Validity

Among adolescent inpatients, scores on the PANSI Negative Ideation scale were found to be positively related to hopelessness, a measure of negative affect, and another measure of suicidal ideation and behavior, and were found to be negatively related to reasons for living and a measure of positive affect (Osman et al., 2002). In high school students, after controlling for the PANSI Positive Ideation Scale scores, scores on the PANSI Negative Ideation scale were found to be related to hopelessness and depression, but not a scale of negative affect (Osman et al., in press). PANSI Negative Ideation scores were higher among inpatient adolescents thought to be at high risk and high school students thought to be at mild risk for suicide relative to high school students thought to be at low risk (Osman et al., in press).

Among adolescent inpatients, scores on the PANSI Positive Ideation scale were found to be positively related to a measure of positive affect and reasons for living, and negatively related to measures of negative affect, hopelessness, and suicidality (Osman et al., 2002). Among high school students, after controlling for PANSI Negative Ideation scores, PANSI Positive Ideation scale scores were found to be related to reasons for living, satisfaction with life, and positive affect (Osman et al., in press). PANSI Positive Ideation scores were higher among high school youths thought to be at low risk for suicide relative to high school students thought to be at mild risk, and adolescent inpatients thought to be at high risk for suicide (Osman et al., in press).

The ability of the PANSI scales to differentiate between different groups of suicidal and nonsuicidal youths also has been examined. Even after considering the contribution of other indices of suicidality, positive and negative affect, hopelessness, and reasons for living, the PANSI Negative Ideation and Positive Ideation scales each contributed unique variance to the classification of adolescent psychiatric inpatients who attempt suicide vs. nonsuicidal youths, and to the classification of youths thought to be at risk for suicide vs. nonsuicidal youths (Osman et al., 2002).

Dimensionality

In two separate studies, one focusing on adolescent psychiatric inpatients, and the other focusing on high school students, confirmatory factor analysis revealed that the PANSI had two factors corresponding to positive and negative ideation as originally envisioned (Osman et al., 2002, in press).

Predictive Validity

No data were found regarding the predictive validity of the PANSI.

Treatment Studies

The PANSI has not been used in treatment studies to date.

Summary and Evaluation

The authors of the Positive and Negative Suicide Ideation Inventory (PANSI) developed the instrument because of the need for a scale which considered both risk and protective factors related to suicidal behavior. The test–retest reliability, dimensionality, and concurrently assessed validity of the PANSI have been examined. This is one of the few scales for which the test developers also examined the incremental validity of the scale (the unique contribution of the scale after considering the contribution of other instruments). However, the PANSI has not yet been used in studies beyond the development and validation samples.

Where to Obtain

Augustine Osman, PhD, Department of Psychology, University of Northern Iowa, 334 Baker Hall, Cedar Falls, IA 50614-0505

PATHOS

Description

PATHOS is a five-item screening questionnaire administered in interview form by clinicians to evaluate which adolescents with intentional overdose are at continued risk for suicidal behavior and are in need of more extensive assessment prior to discharge from an emergency room setting (Kingsbury, 1996). The PATHOS was developed to meet a clinical need—a system for triaging and identifying those youths in most need of thorough evaluation, given that some youths with overdoses are discharged from emergency settings before thorough assessments can be undertaken. The five questions of the PATHOS (on which the acronym is based) are: (a) Have you had *P*roblems for longer than one month?, (b) Were you *A*lone in the house at the time?, (c) Did you plan the overdose for longer than *Th*ree hours?, (d) Are you feeling *HO*peless about the future?, and (e) Were you feeling *S*ad for most of the time before the overdose? ROC analyses in the sample in which the scale was developed post hoc indicated that a score of 2 or greater for the five questions (with each "Yes" answer counting as 1) best identified youths thought to be at risk.

Populations Studied

The PATHOS has been used as a screening instrument for adolescents presenting in emergency settings secondary to overdose (Kingsbury, 1996).

Reliability

No data regarding interrater or test–retest reliability are available.

Internal Consistency

No published data were located.

Concurrent Validity

In a sample of adolescents presenting in an emergency room setting subsequent to overdoses, PATHOS scores were found to be related to independent assessments of hopelessness, depression, suicidal intent, premeditation time, and history of prior overdoses (Kingsbury, 1996). A high-risk group in this same sample was defined as anyone scoring in the top quartile of the depression or hopelessness scales, or assessments of premeditation or suicide intent. A score of 2 on the PATHOS identified these high-risk youths well, with sensitivity of 100% and specificity of 57.9%.

Dimensionality

No published data were located.

Predictive Validity

No published data were located.

Treatment Studies

No published data were located.

Summary and Evaluation

The PATHOS is a clinical screening procedure for identifying adolescents in emergency settings secondary to overdoses who are thought to be at especially high risk and in need of further evaluation. This instrument was developed to meet a clinical need—a system for triaging and identifying those youths in most need of thorough evaluation, given that some youths with overdoses are discharged from emergency settings before thorough assessments can be undertaken. Nonetheless, the ultimate purpose of the screening instrument is unclear because the authors urge that even low-scoring adolescents should be fully evaluated in emergency settings. No interrater reliability data are available for the PATHOS, and the use of the PATHOS in predicting later suicidal behavior has not been demonstrated.

Where to Obtain

The PATHOS can be found in Kingsbury (1996).

Reasons for Living Inventory

Description

The Reasons for Living Inventory (RFL) is a self-report measure designed to assess potential reasons for not committing suicide (Linehan, Goodstein, Nielsen, & Chiles, 1983). As such, the scale is one of the few instruments that assess protective factors or beliefs buffering against suicidal behavior, rather than focusing on risk factors. Different versions of the inventory have different lengths; however, the most commonly used version of the RFL is the RFL–48 (the 48-item version). On the RFL, respondents are asked to rate the current importance of each item as a reason for not killing themselves. Items are scored on a 6-point Likert scale ranging from 1 (*not at all important*) to 6 (*extremely important*). Based on factor analyses with adults, the RFL is thought to assess six domains of reasons for living: (a) survival and coping beliefs, (b) responsibility to family, (c) child-related concerns, (d) fear of suicide, (e) fear of social disapproval, and (f) moral objections. The RFL yields a total score as well as six subscale scores corresponding to each of the above domains. Linehan has noted individual differences in reasons for living and suggested that identification and intervention with maladaptive beliefs (i.e., low reasons for living) may prove useful in treatment of suicidal individuals. Other versions of the RFL include the Brief RFL (BRFL; Ivanoff, Jang, Smyth, & Linehan, 1994), the RFL for Adolescents (RFL–A; Osman et al., 1998) and the Brief RFL for Adolescents (BRFL–A; Osman et al., 1996); these latter two instruments are reviewed separately. The RFL also has been translated into Chinese (Chan, 1995). The RFL is appropriate for clinical research and clinical assessment.

Populations Studied

The RFL has been used with student populations (Cole, 1989b), incarcerated adolescents (Cole, 1989b), and adolescents in inpatient psychiatric settings (Goldston et al., 2001; Pinto et al., 1998).

Reliability

No published data from adolescents were located for the RFL.

Internal Consistency

In a sample of psychiatric inpatients, Pinto et al. (1998) found the RFL (with the Child-Related Concerns deleted) to be internally consistent ($\alpha = .97$). The five scales derived in that study (which were similar but not identical to the original scales) were also internally consistent—Survival and Coping Beliefs: $\alpha = .98$; Responsibility to Family: $\alpha = .91$; Fear of Failure and Social Disapproval: $\alpha = .86$; Moral Objections: $\alpha = .81$; and Fear of Suicide: $\alpha = .72$.

In a sample of Chinese adolescents (Chan, 1995), the RFL scales were found to have moderate to high internal consistency—Survival and Coping Beliefs: $\alpha = .91$; Responsibility to Family: $\alpha = .78$; Fear of Suicide: $\alpha = .64$; Fear of Social Disapproval: $\alpha = .76$; and Moral Objections: $\alpha = 62$.

Concurrent Validity

In a sample of normal high school students, scores on both the RFL Survival and Coping Beliefs and Responsibility to Family scales were negatively related to suicidal ideation, past suicide threats, past suicide attempts, estimated likelihood of future attempts, severity of depression, and hopelessness (Cole, 1989b). In a sample of incarcerated youths (Cole, 1989b), scores on the Survival and Coping Beliefs scale also were negatively related to each of these criterion variables. In contrast, Responsibility to Family scores were related only to past history of attempts among the incarcerated youths. In a similar manner, among students, scores on the Moral Objections scale were negatively related to past suicidal ideation, past attempts, and estimated likelihood of attempting suicide in the future; however, in an incarcerated sample, scores on the Moral Objections scale were unrelated to these variables. Paradoxically, the Fear Suicide scale was modestly *positively* related to depression and hopelessness, and *negatively* related to an index of social desirability.

Most of the expected associations between the Survival and Coping Beliefs and the Moral Objections scales and indices of suicidal behavior and suicide expectations remained significant when controlling (in separate analyses) for severity of depression and hopelessness. In contrast, scores on the Responsibility to Family scale were no longer related to suicidal ideation or past suicidal behavior when controlling for depression or hopelessness (Cole, 1989b).

High school students with no or brief suicidal ideation had stronger reasons for living as assessed with the Survival and Coping Beliefs, Responsibility to Family, and Moral Objections RFL scales than adolescents with "serious" suicidal ideation or a history of suicide attempts (Cole, 1989b). The Fear of Suicide and Fear of Social Disapproval Scales did not differentiate these youths.

Dimensionality

Factor analysis of RFL data from Chinese high school students in Hong Kong (with the Child Concerns items deleted) yielded a five-factor solution that was similar to that obtained with adult samples. The primary differences between the Chinese RFL derived scales and the original scales were (a) the deletion of the Moral Objections scale in the Chinese version of the RFL because of the small number of items and concerns about instability and (b) the splitting of the Survival and Coping Beliefs into two separate scales. Pinto et al. (1998) found that the original five factors identified for the RFL with adult samples did not provide a good fitting model for data from inpatient adolescents. However, in a principal-components analysis, Pinto et al. (1998) identified five very similar factors with eigenvalues greater than 1.0 that accounted for a total of 66.5% of the variance in RFL scores. Although the names of these factors were retained (with the exception of Fear of Social Disapproval, which was renamed Fear of Failure and Social Disapproval), the items loading on these factors differed from the original items.

Predictive Validity

In a sample of psychiatrically hospitalized adolescents with a prior history of suicide attempts (but not among adolescents without such a history), greater Survival and Coping Beliefs as rated on the RFL at index hospitalization predicted *longer* times until posthospitalization suicide attempts (Goldston et al., 2001). Specifically, for inpatient adolescents with a history of attempts, scores of <4.9 on the Survival and Coping Beliefs scale had 83% sensitivity and 48% specificity in predicting suicide attempts within

1 year following discharge. Scores of < 4.9 on the Survival and Coping Beliefs scale or 9 on the BHS yielded 92% sensitivity and 31% specificity in predicting suicide attempts within 1 year of discharge.

Treatment Studies

No published treatment data using the RFL with adolescents were located.

Summary and Evaluation

The RFL is one of the few assessment devices that evaluate deterrents to suicidal behavior or belief systems that theoretically buffer against suicidal behavior. The RFL was developed in adult populations and has been less widely used with adolescents. There is some evidence suggesting that the factor structure of the RFL may not be the same in adult and adolescent populations. Not all of the scales of the RFL appear to have equal use with adolescents; the Survival and Coping Beliefs scale has the most items, has the highest levels of internal consistency, has the most demonstrated convergent validity, and is the only scale of the RFL to have been shown to have some predictive validity with adolescents.

Where to Obtain

Items on the RFL–48 are in Linehan et al. (1983). Information on other versions of the RFL can be obtained from Marsha Linehan, PhD, Department of Psychology, University of Washington, Box 351525, Seattle, WA 98195-1525.

Reasons for Living Inventory for Adolescents and Brief Reasons for Living Inventory for Adolescents

Description

Two self-report measures, the Reasons for Living Inventory for Adolescents (RFL–A; Osman et al., 1998) and the Brief Reasons for Living Inventory for Adolescents (BRFL–A; Osman et al., 1996), were developed to assess the same adaptive or life-maintaining belief system thought to be measured by the original RFL. The RFL–A is a 52-item measure, and the BRFL–A is a 14-item measure. The BRFL–A was developed from items on the original RFL; the RFL–A was developed using both existing items and new items.

Populations Studied

Validation samples for the RFL–A and BRFL–A include both samples of nonclinically ascertained high school students and adolescent psychiatric inpatients (Osman et al., 1996, 1998).

Reliability

No published data were located.

Internal Consistency

In an initial mixed sample of high school students, adolescent psychiatric inpatients, and college freshmen, and in a cross-validation sample of adolescent psychiatric inpatients, the BRFL–A scales were found to be internally consistent—Survival and Coping Beliefs: α = .76 and .74; Responsibility to Family: α = .74 and .85; Fear of Suicide: α = .67 and .70; Fear of Social Disapproval: α = .80 and .76, and Moral Objections: α = .79 and .68 (Osman et al., 1996).

The RFL–A has five factor-analytically derived scales. In two samples of nonclinically referred high school students and another sample of adolescent psychiatric inpatients, the internal consistency of these factor-derived scales was as follows—Future Optimism: α = .91 to .94; Suicide-Related Concerns: α = .93 to .95; Family Alliance: α = .93 to .95; Peer Acceptance and Support: α = .89 to .92; and Self-Acceptance: α = .93 to .95 (Gutierrez, Osman, Kopper, & Barrios, 2000; Osman et al., 1998).

The internal consistency of the entire RFL–A was .96 (Osman et al., 1998) and .97 (Gutierrez et al., 2000) in a sample of nonclinically referred high school students and adolescent psychiatric inpatients, respectively.

Concurrent Validity

In a mixed sample of high school students, adolescent psychiatric inpatients, and college freshmen (Osman et al., 1996), the Survival and Coping Beliefs and Responsibility to Family scales of the BRFL–A were found to correlate negatively with estimated suicide probability, self-rated expectation of later suicide attempts, and current suicidal ideation. The Moral Objections scale was found to be negatively correlated with estimated probability of later suicide attempt and self-rated expectations for later suicide attempts.

However, in this same sample (Osman et al., 1996), the BRFL–A Survival and Coping Beliefs scale was also found to be positively correlated with the Lie and the Defensiveness validity scales of the MMPI–A. The Fear of Social Disapproval Scale was paradoxically negatively related to the Lie Scale of the MMPI–A. The Survival and Coping Beliefs Scale was negatively related to the Depression, Low Self-Esteem, Family Problems, and Negative Treatment Indicators Content Scales of the MMPI–A (following Bonferroni corrections). The Responsibility to Family scale was negatively related to Alienation, Family Problems, and Negative Treatment Indicators. Last, the Moral Objections scale was negatively correlated with the MMPI–A Depression and Negative Treatment Indicators content scales.

In a sample of high school students, the RFL–A total score and scale scores had moderate negative (but statistically significant) correlations with suicidal ideation, suicide threats, estimated likelihood of future attempts as assessed with the Suicidal Behaviors Questionnaire (SBQ), Suicide Probability Scale (SPS) scores, Beck Hopelessness Scale scores, and the depression section of the Brief Symptom Inventory (Osman et al., 1998). All of the correlations (with measures except the Brief Symptom Inventory) remained statistically significant after controlling for general psychopathology as assessed with the Brief Symptom Inventory. In another sample of high school students, reasons for living were found to be positively related to "positive suicide ideation" (ideation thought to be protective against suicide) as assessed with the PANSI (Osman et al., in press).

In psychiatric inpatients, the RFL–A scales again were negatively correlated with SBQ-assessed suicidal ideation, threats, and estimated likelihood of future attempts (Gutierrez et al., 2000; Osman et al., 1998), SPS total scores (Gutierrez et al., 2000; Osman et al., 1998), "negative suicide ideation" on the PANSI (Osman et al., 2002), hopelessness (Gutierrez et al., 2000), and low self-esteem (Gutierrez et al., 2000). RFL–A scores were positively correlated with "positive suicide ideation" on the PANSI (Osman et al., 2002).

In one sample, recently suicidal adolescent psychiatric inpatients had lower scores on each of the RFL–A scales and for the entire RFL–A than psychiatric inpatients without recent suicide attempts and a nonclinically ascertained sample of high school students (Osman et al., 1998). In a second sample of adolescent psychiatric inpatients, both first-time and repeat suicide attempters had lower RFL–A scores than nonsuicidal adolescents (Gutierrez et al., 2000). In yet a third study, adolescents who attempted suicide and were psychiatrically hospitalized had lower RFL–A scores than adolescents thought to be at risk for suicidal behavior (because of their suicidal ideation or threats); these latter adolescents, in turn, had lower RFL–A scores than nonsuicidal adolescents (Osman et al., 2002).

Dimensionality

In a mixed sample of clinically referred adolescents and normal high school students, exploratory and confirmatory factor analyses of the BRFL–A yielded five factors, consistent with the factor structure of the original RFL (Osman et al., 1996).

In a sample of high school students, exploratory factor analysis of RFL–A data yielded five factors, which were interpreted as Future Optimism (by far the largest factor), Suicide-Related Concerns, Family Alliance, Peer Acceptance and Support, and Self-Acceptance (Osman et al., 1998). Confirmatory factor analysis with three additional sets of youths indicated that this factor solution provided an adequate fit for the data (Gutierrez et al., 2000; Osman et al., 1998).

Predictive Validity

No published data were located.

Treatment Studies

No published data were located.

Summary and Evaluation

The RFL–A and the BRFL–A eventually may have greater use with adolescents than the original RFL. However, most of the research with the scales to date has occurred in the context of validation and cross-validation studies, and the predictive validity of both scales has yet to be documented.

Where to Obtain

Items on the RFL–A are in Osman et al. (1998). Items on the BRFL–A are in Osman et al. (1996).

Suicide Probability Scale

Description

The Suicide Probability Scale (SPS) is a 36-item self-report measure designed as a screening instrument to assess suicide risk in individuals ages 14 and older (Cull & Gill, 1988). The impetus for developing this scale was "the lack of empirically validated and generally available measures for predicting suicidal behaviors" (Cull & Gill, 1988, p. 1). Items of the SPS assess four areas: hopelessness, suicidal ideation, negative self-evaluation, and hostility. Respondents are instructed to circle whether each item on the SPS describes them *none or a little of the time, some of the time, good part of the time*, or *most or all of the time*. Interpretation of the SPS is based on individual item analysis, scores on the four subscales (corresponding to the areas above), and the total weighted score (and T score). The authors cautioned that the SPS should not be used as the sole instrument for assessing suicidality when a person is thought to be at risk, and they stated that the SPS is meant to supplement rather than supplant clinical judgment. The scale is appropriate for clinical research and assessment and, according to the authors, screening in "high-risk settings in conjunction with other methods of assessing suicide potential" (Cull & Gill, 1988, p. 3).

Populations Studied

The SPS was validated and standardized with primarily adult samples (Cull & Gill, 1988), but the samples did include 10 to 25 percent adolescents (19 years old and younger). The SPS also has been used with high school students (D'Attilio & Campbell, 1990; D'Attilio, Campbell, Lubold, & Jacobson, & Richard, 1992; Osman et al., 1998; Tatman, Greene, & Karr, 1993), adolescent health clinic attendees (Cappelli et al., 1995), physically abused youths (Kaplan, Pelcovitz. Salzinger, Mandel, & Weiner, 1997), adolescents in a group home setting (Larzelere, Smith, Batenhorst, & Kelly, 1996), and adolescent psychiatric inpatients (Osman et al., 1996).

Reliability

The test–retest reliability of the SPS for two mixed age groups was high ($r = .92$ and $.94$), although the SPS had somewhat lower test–retest reliability in certain subgroups (e.g., $r = .84$ for male Hispanics; Cull & Gill, 1988).

Internal Consistency

In the validation sample of adolescents and (mostly) adults, internal consistency was determined separately for even and odd items and for each subscale—total scale: α = .93 and .93; Hopelessness Scale: α = .85 and .86; Suicidal Ideation Scale: α = .89 and .89; Negative Self-Evaluation Scale: α = .68 and .62; and Hostility Scale: α = .76 and .75 (Cull & Gill, 1988).

In a high school sample, internal consistency was as follows—total scale: α = .90; Hopelessness Scale: α = .78; Suicidal Ideation Scale: α = .86; Negative Self-Evaluation Scale: α = .59; and Hostility Scale: α = .66 (Tatman et al., 1993). It was noted that the item–total correlations of the SPS among the adolescent students (Tatman et al., 1993) was significantly lower than that reported for Cull and Gill's (1988) validation sample.

Concurrent Validity

In a sample of adolescent psychiatric inpatients, the total SPS score was negatively correlated with the Survival and Coping Beliefs, Responsibility to Family, and Moral Objections scales and the total score of the BRFL–A (Osman et al., 1996). In a sample of high school students, SPS scores were found to be negatively associated with all of the RFL–A scales, as well as the total score from that measure (Osman et al., 1998). In student samples, SPS scores also have been found to be associated with decreased social support and death anxiety (D'Attilio & Campbell, 1990; D'Attilio et al., 1992).

In physically abused adolescents, suicide attempters were found to differ from nonsuicidal youths on the Hostility Scale of the SPS (Kaplan et al., 1997). However, in this same sample, the suicide attempters and nonsuicidal youths did not differ on the Negative Self-Evaluation, Suicidal Ideation, or Probability of Suicide Scales, nor with regard to SPS total scores (Kaplan et al., 1997).

Dimensionality

Factor analysis of responses to the SPS revealed six factors with eigenvalues greater than 1.0 (Cull & Gill, 1988). These were interpreted as reflecting Suicidal Ideation, Hopelessness, Positive Outlook, Interpersonal Closeness, Hostility, and Angry Impulsivity. The Positive Outlook factor had only a small cluster of items and was merged with the Interpersonal Closeness factor to form the Negative Self-Evaluation Scale. The Hostility and Angry Impulsivity factors also had a relatively small number of items and were merged to form the Hostility Scale of the SPS.

Factor analysis in a high school sample yielded a factor solution slightly different from that found in the validation sample (Tatman et al., 1993). Essentially, in this sample, three factors were found, which were interpreted as Suicidal Despair (which included modest factor loadings for the hopelessness items), Angry Frustration, and Low Self-Efficacy.

Predictive Validity

In validating this scale, the authors (Cull & Gill, 1988) provided evidence that the items differentiated (in cross-sectional analyses) between individuals who had attempted suicide and individuals who had not attempted suicide. However, in the manual, no evidence about predictive validity (or the ability of the scale to predict suicidal behavior at a later point in time) was offered.

In a sample of adolescents receiving treatment in a group home, SPS scores were predictive (at conventional levels of statistical significance) of future suicide attempts, suicidal verbalizations, and "minor self-destructive behaviors" (Larzelere et al., 1996). However, use of the cutoff for taking suicide precautions cited in the SPS manual would have yielded only 27.6% sensitivity and 89.7% specificity in predicting suicide attempts. Using an alternative cutoff would have yielded sensitivity of 48.3% and specificity of 80.3%.

Treatment Studies

No published studies were located.

Summary and Evaluation

Despite the fact that the SPS was developed in part because of the dearth of available scales predicting suicidal behavior, the manual presents no evidence about the predictive use of the scale. Evidence is mixed as to the scale's usefulness in an adolescent population. One study found SPS scores to be predictive (at statistically significant levels) of later suicidal behavior in a sample of adolescents in a group home. However, in terms of the clinical or practical significance of the findings, the cutoff score recommended in the SPS manual failed to identify even half of the adolescents who eventually attempted suicide.

Where to Obtain

Western Psychological Services, 12031 Wilshire Blvd, Los Angeles, CA 90025-1251

Suicide Resilience Inventory—25

Description

The Suicide Resilience Inventory—25 (SRI–25) is a brief self-report questionnaire for adolescents and young adults for assessing "resilience" to suicide (Gutierrez et al., 2002). The authors define resilience as "the perceived ability, strength, or competence to resist intentional self-harm behaviors when faced with a range of potentially risk-related factors" (Gutierrez et al., 2002, p. 7). The scale has three scales assessing internal protective factors (nine items), external protective factors (eight items), and emotional stability (eight items). SRI items assess areas such as whether the respondents like things about themselves, can resist urges to attempt suicide, can resist urges to engage in self-harm behavior when criticized, and have individuals that they can turn to for support when they are feeling suicidal.

Populations Studied

The SRI–25 has been used with high school students and with adolescent psychiatric inpatients (Gutierrez et al., 2002).

Reliability

No data regarding the test–retest reliability of the SRI–25 was found.

Internal Consistency

In a mixed sample of high school, community college, and university students, in a separate sample of high school students, and in a sample of adolescent psychiatric inpatients, the internal consistency of the total SRI–25 has been found to be high (α = .96, .96, and .97, respectively; Gutierrez et al., 2002). For the three scales, internal consistency in the three samples was as follows: Internal Protective (α = .94, .94, and .95), External Protective (α = .90, .92, and .92), and Emotional Stability (α = .93, .94, and .93; Gutierrez et al., 2002).

Concurrent Validity

The total SRS and three scales were negatively related to past suicide attempts, frequency of suicide ideation, suicide threats, estimated likelihood of future suicide attempts, depression, anxiety, perceived stress, hopelessness, and negative ideation as assessed with the PANSI (Gutierrez et al., 2002). The SRS and three scales were positively related to positive suicide ideation from the PANSI (Gutierrez et al., 2002).

Dimensionality

Confirmatory factor analysis was used to examine the factor structure of the SRS. A 3-factor model was identified which accounted for 62 percent of the data (Gutierrez et al., 2002). These factors, which were allowed to correlate, corresponded to the areas of internal protective factors, external protective factors, and emotional stability (Gutierrez et al., 2002).

Predictive Validity

No evidence of the predictive validity of the SRI–25 was found.

Treatment Studies

The SRI–25 has not yet been used in published treatment studies.

Summary

The Suicide Resiliency Inventory (SRI–25) is a brief inventory developed to measure "resilience" against suicidal behavior. The scale measures internal protective factors, external protective factors, and emotional stability. The scale is internally consistent and has been shown to have concurrent validity. However, the SRS–25 has not yet been used in studies beyond the initial validation samples.

Where to Obtain

Augustine Osman, PhD, Department of Psychology, University of Northern Iowa, 334 Baker Hall, Cedar Falls, IA 50614-0505

Suicide Risk Screen

Description

The Suicide Risk Screen (SRS; Plutchik, van Praag, and Conte, 1989) is a measure composed of items thought to discriminate between patients who have attempted suicide and those who have not in different psychiatric populations. The latest version of the measure (Plutchik et al., 1996) consists of 15 items assessing hopelessness, sleep problems, current depression, feelings of worthlessness, feelings of loss of control, frustration, exposure to suicide, suicidal ideation, and suicide attempts. Plutchik and colleagues have theorized about the interrelationship between suicide risk, impulsivity, and violence risk (Plutchik, 1997; Plutchik et al., 1996; Plutchik et al., 1989b). In this context, it is worth noting that separate scales have been developed for measuring violence risk (Past Feelings and Acts of Violence, Plutchik and van Praag, 1990) and impulsivity (Impulse Control Scale; Plutchik and van Praag, 1989).

Populations Studied

The SRS has been used in studies with hospitalized adolescents (Grilo et al., 1999a, 1999b; Grosz et al., 1994; Soreni et al., 1989).

Reliability

No information about the test-retest reliability of the SRS in adolescents was found.

Internal Consistency

In adolescents, the SRS has been found to be internally consistent, $\alpha =$ .75 (Grosz et al., 1994).

Concurrent Validity

The SRS was found to discriminate between who have made suicide attempts in the past and those who have not (Grosz et al., 1994). SRS scores also were found to be higher among adolescents defined (using another measure) as repeat suicide attempters as contrasted with adolescents without a suicide attempt history (Soreni et al., 1989). Suicide risk as assessed with the SRS was found to be related to violence (Grosz et al., 1994), impulsivity

(Grosz et al., 1994), hopelessness, depression, self-criticism, and childhood abuse in hospitalized adolescents (Grilo et al., 1999a, 1999b).

Dimensionality

No information about the dimensionality of the SRS when used with adolescents was found.

Predictive Validity

No information about the predictive validity of the SRS was found.

Treatment Studies

No published studies were located.

Summary

The Suicide Risk Screen (SRS) is a brief measure composed of items chosen because they were felt to differentiate between suicidal and nonsuicidal individuals. The authors have theorized about the interrelationship between suicidal behaviors, impulsivity, and violence. In this context, the SRS is complemented by two other instruments measuring impulsivity and risk for violence. Results pertinent to the concurrent validity of the SRS has been published, but the test–retest reliability and predictive validity of the measure in adolescents have not been examined.

Where to Obtain

The most recent version of the SRS can be found in the Plutchik et al. (1996) article.

Zung Index of Potential Suicide and Israeli Index of Potential Suicide

Description

The Zung Index of Potential Suicide (IPS) is a rating scale developed 25 years ago for "making predictions about suicide potential and selecting the high risk person . . . [for] early intervention and possible prevention of suicide" (Zung, 1974, pp. 221–222). The scale has two parts: one composed of social and demographic variables associated with risk, and one associated with clinical variables. There are three alternative forms of the clinical portion of the IPS: a form completed by an interviewer, a self-rating form, and a form completed by a significant other.

Items on the interview form are typically rated from 0 (*none, not present or insignificant*) to 4 (*severe in intensity or duration, present most or all of the time in frequency*). Responses on the IPS self-rating form are generally rated from 0 (*none of the time*) to 4 (*most or all of the time*). Social and demographic variables assessed with the IPS include previous hospitalizations, recent moves, recent losses, religion, and number of individual in the household. However, the IPS was developed for use with adults, and several of the sociodemographic variables assessed are not of direct relevance for most adolescents, including marital status (scored 1 if single and 25 years old or older, or widowed, divorced, or separated and 50 years old or older) and education (scored 1 if 17 years of education and over). Variables assessed in the clinical portion of the IPS include depressed mood, symptoms of depression, symptoms of anxiety, substance abuse, aggression, hopelessness, irritability, feelings of confusion, feelings of lack of support, somatic complaints, perceived lack of alternatives to suicide, suicidal ideation, suicide plans, prior suicide attempts, and exposure to suicide.

The 21-item Israeli Index of Potential Suicide (IIPS) was developed on the basis of IPS items that were found to differentiate between suicidal and nonsuicidal individuals (Orbach & Bar-Joseph, 1993). Items were modified from the original IPS because of cultural differences and to ensure their appropriateness for adolescents. Items on the IIPS were rated from 1 (*strongly agree*) to 5 (*strongly disagree*).

Populations Studied

Items extracted from the IPS and administered in self-report format have been used primarily with nonclinically ascertained adolescents (e.g., Cole, 1989a, 1989b). The IIPS has been used with nonclinically ascertained samples, psychiatric samples, and adolescents known to be suicidal (Orbach, Kedem, Gorchover, Apter, & Tyano, 1993).

Reliability

No published test–retest reliability data for the IPS or IIPS were located for adolescent samples.

Internal Consistency

No data on the internal consistency of the IPS when used with adolescents were located. However, the IIPS, a scale based on the IPS, has been described as internally consistent (α = .81 and .91; Orbach & Bar-Joseph, 1993; Orbach et al., 1993).

Concurrent Validity

In a sample of nonclinically ascertained high school students, questions extracted from the IPS regarding suicidal ideation, suicide plans, and suicide attempts were found to be negatively and moderately correlated with the Survival and Coping Beliefs scale of the RFL (Cole, 1989b). There were smaller, but nonetheless statistically significant, negative associations between the ideation and attempt items from the IPS (but not the suicide plans item) and the Responsibility to Family and Moral Objections scales of the RFL. Again, in a high school sample, a "suicide scale" developed by adding the responses to four items extracted from the IPS directly assessing suicidal ideation and behavior was found to be moderately correlated with three measures of depressive symptoms, three measures of hopelessness, and extracted items from the SBQ (Cole, 1989a).

The IIPS (the Israeli modification of the IPS) was found to differentiate between suicidal adolescents and a psychiatric and nonpsychiatric control group (Orbach et al., 1993). Moreover, among suicidal participants (but not among the other youths), suicidal tendencies as assessed with the IIPS were found to be moderately negatively correlated with fear of death (Orbach et al., 1993).

Dimensionality

No published data were located.

Predictive Validity

No published data were located.

Treatment Studies

In a suicide prevention program, suicidal tendencies assessed with the IIPS (the Israeli modification of the IPS) were found to decrease among adolescents in a suicide prevention program (compared with control participants) in four of six schools studied (Orbach & Bar Joseph, 1993). In another school, suicidal tendencies assessed with the IIPS increased in controls but not among participants of the suicide prevention program (Orbach & Bar-Joseph, 1993).

Summary and Evaluation

The IPS was developed 25 years ago for use in the screening of adults. Items extracted from the IPS and administered in self-report form have been used with adolescents. However, little psychometric data, including data regarding reliability and predictive validity, have been published for the IPS items when used with adolescents. A self-report Israeli modification of the IPS (the IIPS) has been developed for which more psychometric data are available. The IIPS also has been used as an outcome measure in a suicide prevention study. However, the predictive validity of this scale also has yet to be examined.

Where to Obtain

The Zung IPS is reproduced in Zung (1974). The IIPS may be obtained from Israel Orbach, PhD, Department of Psychology, Bar-Ilan University, 52900 Ramat-Gan, Israel.

Summary

Reviewed in this chapter were a number of risk assessment instruments. Most have been developed for adolescents. A few (the BHS, FAST, RFL, SPS) were developed for adults or adolescents interchangeably or were developed for adults and then used with adolescents. Relatively few of the instruments (the CASPI, CSPS, and HPLS) were developed specifically for possible use with preadolescents.

Many, but not all, of the risk assessment instruments are linked to theory. For example, hopelessness is the focus of two scales, the BHS and the HPLS. A pessimistic view of the future (of which hopelessness could be considered to be an extreme example) is part of the cognitive triad of characteristics typified by depressed individuals, as described in Beck's cognitive theory and therapy for depression. The LAS is based on notions that there are interrelationships between various life-enhancing and life-threatening behaviors. Likewise, the MAST focuses on the relationship between suicidal behavior and the "basic conflict among attitudes of life and death." Emphasizing the positive, the versions of the RFL focus on the protective effects of having strong reasons for not committing suicide, or for living. The Expendable Child Measure is predicated on the notion that youths' suicidality is related to their perception of their parents' rejection of them. The FAST similarly is based on theory that self-destructive voices, in part introjected from one's parents, are related to suicidal tendencies. The CSPS is also grounded in part in psychodynamic and developmental theory, with a section related to ego functioning and defense mechanisms.

Every instrument in this section with the exception of the Adapted SAD PERSONS scale has evidence of concurrently assessed construct validity. However, only four (BHS, HPLS, RFL, and SPS) have been found to have predictive validity. Of these, scores on two (BHS and RFL) were found to be predictive only among individuals with prior histories of suicidal behavior, and the predictive use of the SPS, while statistically significant, was not strong. This does not mean that these risk scales should not be used to aid in the evaluation of suicidal youths. It simply underscores the reality that more research has to be conducted to demonstrate the usefulness of many of these risk instruments in suicide assessment. (Please refer to Table 7.1 for a complete instrument-by-instrument comparison.)

Interventions for suicidal youths can focus on reducing suicidal ideation and behavior or can focus also on reducing the factors that theoretically increase the chances of suicidal behavior, while bolstering those factors thought to buffer against suicidal behavior. In this regard, four of the risk assessment instruments have been used as outcome measures in treatment studies: the BHS, HPLS, ISO–30, and IIPS. Unfortunately, too few controlled outcome studies of suicide prevention and treatment interventions have been conducted with youths to make a determination of which risk factor assessments are of most use in this context.

Table 7.1

Characteristics of Risk Assessment Instruments

Instrument	Populations in which risk factors examined[a]	Reliability	Internal consistency	Dimensionality	Concurrent validity evidence	Predictive validity evidence	Used as outcome measure
Adapted SAD PERSONS	Not tested	–	–	–	–	–	–
BHS	Clin, ER, Sch, Homeless	+	+	+	+	+	+
CASPI	Clin, Sch	+	+	+	+	–	–
CSPS	Clin, ER, Sch	+	+	–	+	–	–
CSRA	Res	–	+	+	+	–	–
Expendable Child Measure	Clin	–	+	–	+	–	–
FAST	Clin	+	+	+	+	–	–
HPLS	Clin, ER, Incar, Sch	+	+	+	+	+	+
ISO–30	Clin, Sch	+	+	–	+	–	+
LAS	Clin, Sch	+	+	+	+	–	–
MACI Suicidal Tendencies Scale	Clin	+	+	–	+	–	–
MAST	Bereaved, Clin, Sch	–	+	+	+	–	–
PANSI	Clin, Sch	+	+	+	+	–	+
PATHOS	ER	–	–	–	+	–	–
RFL	Clin, Incar, Sch	–	+	+	+	+	–
RFL–A, BRFL–A	Clin, Sch	–	+	+	+	–	–
SPS	Abuse, Clin, Med, Res, Sch	+	+	+	+	+	–
SRI–25	Clin, Sch	–	+	+	+	–	–
SRS	Clin	–	+[b]	–	+	–	–
Zung IPS	Clin, Sch	–	–	–	+	–	+

Note. The instruments are as follows: Adapted SAD PERSONS is an acronym for Sex, Age, Depression or affective disorder, Previous attempts, Ethanol-drug abuse, Rational thinking loss, Social supports lacking, Organized plan, Negligent parenting, family stresses, or modeling of suicide by family members, and School problems; BHS = Beck Hopelessness Scale; CASPI = Child–Adolescent Suicidal Potential Index; CSPS = Child Suicide Potential Scales; CSRA = Child Suicide Risk Assessment; FAST = Firestone Assessment of Self-Destructive Thoughts; HPLS = Hopelessness Scale for Children; ISO–30 = Inventory of Suicide Orientation—30; LAS = Life Attitudes Schedule; MACI = Millon Adolescent Clinical Inventory; MAST = Multi-Attitude Suicide Tendency Scale for Adolescents; PANSI = Positive and Negative Suicide Ideation Inventory; PATHOS, which is based on an acronym for the following questions to respondents: Have you had Problems for longer than 1 month? Were you Alone in the house at the time? Did you plan the overdose for longer than Three hours? Are you feeling HOpeless about the future? and Were you feeling Sad for most of the time before the overose?; RFL = Reasons for Living Inventory; RFL–A = Reasons for Living Inventory for Adolescents; SPS = Suicide Probability Scale; SRI–25 = Suicide Resilience Inventory; SRS = Suicide Risk Screen; Zung IPS = Zung Index of Potential Suicide.

[a]Clin = inpatient and/or outpatient psychiatric clinically referred or treatment-seeking youths; ER = youths in emergency department setting; Sch = school or community samples (including nonpatient control in research studies); Homeless = homeless youths; Res = youths in residential treatment; Incar = incarcerated youths; Bereaved = bereaved children; Abused = abused children or children with posttraumatic stress disorder; Med = medically ill youths.

[b]For the Israeli adaptation of the Zung IPS (IILPS).

Assessing Risk of Suicidal Behaviors: Multitiered Screening Assessments

Four sets of instruments used in multitiered screening assessments for suicide risk are reviewed in this chapter. The multitiered screening assessments reviewed are all designed to identify (and target for prevention efforts) high-risk populations of adolescents. Youths considered at risk because of their responses to initial screenings are evaluated further with a more individualized, interview-based, or comprehensive screening. This latter screening may be followed by interview or intervention with a trained professional.

Multitiered screening systems are generally predicated on the notion that targeted or "indicated" prevention efforts (for youths identified as high risk) are likely to have greater impact than universal prevention efforts that are targeted at all youths. The multitiered systems are generally used in an effort to increase the efficiency of screenings, reducing false positives in an effort to more accurately identify those youths at highest risk or in most need of intervention. The multitiered screening assessment systems are, by the definitions provided in this text, risk assessment instruments (or sets of instruments). However, unlike the majority of the risk assessment questionnaires, each of these systems also includes questions directly assessing the presence or absence of suicidal behavior. For this reason, the consistency of the queries about suicidal ideation and behavior with O'Carroll et al.'s (1996) recommended operational definitions is noted for each of these instruments.

Four multitiered screening systems are reviewed: (a) the Columbia Teen Screen (Shaffer, Wilcox et al., 1996) used in conjunction with the

Diagnostic Interview Schedule for Children (DISC), (b) the High School Questionnaire (and embedded Suicide Risk Screen) and Measure of Adolescent Potential for Suicide (Eggert et al., 1994), (c) the Suicide Ideation Questionnaire used in conjunction with the Suicidal Behaviors Interview (Reynolds, 1991), and (d) the Evaluation of Suicide Risk Among Adolescents and Imminent Danger Assessment (Bradley & Rotheram, 1990; Rotheram-Borus, 1987, 1989). The first three of these assessment systems have been developed for mass screenings in school settings, although they could potentially be used in other settings as well. The last multitiered screening assessment system (Evaluation of Suicide Risk Among Adolescents and Imminent Danger Assessment) has been used mostly in individual screenings with adolescents thought to be at high risk for suicidal and life-endangering behaviors (e.g., runaway youths, youths seeking crisis services, gay and bisexual adolescent males seeking services).

Columbia Teen Screen and Diagnostic Interview Schedule for Children

Description

The Columbia Teen Screen was developed as a rapid (11-item) self-report screening questionnaire for assessing risk of suicidal behaviors (Shaffer, Wilcox, et al., 1996; Shaffer & Craft, 1999). This measure includes four stem items regarding current and past suicidal ideation and attempts and stem questions about depression and alcohol and substance abuse. If the respondent answers positively to the Yes/No stem questions about suicidal behavior, he or she is then directed to a series of Yes/No questions assessing the seriousness of the problem, whether help is being received for this problem, and whether the respondent would like to have help with this problem. The stem questions for depression and about alcohol and drug abuse ask the respondent how much of a problem he or she is having with these areas on a 1 (*no problem*) to 5 (*very bad problem*) scale. If the problem is rated as a "bad problem" or a "very bad problem," respondents are then asked Yes/No questions about whether they are concerned about the problem, have seen a mental health professional, or have an appointment to see a mental health professional. In this measure, adolescents who report one of the following are assumed to be at risk for suicidal behavior: (a) suicidal ideation; (b) past suicide attempts; (c) a "bad" or "very bad" problem with depression, substance, or alcohol use; or (d) a need for help with depression, substance, or alcohol use.

Those youths who screen positive with the Columbia Teen Screen are typically assessed more fully in a second-stage screening with the DISC, administered either by computer or in person by a trained staff member. On the basis of these screenings, students considered to be at risk or in need of a referral for treatment meet with a clinician. Thereafter, referrals for treatment and contacts with parents are made as needed.

Populations Studied

In one study (D. Shaffer, personal communication, October 1999), the Columbia Teen Screen was used to screen for at-risk youths in eight high schools in the New York City area (one of which withdrew consent in mid-screening and was removed from analyses). These schools initially included two suburban and six urban schools, two single-sex schools (one all female and one all male), two parochial schools, one vocational-technical school, and five unspecialized public schools.

Assessment and Definitions of Suicidal Behaviors

The two stem questions on the Columbia Teen Screen regarding suicidal ideation (whether respondents have thought about suicide during the past 3 months) and suicide attempts (whether they ever tried to commit suicide) implicitly refer to nonzero intent to die and are consistent with the operational definitions proposed by O'Carroll et al. (1996). The suicidal ideation and behavior queries of the DISC were reviewed in chapter 3.

Reliability

From a much larger school-based sample (D. Shaffer, personal communication, October 1999), 85 students were readministered the Columbia Teen Screen 14 days after its initial administration. Test–retest reliability was as follows—suicidal ideation in last 3 months: $\kappa = .48$; frequent suicidal ideation: $\kappa = .42$; "seriously" thought about killing self: $\kappa = .56$; suicidal ideation for "a long time": $\kappa = .39$; lifetime suicide attempts: $\kappa = .58$; problems with depression: $\kappa = .36$; and problems with alcohol or drugs: $\kappa = .48$.

The reliability of the suicide assessment queries of the DISC was reviewed in chapter 3. The reliability of the diagnostic assessment of the DISC is reviewed in Shaffer et al. (2000).

Internal Consistency

No published data regarding internal consistency of the screeners were located.

Concurrent Validity

From a larger school-based sample, 319 adolescents who screened positive on the Columbia Teen Screen and 322 students who endorsed none of the items associated with risk were interviewed with the DISC–2.3 (D. Shaffer, personal communication, October 1999). Endorsement of the item regarding suicidal ideation was associated with an 11.6-fold increase in the likelihood of a prior attempt (assessed with the DISC), 3.6-fold increase in the likelihood of any DISC diagnosis, and a 4.9-fold in the increase of a DISC mood disorder diagnosis. Endorsing the item regarding "often thought about suicide" was associated with a 13.2-fold increase in the likelihood of past attempt (as assessed with the DISC), a 4.3-fold increase in the rate of any DISC-assessed diagnosis, and a 4.2-fold increase in the likelihood of a current mood disorder. Endorsing the item "seriously thought about suicide" was associated with a 21.9-fold increase in the rate of prior attempts (assessed with the DISC), a 4.6-fold increase in the rate of any DISC-assessed disorder, and a 4.7-fold increase in the odds of having a mood disorder. In this same sample, the screening item regarding suicidal ideation in the last 3 months had 61% sensitivity and 88% specificity in "predicting" past suicide attempts as assessed with the DISC.

Dimensionality

No published data were located.

Predictive Validity

In the New York metropolitan area, a large number of high school students were screened with instruments including the Columbia Teen Screen (D. Shaffer, personal communication, October 1999). Students were considered to be at risk on the basis of their responses to the Columbia Teen Screen. A large sampling of students, approximately half of whom were thought to be at risk, were followed up approximately 3 to 4 years later. A classification of "at risk" on the Columbia Teen Screen was found to have 71% sensitivity and 51% specificity in predicting suicidal ideation within the last year according to the DISC administered at the second assessment. Questions regarding suicidal ideation and attempts on the Columbia Teen Screen generally were less sensitive, although more specific in their relationship to later suicidal ideation.

In this same study, the Columbia Teen Risk classification of "at risk" yielded 78% sensitivity and 53% specificity in predicting suicide attempts since the initial screen (D. Shaffer, personal communication, December 1999). Again, questions regarding ideation and attempts at the initial screening were generally less sensitive but more specific in their relationship to later attempts.

Treatment Studies

The Columbia Teen Screen and DISC have not been used in published treatment studies.

Summary and Evaluation

The Columbia Teen Screen is a brief instrument that has been promoted for use as part of a multitiered screening program for identifying high-risk youths for school-based prevention programs. Preliminary indications are that the instrument has excellent concurrent validity. More importantly, the classification of "at risk" from the instrument not only has been shown to be predictive of later suicide ideation and attempts but is more sensitive as a screener than prior history of suicidal ideation/behavior by itself.

Where to Obtain

Division of Child and Adolescent Psychiatry, New York State Psychiatric Institute, 1051 Riverside Drive, New York, NY 10032

Evaluation of Suicide Risk Among Adolescents and Imminent Danger Assessment

Description

The Evaluation of Suicide Risk Among Adolescents and Imminent Danger Assessment is a two-stage screening interview for the evaluation of suicidal behaviors and risk (Bradley & Rotheram-Borus, 1990; Rotheram-Borus, 1987, 1989). The first-stage screener, the Evaluation of Suicide Risk Among Adolescents, is used for the identification of youths thought to be at risk, including youths who directly report suicidal ideation and attempts, and hence, are in need of closer evaluation. This screen consists of questions about thoughts of wanting to die, suicidal ideation, and suicide attempts in the last week; lifetime suicidal ideation and attempts; exposure to suicidal behavior in close friends or family members; feelings of anger and dysphoria and symptoms of depression; and symptoms of conduct disorder.

If adolescents are considered to be at risk on the basis of an algorithm for combining the risk factors (youths with current suicidal ideation or plan are automatically considered to be at risk), they are administered the second-stage screening interview, the Imminent Danger Assessment. This screen is predicated on the notion that youths who are in imminent danger of harming themselves should not be able to complete five clinical tasks "incompatible with suicide." It should be noted that the completion of these tasks in and of itself may be therapeutic for youths. These tasks include making three self-referent positive statements (self-compliments), identifying (using a "feeling thermometer") situations associated with suicidal feelings and behaviors, articulating or generating a list of alternative actions to suicidal behaviors in the context of the above situations, identifying three resource people who can help the youth cope with suicidal feelings, and promising to not engage in suicidal behavior for a discrete period of time and to contact someone if feeling suicidal. If adolescents are unable to complete any of these five tasks, they are evaluated for possible psychiatric hospitalization (emergency referral). Otherwise, they are referred for follow-up care (preventative referral).

Populations Studied

Items from the Evaluation of Suicide Risk Among Adolescents have been used to screen primarily African American and Hispanic runaway teenagers (Rotheram-Borus & Bradley, 1991) and gay and bisexual adolescent males seeking services (Rotheram-Borus, Hunter, & Rosario, 1994), as well as primarily Caucasian middle-class adolescents seeking crisis services (Rotheram-Borus, Walker, & Ferns, 1996).

Assessment and Definitions of Suicidal Behaviors

The Evaluation of Suicide Risk Among Adolescents includes several queries for the assessment of suicidal behavior. Respondents are asked whether they have thought about hurting or killing themselves in the last week and whether they have ever seriously thought about killing themselves (with *seriously* meaning every day for a week, or more). The wording of the former question is such that it may elicit responses about thoughts of nonsuicidal self-harm behavior (hurting themselves) in addition to suicidal behavior. The wording of the latter question is also problematic. To the authors' credit, they define the word *seriously* for respondents (which most instruments using this wording do not do); however, although a subset of adolescent suicidal behavior is deliberated for a considerable period of time, other suicidal behavior is more impulsive, certainly considered for less than a week. Hence, this question is likely to yield a conservative estimate of youths considering suicide. As a screener, the question may miss youths who have been thinking of suicide for less than 1 week.

The primary questions regarding suicide attempts ask respondents whether they have ever hurt or tried to kill themselves and the last time they engaged in that behavior. Both of these questions are likely to elicit responses not only about suicidal behavior (with at least some intent to die) but also about nonsuicidal self-harm behavior. As such, these questions are not consistent with definitions of suicidal ideation and attempts recommended by O'Carroll et al. (1996).

Reliability

Interrater reliability of videotaped vignettes of suicidal youths being evaluated with the two-stage interview was high, ranging from an average of .94 for staff members in runaway shelters to .98 for clinical supervisors to .93 for the research team (Rotheram-Borus & Bradley, 1991).

Internal Consistency

No published data were located.

Concurrent Validity

For the questions regarding suicidal ideation and attempts used in the Evaluation of Suicide Risk Among Adolescents, a high rate of lifetime suicide attempts, recent attempts, suicidal ideation within the last week, and exposure to suicidal behavior was found among primarily Hispanic and African American gay and bisexual adolescent males seeking services (Rotheram-Borus et al., 1994), In this study, suicide attempters were found to have higher levels of gay-related stresses, were more likely to drop out of school and live outside of the home, and were more likely to have friends and family members who had attempted suicide (Rotheram-Borus et al., 1994).

Dimensionality

No published data were located.

Predictive Validity

No published data were located.

Treatment Studies

The Evaluation of Suicide Risk Among Adolescents and Imminent Danger Assessment screening procedures were used to screen 741 primarily African American and Hispanic runaway teenagers for suicidal behavior over a 30-month period (Rotheram-Borus & Bradley, 1991). Although the numbers are small, there were nine suicide attempts in the 3 months prior to implementation of the screening in the runaway shelters, in contrast to two attempts in these settings in the 18 months following implementation of the screening program.

Summary and Evaluation

The Evaluation of Suicide Risk Among Adolescents and Imminent Danger Assessment is a two-stage screening interview for the evaluation of suicidal behaviors and risk. This assessment system has much intuitive appeal as a method for clinical screening and approach for dealing with high-risk youths. However, the assessment questions for suicidal ideation and attempts in the Evaluation of Suicide Risk are not consistent with recommended definitions of these terms by O'Carroll et al. (1996). Moreover, little psychometric data have been published for the Evaluation of Suicide Risk Among Adolescents and Imminent Danger Assessment.

Where to Obtain

Address for publisher of the Bradley and Rotheram-Borus (1990) manual: National Resource Center for Youth Services, 2020 West Eighth Street, Tulsa, OK 74119. The Evaluation of Suicide Risk Among Adolescents and Imminent Danger Assessment may also be obtained from Mary Jane Rotheram-Borus, PhD, UCLA Neuropsychiatric Institute, 10920 Wilshire Blvd., Suite 1103, Los Angeles, CA 90024.

High School Questionnaire/Suicide Risk Screen and Measure of Adolescent Potential for Suicide

Description

The Suicide Risk Screen (SRS) and the Measure of Adolescent Potential for Suicide (MAPS) are instruments used in a two-stage screening procedure for identifying youths with a high probability of suicidal behavior (Eggert et al., 1994; Eggert, Thompson, Herting, & Nicholas, 1995; Thompson & Eggert, 1999). Part I consists of a preliminary questionnaire, the High School Questionnaire (Eggert et al., 1994). Within the High School Questionnaire are items related to the classification of risk in accordance with the SRS. The SRS includes questions about three areas pertinent to risk for future suicidal behaviors: current suicidal ideation and behaviors, depression, and alcohol/drug use.

Part II of this screening procedure involves a computer-assisted face-to-face interview, the MAPS (Eggert et al., 1994; Eggert et al., 1995; Thompson & Eggert, 1999). The MAPS (which takes approximately 2 hours) assesses three areas in evaluating suicide risk: (a) direct suicide risk factors, (b) related risk factors, and (c) protective factors. Assessment of direct suicide risk factors is accomplished with questions about exposure to suicide, attitudes and beliefs about suicide, suicidal ideation, suicidal behaviors (including planning, behavioral preparation, number of prior attempts, and lethality of prior attempts), and estimation of the degree of current threat of suicidal behaviors. Degree of related risk factors is assessed with items focusing on depression, hopelessness, anxiety, anger, perceived stress, current stresses, victimization or abuse, drug/alcohol use, school problems and likelihood of dropping out, and risk-taking behaviors. Protective factors are assessed with questions about self-esteem, personal control, coping strategies, and availability of support.

Populations Studied

The MAPS screening system has been used to identify youths in the school system thought to be at risk for suicidal behavior (Eggert et al., 1994; Eggert, Thompson, Herting, & Nicholas, 1995; Thompson & Eggert, 1999; Thompson, Eggert, & Herting, 2000; Thompson, Eggert, Randell, & Pike, 2001).

Reliability

Interrater reliability (based on three videotaped MAPS interviews) ranged from .73 to .91 (Eggert et al., 1994). No published data regarding the test–retest reliability of the SRS were located.

Internal Consistency

Among youths considered at risk for school drop-out and suicide, the internal consistency of the scales on the MAPS ranged from moderate to high (α = .53 to .92; Eggert et al., 1994). In another sample of high-risk students, the internal consistency of the SRS was .81 (Thompson & Eggert, 1999).

Concurrent Validity

Interviewer global ratings for each scale on the MAPS correlated between .52 and .79 with ratings on the Los Angeles Suicide Potential Scale (Eggert et al., 1994). Ratings of risk based on the SRS were related to clinicians' overall ratings of suicide risk (Eggert et al., 1994; Thompson & Eggert, 1999) and more severe suicidal ideation as assessed with the SIQ–JR (Thompson & Eggert, 1999).

Most of the other evidence regarding the convergent and discriminant validity of the different scales of the High School Questionnaire and MAPS is provided by the intercorrelations (and lack of correlations) between different scales on these instruments rather than by examination of correlations with other measures. For example, in one study, youths considered to be at high risk for suicidal behavior by virtue of assessment with the SRS reported more related risk (e.g., anger, anxiety, family distress) and lower protective (e.g., problem-solving coping, social and family support) factors, and higher scores on the Direct Risk Assessment Scale of the MAPS than youths not thought to be at risk (Thompson & Eggert, 1999). In one study focused on adolescent activity involvement, youths thought to be at risk for suicide (based on the SRS) were found to be involved in more solitary activities (assessed with an instrument other than the MAPS) than nonsuicidal youths (Mazza & Eggert, 2001).

Dimensionality

No published data were located.

Predictive Validity

The predictive validity of the MAPS has not been examined (in the sense of predicting future suicidal behavior).

Treatment Studies

The MAPS was used as a treatment outcome measure in a school-based prevention program with adolescents thought to be at risk for suicidal behaviors and school dropout (Eggert et al., 1995). However, the two intervention groups and the control group both evidenced significant reductions in suicidal ideation and other risk factors (e.g., depression, hopelessness, anger, stress). The authors interpreted this as possibly indicating that the MAPS assessments in and of themselves may have had a therapeutic effect.

In a second study, Thompson et al. (2001) compared the efficacy of two suicide prevention interventions with usual care for adolescents considered to be at risk for school dropout and suicidal behavior. There were reductions in suicidal ideation, favorable attitude toward suicide, depression, and hopelessness in all interventions, although there was a greater rate of reduction in the two intervention groups under study. Differential treatment effects depending on gender were found for anxiety and anger (with girls responding better to a skills-building group than boys). Two protective factors (perceived personal control and problem-solving coping) showed greater enhancement following the skills-building group than following the other interventions. Because of the similar trends in several of the outcome measures in both studies after initial assessment across all conditions, the possibility needs to be ruled out that there is artifactual attenuation in responding with repeated administrations of the MAPS (although specific treatment effects were noted in the Thompson et al., 2001 study).

Summary and Evaluation

The SRS and the MAPS are used together in a two-stage screening procedure for identifying youths with a high probability of suicidal behavior. In one suicide prevention intervention study, specific treatment effects were found on several indices assessed with the MAPS. However, no data have been published pertaining to test–retest reliability and the possible attenuation in responses with repeated administration of the MAPS. In addition, the ability of this screening procedure to identify youths who will make future suicide attempts has not yet been evaluated.

Where to Obtain

Leona L. Eggert, PhD, RN, FAAN, or Elaine A. Thompson, PhD, RN, Department of Psychosocial and Community Health, University of Washington, Box 357263, Seattle, Washington 98195-7263

Suicidal Ideation Questionnaire and Suicidal Behaviors Inventory

Description

Reynolds (1991) described the utility of a two-tiered screening strategy consisting of the Suicidal Ideation Questionnaire (SIQ) and the Suicidal Behaviors Inventory (SBI). The procedure described by Reynolds focuses more specifically on suicidal ideation and behavior than the other school-based strategies. The first relatively brief screening with the SIQ focuses on suicidal ideation. This stage of screening has been noted to identify 9% to 11% of youths (Reynolds, 1991). The second-stage survey with the SBI is individualized and interview-based, and focuses on both suicidal ideation and attempts, as well as general distress and social support. In one pilot study, the SBI identified approximately 25% of students scoring at or above a conservative cutoff score of 30 on the SIQ, and approximately 33% of students scoring at or above a cutoff score of 41 on the SIQ, as being at risk and in need of evaluation (Reynolds, 1991).

Populations Studied

The SBI also has been used in conjunction with the SIQ in a two-stage screening approach to the identification of youths at risk for suicidal behavior (Reynolds, 1991).

Assessment and Definition of Suicidal Behaviors

The queries of the SBI and SIQ are described in chapters 4 and 5, respectively.

Reliability

The reliability of the SBI and SIQ are described in chapters 4 and 5, respectively.

Internal Consistency

The internal consistency of the SBI and SIQ are described in chapters 4 and 5, respectively.

Concurrent Validity

Evidence regarding the concurrent validity of the SBI and SIQ are described in chapters 4 and 5, respectively.

Dimensionality

Results from factor analyses of the SBI and SIQ are described in chapters 4 and 5, respectively.

Predictive Validity

The predictive validity of the SIQ is described in chapter 5. No published data regarding the predictive validity of the SBI were located.

Treatment Studies

The prior use of the SIQ in treatment studies is described in chapter 5. The SBI apparently has not been used in treatment studies.

Summary and Evaluation

Reynolds (1991) recommended the use of the SBI in conjunction with the SIQ in a two-stage screening procedure for the identification of youths at risk for suicidal behaviors. The SIQ and SBI are both highly reliable instruments, the first being a brief screen and the second being an individualized interview focusing on both suicidal ideation and behavior. Together, these instruments offer an efficient method of screening for suicidality in student populations. The primary drawback of this screening procedure is that the first stage focuses solely on suicidal ideation, which can wax and wane over time. Youths with no suicidal ideation at the time of the screening but a history of suicide attempts will be missed with this screening procedure.

Where to Obtain

The SIQ can be obtained from Psychological Assessment Resources, Inc., P.O. Box 998, Odessa, FL 33556. The SBI can be obtained by writing

William M. Reynolds, PhD, Department of Psychology, Humboldt State University, Arcata, CA 95521.

Summary

The four screening systems in this chapter differ in their foci. Implicit in the Columbia Teen Screen and follow-up DISC is an emphasis on psychiatric disorders as the primary risk factors for suicide. Although some prevention workers may be uncomfortable with this emphasis, it is well established that the great majority of suicide attempts and completed suicides occur in the context of diagnosable (and treatable) psychiatric disorders. The Evaluation of Suicide Risk Among Adolescents and MAPS also include assessments of psychopathology, but not to the same degree as the Columbia Teen Screen and DISC. The SIQ as an initial screen does not focus on psychiatric disorder at all, focusing instead on thoughts of death and suicidal ideation, and the SBI (in the second tier of screening) includes questions only about general distress (in addition to in-depth information about suicidal thoughts and behavior). (Please refer to Table 8.1 for a complete instrument-by-instrument comparison.)

Unlike the other assessment systems, the SIQ as an initial screen does not include questions about past suicide attempts. Previous suicide attempts are one of the best predictors, if not the best predictor, of future suicidal behavior. The practical implication of this assessment strategy is that youths who have made suicide attempts in the past but who are not currently evidencing suicidal ideation will not be identified at initial screening.

For efficiency, each of the multitiered screening systems uses a brief or self-report assessment at the initial screening. The Columbia Teen Screen, SRS (embedded in the High School Questionnaire), and SIQ are all brief questionnaires. The Evaluation of Suicide Risk Among Adolescents is a brief interview that takes approximately 10 minutes.

The Columbia Teen Screen (and DISC) is the only one of the four assessment systems that does not include any assessment of potential protective factors. In contrast, the Imminent Danger Assessment in a second-stage assessment not only assesses protective factors but also forces respondents to actively demonstrate that they are not at imminent risk (by asking for alternatives to suicidal behavior, for specific support people, etc.).

In addition to psychometric properties and the efficiency of screening, there also are a number of practical issues that should be considered in the

Table 8.1

Characteristics of Multitiered Screening Assessments

First screening instrument	Second screening instrument	Focus of first screening instrument	Focus of second screening instrument	Populations in which youths have been screened[a]	Reliability of first instrument	Reliability of second instrument	Concurrent validity of first instrument	Concurrent validity of second instrument	Predictive validity of first instrument	Predictive validity of second instrument
Columbia Teen Screen	DISC	Suicidal ideation and attempts, depression, substance abuse	Psychiatric diagnostic interview (administered via computer or staff)	Sch	+	+	+	+	+	+
Evaluation of Suicide Risk Among Adolescents	Imminent Danger Assessment	Suicidal ideation and attempts, risk factors	Ability to complete tasks incompatible with suicide	Clin, GLB, Runaway	+	+	+	−	−	−
HSQ (Including Suicide Risk Screen)	MAPS	Suicidal ideation and attempts, depression, substance abuse	Computer assessment of risk and protective factors	Sch	−	+	+	+	−	−
SIQ	SBI	Suicidal ideation	Suicidal ideation and attempts, risk, and protective factors	Sch	+	+	+	+	+	−

Note. The instruments are as follows: DISC = Diagnostic Interview Schedule for Children; HSQ = High School Questionnaire; MAPS = Measure of Adolescent Potential for Suicide; SIQ = Suicide Ideation Questionnaire; SBI = Suicidal Behaviors Inventory.

[a]Sch = school or community samples; Clin = inpatient and/or outpatient psychiatric clinically referred or treatment-seeking youths; GLB = gay, lesbian, and bisexual youths; Runaway = runaway youths.

choice of multitiered screening assessments but that are beyond the scope of this book. These include total costs for implementation, training and personnel needs, time involved in administering the assessments, and how to get youths into treatment who are determined on the basis of the screenings to be at high risk.

Assessing Intent and Lethality of Suicidal Behavior

This chapter focuses on instruments and questions developed for assessing the intent and medical lethality of suicidal behavior. There are potentially several reasons for trying to assess these clinical characteristics of suicidal behavior.

First, suicidal behavior with one set of clinical characteristics may predict later behavior better than suicidal behavior with different characteristics. There are suggestions of such possibilities in the adult literature and in the clinical impressions of practitioners. However, none of the instruments assessing the clinical characteristics of adolescent suicidal behavior have been demonstrated to be useful in predicting later suicidal behavior among youths.

For example, it has been found that adult alcoholics who take precautions to prevent intervention in a suicide attempt are more likely to eventually complete suicide than alcoholics who do not take such action (Beck, Steer, & Trexler, 1989). However, it has yet to be demonstrated that adolescents who take precautions to prevent discovery during a suicide attempt also have a worse prognosis. In a similar manner, Peruzzi and Bongar (1999) found that psychologists consider medical lethality of past suicide attempts to be one of the most important predictors of future risk for completed suicide. However, researchers have not found that adolescents who make suicide attempts with more severe medical lethality are more likely to eventually complete suicide or make future attempts than adolescents who make attempts with less severe medical lethality.

The second reason for assessing the clinical characteristics of suicidal behavior is that clinicians may want to incorporate information about intent and lethality of suicidal behavior into their treatment-planning process. In this vein, it would be important to show that suicidal behavior with specific clinical characteristics has a different course or responds to certain treatments in a different manner than suicidal behavior with other clinical characteristics. That is, it is important to ask questions such as, "Is there an empirical basis for treating a suicide attempt that almost caused death any differently from a suicide attempt with the same intent, but less serious medical consequences?" Unfortunately, there has been a dearth of systematic research addressing questions such as these.

Third, researchers may focus on the clinical characteristics of suicidal behavior as a targeted outcome in interventions, particularly with chronically suicidal patients (or patients who can be expected to continue engaging in suicidal behavior). For example, among adults, there has been some indication that dialectical behavior therapy can reduce the medical lethality of self-harm behavior (Linehan, Armstrong, Suarez, Allmon, & Heard, 1991). To date, clinical characteristics of suicidal behavior have not yet been targeted in published clinical trials with youths.

The final reason for assessing the clinical characteristics of suicidal behavior is description. Information about intent and medical lethality helps clinicians and researchers communicate efficiently about the similarities and differences of suicidal behaviors under study.

Beck Suicide Intent Scale

Description

The Beck Suicide Intent Scale (SIS) is a semistructured 15-item interviewer rating scale that is used to evaluate the severity of suicidal intent for a previous suicide attempt, usually an attempt immediately preceding the interview (Beck, Schuyler, & Herman, 1974). There are two sections in the SIS: one assesses objective characteristics of the suicide attempt (such as precautions taken against discovery, degree of planning, taking precautions against discovery), and the other assesses subjective characteristics (such as expectation of fatality, perceived seriousness of the attempt, etc.). Although developed for use with adults, the SIS has been recommended as appropriate for research with adolescents (Steer & Beck, 1988).

The SIS was included in the Suicide Circumstances Schedule, a compilation of instruments assessing suicidal behaviors (Brent et al., 1988, see chap. 10). A Physician ED (Emergency Department) measure for evaluating suicidal behavior, based largely on the SIS, has also been developed (Spirito, Lewander, Levy, Kurkjian, & Fritz, 1994).

Populations Studied

The SIS has been used with medically hospitalized patients who have attempted suicide (L. Brown et al., 1991; Groholt et al., 2000; Hawton et al., 1999; Spirito et al., 1996, 2002), psychiatrically hospitalized patients who have attempted suicide (Enns et al., 1997; Nasser & Overholser, 1999; Nock & Kazdin, 2002; Overholser et al., 1997; Spirito et al., 1996), youths presenting in an emergency department (Kingsbury, 1993; Spirito et al., 1994, 2002), Aboriginal youths (Enns et al., 1997), and sexually and other physically abused adolescents (Shaunesey et al., 1993).

Reliability

There was substantial interrater agreement on the SIS in a small sample of adolescent psychiatric inpatients and their parents, as well as parents of adolescents who completed suicide (intraclass correlation coefficients ranging from .83 to 1.00; Brent et al., 1988).

Internal Consistency

In a sample of adolescents who attempted suicide, the total SIS was found to be internally consistent ($\alpha = .85$; Spirito et al., 1996). The subjective portion of the scale was found to have higher internal consistency than the objective portion of the scale ($\alpha = .85$ and .60, respectively). The item–total correlations for items in the objective portion of the scale ranged from .12 (*ns*) to .56; Item 8 on the SIS regarding prior communication was the only item without a statistically significant item–total correlation. Item–total correlations for the subjective portion of the scale ranged from .57 to .81.

The internal consistency of the entire SIS was replicated in two samples of adolescents with recent attempts ($\alpha = .74$ and .79, respectively; Kingsbury, 1993; Nassar & Overholser, 1999). However, Kingsbury (1993) noted the two sections of the SIS were not highly correlated ($r = .24$).

Concurrent Validity

In various clinically referred samples, higher SIS total scores have been found to be related to intent to die (Groholt et al., 2000), greater severity of depression (DeMaso et al., 1994; Enns et al., 1997; Nock & Kazdin, 2002; Overholser et al., 1997; Spirito et al., 1996), greater anhedonia (Nock & Kazdin, 2002), greater degree of hopelessness (Enns et al., 1997; Nock & Kazdin, 2002; Spirito et al., 1996), more severe anxiety (Enns et al., 1997), and more severe suicidal ideation as assessed with the SIQ (Spirito et al., 1996). Longer premeditation before suicidal attempts (assessed with two items on the SIS) was related to greater depression and hopelessness (L. Brown et al., 1991). Mixed results have been reported regarding the relationship between suicide intent scores and medical lethality (DeMaso et al., 1994; Groholt et al., 2000; Nasser & Overholser, 1999)

Dimensionality

From data collected from adolescents who had taken intentional overdoses, Kingsbury (1993) extracted four factors from the SIS; these factors were variously interpreted as Belief About Intent, Preparation Before Overdose, Prevention of Discovery, and Communication. The last factor included only two SIS items. In contrast, in a sample of medically and psychiatrically hospitalized adolescents who attempted suicide, Spirito et al. (1996) extracted a three-factor solution, interpreted as Expected Outcome, Isolation Behaviors, and Planning Activities. Items 7 (regarding the presence of a suicide note) and 8 (regarding prior communication) did not load on any of the factors.

Predictive Validity

In a 1-year follow-up study, Hawton et al. (1999) did not find that suicide intent as assessed with the SIS differentiated adolescents who had a history of repeat attempts or attempted suicide during the follow-up from those who attempted once. Similarly, using the Physician ED measure (based largely on the SIS), Spirito et al. (1994) did not find that suicide intent was related to repeat suicidal behavior among adolescents in a 3-month follow-up (although length of planning the attempt was positively related to compliance with outpatient psychiatric treatment).

Treatment Studies

The SIS apparently has not been used as an outcome variable in treatment trials with adolescents. Suicidal intent assessed with the SIS was examined as a potential moderator variable in a clinical trial examining a problem-solving intervention for improving aftercare utilization following suicide attempts (Spirito et al., 2002). SIS scores, however, were not found to be significantly related to the number of therapy sessions attended (Spirito et al., 2002).

Summary and Evaluation

The SIS was initially developed for adult populations, and its use with adolescents is still being evaluated. The scale correlates as expected with constructs such as depression and hopelessness, but data regarding the relationship between intent and medical lethality of attempts are mixed. Although the SIS appears to be useful as a research instrument, and aspects of suicide intent (e.g., precautions against discovery) have been shown to have predictive value in adults, it is not clear whether the SIS conveys any unique information about prognosis or treatment considerations in adolescents.

Where to Obtain

The SIS is in Beck, Schuyler, and Herman (1974). The Physician ED measure based on the SIS can be obtained from Anthony Spirito, PhD, Child and Family Psychiatry, Rhode Island Hospital, 593 Eddy Street, Providence, RI 02903.

Child and Adolescent Psychiatric Assessment Clinical Characteristics Questions

Description

The Child and Adolescent Psychiatric Assessment (CAPA; Angold & Costello, 2000; Angold, Cox, et al., 1995; Angold, Prendergast, et al., 1995) was described earlier (see this volume, chap. 3). In the CAPA, there are separate questions regarding method of suicide attempt, suicide intent (coded on a 3-point scale from minimal intention to absolute [or almost absolute] intention to commit suicide), lethality of suicidal attempt (coded on a 3-point scale from mild or requiring no medical attention to serious, resulting in unconsciousness, resuscitation, etc.), and alcohol or drug intoxication at the time of the attempt.

Populations Studied

No published studies using the CAPA questions regarding clinical characteristics of suicidal behavior were located.

Reliability

No published data were located regarding the test–retest and interrater reliability of the clinical characteristics items.

Internal Consistency

No published data were located.

Concurrent Validity

No published data were located.

Dimensionality

No published data were located.

Predictive Validity

No published data were located.

Treatment Studies

No published data were located.

Summary and Evaluation

The questions regarding clinical characteristics of suicidal behavior on the CAPA are straightforward and are likely useful for descriptive purposes. Their use in clinical decision making and in research regarding suicidal behaviors has not been demonstrated.

Where to Obtain

Adrian Angold, MRCPsych, Developmental Epidemiology Program, Department of Psychiatry and Behavioral Sciences, Duke University Medical Center, DUMC Box 3454, Durham, NC 27710

Interview Schedule for Children and Adolescents Clinical Characteristics Questions

Description

The Interview Schedule for Children and Adolescents (ISCA; Kovacs, 1997) was described earlier (see this volume, chap. 3). In the ISCA, there are questions assessing methods (and contemplated methods) of suicide attempts, the purpose or "idea" associated with attempts or contemplated attempts, whether inpatient or ambulatory medical care was needed for suicide attempts, and psychological intent (wish to die vs. wish to live) at the time of the attempts.

Populations Studied

No studies using the ISCA questions regarding clinical characteristics of suicidal behavior were located.

Reliability

No published data were located regarding the test–retest and interrater reliability of the clinical characteristics items.

Internal Consistency

No published data were located.

Concurrent Validity

No published data were located.

Dimensionality

No published data were located.

Predictive Validity

No published data were located.

Treatment Studies

No published data were located.

Summary and Evaluation

The questions regarding clinical characteristics of suicidal behavior on the ISCA are straightforward and are likely useful for descriptive purposes. Their use in clinical decision making and their predictive validity have not been demonstrated.

Where to Obtain

Maria Kovacs, PhD, Western Psychiatric Institute and Clinic, University of Pittsburgh School of Medicine, 3811 O'Hara Street, Pittsburgh, PA 15213

Schedule for Affective Disorders and Schizophrenia for School-Age Children Medical Lethality and Intent Questions

Description

The various versions of the Schedule for Affective Disorders and Schizophrenia for School-Age Children (K–SADS) were described earlier (see this volume, chap. 3). In the K–SADS–P IVR (Ambrosini & Dixon, 1996) and K–SADS–L (Klein, 1994), the rating scale corresponding to questions about the presence of suicidal ideation or attempts requires some judgment about the intent and medical lethality of suicidal behavior. Specifically, suicide attempts judged to be primarily communicative or "gestures" are not rated as highly as suicide attempts associated with medical harm or "definite intent to die."

In addition, there are highly similar sets of questions with corresponding 0-to-6 rating scales in the K–SADS–P IVR (Ambrosini & Dixon, 1996), K–SADS–L (Klein, 1994), and K–SADS–E (Orvaschel, 1994) specifically assessing medical lethality and intent associated with suicide attempts. In the K–SADS–PL (Kaufman et al., 1996), there is an analogous, but compressed (0-to-3 instead of 0-to-6) rating scale. Responses to the questions regarding "seriousness" (intent) are rated from "obviously no intent/purely manipulative gesture" to "every expectation of death." Responses to the questions regarding medical lethality are rated from "no danger" to "extreme, e.g., respiratory arrest, prolonged coma."

Because of the correlation ($r = .66$) between K–SADS ratings of intent and medical lethality (using the Lethality of Suicide Attempt Rating Scale, to be described next) in a large community sample of adolescents (a finding that has not been demonstrated to be consistent across instruments and studies; see, e.g., DeMaso et al., 1994; Nasser & Overholser, 1999; Plutchik, van Praag, Picard, Conte, & Korn, 1989), Lewinsohn et al. (1996) recommended computing the cross-product of the responses to these answers (Intent × Lethality) to generate a single index of "seriousness of an attempt."

Populations

The K–SADS intent and lethality items have been used to assess the clinical characteristics of suicide attempts in a community sample of adolescents (Lewinsohn et al., 1996).

Reliability

No published data were located regarding the interrater and test–retest reliability for these items.

Internal Consistency

No published data were located.

Concurrent Validity

In a community sample of adolescents, Lewinsohn et al. (1996) found higher K–SADS intent scores to be associated with more severe depression, internalizing and externalizing behaviors, and poor coping skills. Suicidal intent was also related to male gender, poorer social support, and lower interviewer ratings of attractiveness. Seriousness of past attempt (the cross-product of intent and lethality ratings using a different measure) was correlated with current depression ($r = .23$; Lewinsohn et al., 1993).

Dimensionality

No published data were located.

Predictive Validity

No published data were located.

Treatment Studies

No published treatment studies were located in which the K–SADS intent and medical lethality items were used.

Summary and Evaluation

The K–SADS intent and lethality items show promise for research. However, similar to ratings from other interviews, the data regarding lethality and intent have not been shown to have use in treatment planning and have not been shown to have predictive validity.

Where to Obtain

K–SADS–E: Helen Orvaschel, PhD, Center for Psychological Studies, Nova Southeastern University, 3301 College Avenue, Ft. Lauderdale, FL 33314

K–SADS–L: Rachel G. Klein, PhD, Department of Psychiatry, New York State Psychiatric Institute, 1051 Riverside Drive, New York, NY 10032

K–SADS–P IVR: Paul J. Ambrosini, MD, MCP Hahnemann University, EPPI, 3200 Henry Avenue, Philadelphia, PA 19129

K–SADS–PL: Joan Kaufman, PhD, Department of Psychology, Yale University, P.O. Box 208205, New Haven, CT 06520. Also at http://www.wpic.pitt.edu/ksads

---

Lethality of Suicide Attempt Rating Scale

Description

The Lethality of Suicide Attempt Rating Scale (Smith, Conroy, & Ehler, 1984) is a measure used to evaluate the severity of medical lethality of suicide attempts. Items are scored on an 11-point scale, ranging from 0 (*death is an impossible result of the suicidal behavior*) to 10 (*death is almost a certainty*). The scale is supplemented by tables describing the lethality of different medications.

Populations Studied

The Lethality of Suicide Attempt Rating Scale has been used in a community sample of adolescents (Lewinsohn et al., 1993, 1994, 1996), with adolescent psychiatric inpatients (Nasser & Overholser, 1999), and with adolescents who have attempted suicide in a group home (Handwerk, Larzelere, Friman, & Mitchell, 1998).

Reliability

Interrater reliability of 24 mental health staff in judging the medical lethality depicted in 24 suicide attempt vignettes was found to be high (ICC from .81 for social workers to .88 for psychologists; Smith et al., 1984). Interrater reliability for the medical lethality ratings of adolescent psychiatric inpatients who attempted suicide also was found to be high ($r = .90$; Nasser & Overholser, 1999). Six-month test–retest reliability in ratings was .72 (Nasser & Overholser, 1999).

Internal Consistency

Not applicable because of the single item.

Concurrent Validity

In a community sample of adolescents, medical lethality ratings were found to be correlated with the number of major life events, earlier physical maturation, severity of depression, internalizing and externalizing behavior problems, and poor coping skills (Lewinsohn et al., 1996). Seriousness of past attempt (the cross-product of K–SADS-rated intent and lethality ratings) was correlated with current depression ($r = .23$; Lewinsohn et al., 1993). In addition, in youths who attempted suicide at a group home, the number of prior communications regarding suicidality was inversely related to ratings of medical lethality (Handwerk et al., 1998).

Adolescent psychiatric inpatients whose suicide attempts were rated as "high lethality" also reported higher levels of suicide intent on the SIS than youths with suicide attempts that were not rated as lethal (Nasser & Overholser, 1999). Specifically, adolescents with more lethal suicide attempts were more likely to time their attempts so that they would not be discovered, did not see the results of the attempts as being reversible, were less likely to communicate about the attempts, were more likely to expect that they would die, and said that they wanted to die more than youths with less lethal attempts. The adolescents with suicide attempts of differing levels of lethality did not differ with respect to severity of depression, hopelessness, self-esteem, or substance abuse.

Dimensionality

Not applicable because of the single rating.

Predictive Validity

No published data were located.

Treatment Studies

No published data were located.

Summary and Evaluation

The Lethality of Suicide Attempt Rating Scale is a promising measure of the medical lethality of suicide attempts that is being used in an increasing number of studies. Unlike some previous measures of medical lethality, this instrument seems to be related to ratings of suicide intent among adolescents. The use of the scale in clinical decision making and the predictive validity of the scale have not yet been evaluated.

Where to Obtain

The Lethality of Suicide Attempt Rating Scale is in Smith et al. (1984).

Pierce Suicide Intent Scale

Description

In developing the Pierce Suicide Intent Scale (Pierce, 1977), the author wanted to design and test "a more objective scale for measuring suicidal intent" (p. 378) than the Beck Suicide Intent Scale (SIS) discussed earlier in the chapter. Nonetheless, the Pierce Scale is essentially a modification of the Beck Scale in that the first 6 of 12 items, as well as the 8th item on this semistructured interview, were taken directly from the Beck Scale. Other items on this 12-item scale are modifications of items on the Beck SIS. Although they are summed with the other items to determine an estimate of intent, the last 2 items on the Pierce Scale do not really measure intent at all, but rather measure medical risk or lethality associated with the suicide attempt. There are three scales on the Pierce Suicide Intent Scale: The first 6 items are summed to yield a circumstances score, Items 7 through 10 are summed to yield a self-report score, and the last 2 items are summed to yield a medical risk score. The Pierce Suicide Intent Scale was developed with a sample of primarily adults, although the youngest individual in the sample who attempted suicide was 13.

Populations Studied

The Pierce Suicide Intent Scale has been used with mixed samples of adults and adolescents (Pierce, 1977), adolescents recruited from an emergency room setting (Rotheram-Borus & Trautman, 1988, 1990; Trautman, Rotherum-Borus, Dopkins, & Lewin, 1991), adolescents in outpatient psychiatric settings (Rotheram-Borus & Trautman, 1988), Mexican American adolescents (Ng, 1996), and samples of primarily Hispanic and African American adolescents (Rotheram-Borus & Trautman, 1988, 1990; Trautman et al., 1991).

Reliability

In an initial sample, the interrater reliability of the suicide intent of 16 patients (ages unspecified) was .97 (Pierce, 1977). With a sample of primarily Hispanic and African American adolescents who attempted suicide, interrater reliability of the Pierce Suicide Intent Scale was .85 (Rotheram-Borus & Trautman, 1990).

Internal Consistency

In a mixed sample of adults and adolescents, item–total correlations ranged from .29 to .66 (Pierce, 1977). In a sample totally composed of adolescents, the internal consistency of the scale (as measured with Cronbach α) was .73 (Rotheram-Borus & Trautman, 1990).

Concurrent Validity

In a mixed sample of adolescent and (primarily) adult suicide patients, scores from the Pierce Scale were highly correlated with the Beck Scale scores ($r = .93$; Pierce, 1977). Pierce Suicide Intent Scale scores were higher for patients with multiple suicide attempts and for patients who had received prior psychiatric treatment (Pierce, 1977). Similarly, in a sample of Mexican American adolescents, suicide attempts with high intent were associated with a greater number of previous attempts than suicide attempts with lower intent (Ng, 1996). In a sample of primarily Hispanic and African American adolescents who attempted suicide , scores on the Pierce Suicide Intent Scale were not related to either severity of depression or hopelessness (Rotheram-Borus & Trautman, 1988).

Dimensionality

No published data were located.

Predictive Validity

No data pertaining to predictive validity with youths were located.

Treatment Studies

The Pierce Suicide Intent Scale has not been used in treatment studies with adolescents.

Summary and Evaluation

The Pierce Suicide Intent Scale is not appreciably different from the more widely used Beck SIS. The scale confounds issues of intent and medical lethality by including two items regarding the medical consequences of suicide attempts. The use of the scale in clinical decision making and the predictive validity of the scale have not yet been evaluated.

Where to Obtain

The Pierce Suicide Intent Scale is in Pierce (1977).

Risk–Rescue Rating Scale

Description

The Risk–Rescue Rating Scale (Weisman & Worden, 1972) was originally developed for assessing the medical lethality of suicidal behavior in adults. It has been included in the Suicide Circumstances Schedule, a compilation of instruments assessing suicidal behaviors (Brent et al., 1988, see chap. 10). The clinician-rated scale has a section devoted to medical Risk and a section devoted to likelihood of Rescue. The Risk Scale includes five questions pertaining to the lethality of the method used, level of impaired consciousness, lesions/toxicity of the attempt, potential for medical reversibility versus lasting damage, and treatment required. The Rescue Scale includes five questions assessing whether or not the location of the attempt was remote or isolated, the person (if any) initiating the rescue, the probability of eventual discovery, accessibility to rescue, and time delay until discovery. Each item on the Risk and Rescue scales is scored 1 to 3; the scores on each of the scales is then summed and combined to yield a total classification based on the Risk–Rescue score.

Populations Studied

The Risk–Rescue Rating Scale has been used to assess medically hospitalized adolescents secondary to suicide attempts (Groholt et al., 2000; Spirito, Brown, Overholser, Frtiz, & Bond, 1991; Swedo et al., 1991), adolescents in outpatient psychiatric settings who have attempted suicide (DeWilde, Kienhorst, Diekstra, & Wolters, 1992, 1993), and adolescents in school settings who have attempted suicide (DeWilde et al., 1992, 1993).

Reliability

In a small sample of suicidal inpatients and their parents, and parents of adolescents who completed suicide, Brent et al. (1988) found acceptable agreement with the Risk–Rescue Rating Scale (intraclass correlation coefficients ranging from .91 to 1.00). In contrast, Spirito et al. (1991) documented considerable difficulty in obtaining reliable ratings with the Risk–Rescue Rating Scale in adolescents. After devising a set of decision rules because of ambiguity about how items should be rated, graduate student raters were still only able to achieve 81% agreement ($\kappa = .72$) for the Risk Scale and 74% agreement ($\kappa = .61$) for the Rescue Scale. A second test–retest study was undertaken for the most discrepant cases rated in the first study. Between a child psychiatrist and a child psychologist, there was only 70% agreement ($\kappa = .47$) on the Risk Scale and 43% agreement ($\kappa = .07$) on the Rescue Scale.

Internal Consistency

No data are available for adolescents.

Concurrent Validity

In a chart review of medically hospitalized adolescents (secondary to suicide attempts), Brent (1987) found greater medical lethality to be associated with male gender, diagnosis of affective disorder, affective disorder in combination with substance use disorder, family history of affective disorder, and higher suicide intent. Medical lethality was not found to be related to hopelessness. Groholt et al. (2000) found greater medical lethality to be associated with suicide attempts motivated primarily by a desire to die. Risk–Rescue ratings were higher for a mixed sample of adolescents and young adults classified with another medical lethality instrument as having "near lethal" suicide attempts compared with those whose attempts were not classified as "near lethal" (Potter et al., 1998).

Dimensionality

No published data were located.

Predictive Validity

No published data were located.

Treatment Studies

No published data were located.

Summary and Evaluation

The Risk–Rescue Rating Scale was developed to assess medical lethality. Spirito et al. (1991) raised questions about its appropriateness with adolescents and documented difficulties in obtaining reliable ratings with the scale. The clinical and predictive use of the scale has not been demonstrated.

Where to Obtain

The Risk–Rescue Rating Scale is in Weisman and Worden (1972).

Self-Inflicted Injury Severity Form

Description

The Self-Inflicted Injury Severity Form (SIISF) is an "epidemiological research tool for identifying individuals in hospital emergency departments who have life-threatening self-inflicted injuries . . . [that is,] cases of attempted suicide who would have died from suicide-related injuries had they not received rapid and effective prehospital care or other emergency treatment" (Potter et al., 1998, pp. 174–175). The SIISF was validated using a sample of 13- to 34-year-olds who attempted suicide. On the SIISF, self-inflicted injuries are classified first according to method: 1 = gunshot; 2 = jumping or blunt trauma; 3 = hanging; 4 = suffocation; 5 = laceration or stabbing; 6 = ingestion, inhalation, or injection; and 7 = other. For each of the specified methods, injuries are then classified on a 1-to-3 or 1-to-4 rating scale according to medical lethality. For example, injuries with a gun are classified as 1 = "gun fired, bullet missed patient," 2 = "gun fired, bullet wound limited to skin and subcutaneous tissue," or 3 = "gun fired, bullet penetrated muscle, bone, and/or internal organ."

Populations Studied

The SIISF has been used in emergency room settings in classification of self-injuries among adolescents and adults (ages 13–34; Kresnow et al., 2001; Potter et al., 1998; Powell et al., 2001).

Reliability

Interrater agreement as to the classification of suicide attempt method on the SIISF was high ($\kappa = .94$; Potter et al., 1998). Using the classification of "near-fatality," agreement as to case status by independent reviewers was also high ($\kappa = .93$), with poisoning being the only method associated with disagreements. Agreement as to level of severity could not be reliably computed for attempts with guns, jumping, hanging, or drowning/suffocating because of the small sample size. There was substantial agreement for severity of injury associated with laceration/stabbing ($\kappa = .71$) and ingestion ($\kappa = .73$ for level of consciousness; $\kappa = .78$ for physiological symptoms).

Internal Consistency

No published data were located.

Concurrent Validity

There was high agreement as to method of self-injury between the SIISF and the Risk–Rescue Rating Scale (Potter et al., 1998). Injuries classified as cases according to the SIISF (because of their near-fatality) had higher Risk–Rescue Rating Scale scores than injuries classified as noncases. Nearly lethal cases also had higher rates of alcoholism and were more likely to have been drinking in the 3 hours prior to the suicide attempt than those whose attempts were less lethal(Powell et al., 2001). Those classified as having nearly lethal suicide attempts were paradoxically differentiated from those whose suicide attempts were "less lethal" by their lower rates of previous attempts, less severe levels of depression and hopelessness, and lower rates of previous help-seeking (Swahn & Potter, 2001).

Dimensionality

No published data were located.

Predictive Validity

No published data were located.

Treatment Studies

No published data were located.

Summary and Evaluation

The SIISF is an instrument for identifying individuals who made "near-lethal" suicide attempts. As of yet, the instrument has not been used in published studies beyond the original validation sample. The intended purpose of the instrument, identifying "near-fatal" suicide attempts, is a questionable one for adolescents, given that the predictive validity and clinical use of ratings of medical lethality of suicide attempts among adolescents have yet to be demonstrated.

Where to Obtain

The SIISF is in Potter et al. (1998).

Summary

Perhaps the most important thing to remember about assessments of the subjective intent or medical lethality of suicide attempts is that *none* of them have been shown to have evidence of predictive validity. That is, despite the fact that mental health professionals tend to give weight to the clinical characteristics of suicidal behavior when estimating the risk of future suicidal behavior (Peruzzi & Bongar, 1999), intent and lethality ratings have yet to be demonstrated in the empirical literature to have use in predicting future behaviors or response to treatment among adolescents. This does not mean that subjective intent and medical lethality do not have predictive validity; rather, this is a matter of future empirical test. With that caveat, probably the best current uses of instruments assessing the clinical characteristics of suicidal behavior are for clinical research and as a means of describing suicidal behavior. As interventions for chronically suicidal patients, such as dialectical behavioral therapy, become more widely used, such instruments may also have use as outcome measures in treatment studies.

Several diagnostic interviews contain screening items regarding the clinical characteristics of suicidal behavior. However, the instruments devoted specifically to measuring these domains have been much better studied than the screening items. The Beck and Pierce Suicide Intent Scales are both reliable instruments for assessing intent, but the Beck instrument offers a "purer" assessment of intent because it does not include items regarding lethality of attempt. Questions have been raised about the ease with which the Risk-Rescue Rating Scale can be used reliably as a measure of lethality. The SIISF has been demonstrated to be highly reliably and also has been found to be strongly correlated with the Risk–Rescue Rating Scale; hence, it may offer a reasonable and easier-to-use alternative for assessing lethality than the Risk–Rescue Rating Scale. Nonetheless, at the time of this writing, the SIISF had not yet been evaluated beyond initial validation samples. The Lethality of Suicide Attempt Rating Scale also has demonstrated interrater reliability and concurrent validity and may prove useful in assessment of medical lethality of suicidal behavior among youths. (Please refer to Table 9.1 for a complete instrument-by-instrument comparison.)

Table 9.1

Characteristics of Instruments and Items for Clinical Characteristics of Suicidal Behavior

Instrument	Focus of Instrument	Reliability	Concurrent validity	Predictive validity
Beck SIS	Intent	+	+	—
CAPA Clinical Characteristics items	Intent, medical lethality	—	—	—
ISCA Clinical Characteristics items	Intent, need for medical attention	—	—	—
K–SADS Clinical Characteristics items	Intent, medical lethality	—	+	—
Lethality of Suicide Attempt Rating Scale	Medical lethality	+	+	—
Pierce SIS	Intent	+	+	—
Risk–Rescue Scale	Medical lethality, likelihood of rescue	+	+	—
SIISF	Medical lethality	+	+	—

Note. The instrument are as follows: Beck SIS = Suicide Intent Scale; CAPA = Child and Adolescent Psychiatric Assessment; ISCA = Interview Schedule for Children and Adolescents; K–SADS = Schedule for Affective Disorders and Schizophrenia for School-Age Children; Pierce SIS = Suicide Intent Scale; SIISF = Self-Inflicted Injury Severity Form.

10

Other Sucide-Related Instruments

This section of the book is devoted to instruments that assess areas related to suicidality not covered elsewhere. These include the following:

- instruments assessing attitudes toward suicidal behaviors
- instruments assessing the circumstances of exposure to suicide or death
- compilations of instruments
- forms for recording information from clinical interviews about suicidal behaviors
- "process" instruments and projective instruments for assessing suicidality
- interviews for survivors of suicide

Many of these instruments have not been evaluated extensively from a psychometric perspective; when information about psychometric properties is available, I have described it. Because of the variety of these types of instruments and because many of these instruments do not lend themselves to the same type of critique as the other instruments reviewed in this book, I have provided the descriptive information for information purposes only.

Attitudes Toward Suicide List

Description

The Attitudes Toward Suicide List is a 20-item measure designed to assess attitudes about personally engaging in suicidal behavior (DeWilde et al., 1993; Diekstra & Kerkhof, 1989). The items on this scale are rated on a 5-point scale, ranging from *certainly yes* to *certainly no*. The Attitudes Toward Suicide List has been found to be internally consistent, α = .81 (Diekstra & Kerkhof, 1989). Factor analysis of this scale has yielded five factors interpreted as follows: "(1) restrictive/permissive attitude toward suicide as a consequence of social/relational loss, (2) restrictive/permissive attitude toward suicide as a consequence of serious physical suffering, (3) moral judgment of suicide, (4) restrictive/permissive attitude toward suicide as a consequence of losing or not acquiring nuclear family, and (5) consequences of suicide (for society or relatives)" (DeWilde et al., 1993, p. 53). The Attitudes Toward Suicide List has been studied both on the item level (Kienhorst, DeWilde, Diekstra, & Wolters, 1991) and on the factor level (DeWilde et al ., 1993). In one study of adolescents in the Netherlands, suicidal adolescents were found to differ from nonsuicidal youths, but not depressed youths, in terms of the attitudes about suicide in response to loss, attitudes about suicide in response to personal suffering, and moral judgments about suicide (DeWilde et al., 1993).

Where to Obtain

Erik J. De Wilde, PhD, Department of Clinical, Personal and Health Psychology, University of Leiden, Wassenaarseweg 52, 2333 AK Leiden, The Netherlands

---

Attitudes Toward Suicide and Suicidal Ideation

Description

The Attitudes Toward Suicide and Suicidal Ideation questionnaire (Stein, Brom, Elizur, & Witztum, 1998) was developed to examine adolescents' attitudes toward suicide and the relationship between these attitudes and other factors thought to be risk factors for suicidal behavior. The Attitudes Toward Suicide and Suicidal Ideation questionnaire consists of 156 multiple-choice questions examining the attitudes regarding suicidal behavior and personal experiences with suicidal ideation and suicidal behavior. Many of the items on this instrument were excerpted from other questionnaires; the remainder were developed by a group of professionals specializing in suicide. Factor analysis of data from a sample of Israeli 16- to 17-year-olds undergoing evaluations prior to being drafted for military service revealed that the attitudes fell into four groups: (a) society's right to prevent suicide (e.g., suicidal individuals should be helped even when they do not want help, individuals who assist others with suicide need to be punished), (b) suicide as reflecting mental illness (e.g., suicidal individuals need treatment, individuals who attempt suicide have mental illness), (c) the right to discuss suicide (e.g., suicidal behavior should be concealed, discussions in school about suicide may reduce suicidal problems), and (d) the seriousness of suicidal talk and behavior (e.g., suicidal threats by an adolescent should be taken seriously, individuals who attempt suicide want to die, individuals who attempt suicide may do so again).

Where to Obtain

Daniel Stein, MD, Abarbanel Mental Health Center, 15 Keren Kayemet Street, Bat-Yam 59100 Israel

---

Characteristics of Exposure to Death

Description

The Characteristics of Exposure to Death (CED) Scale (Brent et al., 1992; Brent, Perper, Moritz, Liotus, et al., 1994; Brent, Perper, Moritz, Liotus, et al., 1993; Brent et al., 1995) is an interview measure consisting of 30 items designed to evaluate the experience of the respondent "just before, during, and after the death of a peer." Four areas are specifically assessed: the circumstances of death, direct exposure (i.e., what was witnessed), indirect exposure (e.g., visiting scene of death), and events following death. More specifically, respondents are asked whether they saw the injury, whether they were at the scene of the injury/death prior to the victim being removed, whether they saw the victim die, whether they discovered the victim, whether they heard through the media about the death, whether they attended the funeral, whether the casket was open, whether there was anything that may have suggested the victim's plans, whether they thought they could have done something to prevent the death, and the last time they spoke with the deceased individual. Interviewer agreement with the CED has been found to be high ($\kappa = .97$).

Using the CED, it was found that adolescents exposed to a friend's suicide had greater lifetime history of exposure to suicidality, including completed suicide (excluding the friend's suicide), compared with psychiatrically and demographically matched control adolescents (Brent et al., 1992). In addition, adolescents with a peer who committed suicide were much more likely to develop posttraumatic stress disorder if they saw the scene of death, were witness to the suicide, discovered the body, knew of the suicide plans beforehand, or had a conversation with the victim on the day of the suicide (all assessed with the CED; Brent et al., 1995).

Where to Obtain

David A. Brent, MD, University of Pittsburgh School of Medicine, Western Psychiatric Institute and Clinic, 3811 O'Hara Street, Pittsburgh, PA

Columbia/Ruane Initial Evaluation Form for Child and Adolescent Suicide Attempters/Ideators

Description

The Columbia/Ruane Initial Evaluation Form is an evaluation form developed for emergency room settings, crisis service settings, or the initial interview with patients who attempt suicide (Shaffer, Trautman, Mufson, Piacentini, & Grae, 1997). The form was developed to ensure that in evaluation settings all pertinent questions are asked of patients who have attempted suicide. Questions include method of attempt, whether the patient was intoxicated at the time of the attempt, symptoms of mania, psychosis, drug use, impulsivity, antisocial behavior, history of prior suicide attempts, mental health treatment history, family history of suicidal behavior, items from the Hamilton Depression Rating Scale, and items similar to those of the Beck Suicide Intent Scale regarding isolation, timing, precautions against discovery, final acts in anticipation of death, degree of premeditation, and reported intent at the time of the attempt.

Where to Obtain

Division of Child and Adolescent Psychiatry, Columbia University— New York State Psychiatric Institute, 1051 Riverside Drive, New York, NY 10032

Completed Suicide Event Interview

Description

The Completed Suicide Event Interview (Shaffer, Gould, et al., 1996) is an extensive semistructured interview examining the details of a completed suicide. Included are questions about method of suicide, source of the method, location of the suicide and degree of isolation, details of the discovery of the suicide victim, mood at the time of the suicide, evidence of suicide planning, precipitants of the suicide, exposure to suicide and suicidal behavior among family and peers, other exposure to suicide, degree of morbid preoccupation, and participation in suicide prevention programs. No psychometric data are available for the Completed Suicide Event Interview. A revision of the Completed Suicide Interview has been developed by Madelyn Gould, PhD; studies of the psychometric properties of that version of the interview are in progress.

Where to Obtain

Division of Child and Adolescent Psychiatry, Columbia University—New York State Psychiatric Institute, 1051 Riverside Drive, New York, NY 10032

Psychological Pain Assessment Scale

Description

The Psychological Pain Assessment Scale (PPAS; Shneidman, 1999) is the only projective personality assessment device described in this book. The PPAS is fashioned after the Thematic Apperception Test of Henry Murray, and it has been developed in the context of Shneidman's theoretical notions about psychological pain or "psychache"—the unmet psychological needs and the negative emotions associated with such needs that are thought to be of central importance in the genesis and understanding of suicidal behavior. The PPAS is designed to elicit expressions of psychological pain and to provide the opportunity for "explorations of relationships between heightened psychache and suicidal acts" (Shneidman, 1999, p. 287). As such, the PPAS is not a hypothesis-testing so much as a hypothesis-generating tool for clinicians. At the beginning of the PPAS is an eloquent definition of psychological pain and a question asking respondents to rate their current level of psychache. After this rating, respondents are asked to look at five emotionally evocative pictures and to rate the psychological pain depicted in each. Respondents are also asked to consider the "worst mental pain" they have ever experienced, and they are asked to circle the three feelings (corresponding to unmet needs) most prominent at the time of that pain. Respondents are also asked whether they ever made a suicide attempt and how close to death they came as a result of the attempt. In the last part of the PPAS, respondents are asked to describe in prose the "worst psychological pain felt," the circumstances of this pain, and how the incident "worked out." The PPAS has been administered to both adults and adolescents (E. Shneidman, personal communication, September 1999).

Where to Obtain

Edwin S. Shneidman, PhD, Professor of Thanatology Emeritus, University of California, Los Angeles, 11431 Kingsland Street, Los Angeles, CA 90066

Reasons for Suicide Attempts and Reasons for Overdose

Description

Different from questions of suicidal intent (usually conceptualized in terms of whether or how much someone wants to die) are the reasons or motivations for attempting suicide. The Reasons for Suicide Attempts and Reasons for Overdose instruments have been developed to address these issues. The original articles focusing on reasons or motivations for overdose were published in the 1970s and were focused on primarily adult populations (Bancroft et al., 1979; Bancroft, Skrimshire, & Simkin, 1976). Boergers et al. (1998) modified the procedures for administering the Reasons for Overdose list (turning the items into a self-report scale as opposed to cue cards to be administered in interview, asking participants to indicate their "primary" motivation after choosing all reasons for their suicidal behavior, and adding the item "to die" to the list of reasons). Using this scale, Boergers et al. (1998, p. 1289) found that the most commonly endorsed motivations for adolescent suicide attempts were "to die," "to get relief from a terrible state of mind," "to escape for a while from an impossible situation." The latter two reasons are similar to those cited by British (Hawton, Cole, O'Grady, & Osborn, 1982) and Dutch (Kienhorst, DeWilde, Diekstra, & Wolters, 1995) suicidal youths, although the samples did differ in how often the item "to die" was cited as a motivation for suicide (Boergers et al., 1998).

The Bancroft et al. (1976, 1979) Reasons for Overdose also were translated into Dutch by Kerkhof (1985, cited in Kienhorst et al., 1995). Instead of endorsing or not endorsing various reasons for suicide attempts, the Dutch version of this instrument ("Reasons for Attempting Suicide") asks respondents to rate each reason for overdose from 1 (*was certainly not so*) to 7 (*was certainly so*). Factor analysis of these items indicated that the motivations for adolescent suicide attempts fell roughly into five groups: (a) appeal to others, (b) relief or cessation of consciousness, (c) escape or losing self-control, (d) revenge, and (e) considering suicide as the only option left (Kienhorst et al., 1995).

Where to Obtain

Items for Reasons for Suicide Attempts and Reasons for Overdose can in found it Boergers et al. (1998) and Kienhorst et al. (1995).

Self-Injury Inventory

Description

The Self-Injury Inventory (SII; Zlotnick, Donaldson, Spirito, & Pearlstein, 1997; Zlotnick et al., 1996; Zlotnick, Wolfsdorf, Johnson, & Spirito, in press) is a self-report scale developed to assess nonsuicidal self-mutilation and other nonsuicidal self-injurious behaviors. This scale may be useful in assessing those self-harm behaviors that are frequently confused with suicidal behaviors and are motivated by reasons other than a desire to die, such as anxiety reduction. Self-injurious behaviors assessed include cutting, scratching, burning, and hitting oneself (Zlotnick et al., 1997). Also assessed are other classes of typically impulsive risk-taking behaviors such as driving recklessness, binge eating, binge drinking, physical violence, and having unprotected sex. The SII has been used in the assessment of adolescents and adults in inpatient settings.

Where to Obtain

Caron Zlotnick, PhD, Butler Hospital, Brown University Department of Psychiatry and Human Behavior, Providence, RI 02906

Suicidal Behavior History Form

Description

The Suicidal Behavior History Form (SBHF; Reynolds & Mazza, 1992a, 1992b) is a form for systematically recording information about suicidal behaviors from a clinical interview. Similar to the Columbia/Ruane Initial

Evaluation Form, the form's queries can serve as a series of prompts to clinicians to obtain certain information about suicidal behaviors. Indeed, the SBHF manual states that it should be administered as a "semistructured interview" (Reynolds & Mazza, 1992b, p. 6). On the SBHF, there are sections for recording information about general history of suicide attempts, description of the most recent attempt (including place, circumstances, proximity of others), reasons for the suicide attempt, consequences of the attempts, presence of suicide notes, preparations for death (e.g., writing a will), history of mental health treatment, prior attempt history (including methods, places, circumstances, and consequences of prior suicide attempts), and current status (including access to means of suicide such as firearms or medications and exposure to suicidal behavior in the family, expectations of later suicide attempts, and current suicidal ideation). The SBHF manual states that this instrument should not be used to determine "current risk" and should be used in conjunctions with other specific measures of current suicidal behaviors such as the Suicidal Ideation Questionnaire or the Suicidal Behaviors Interview.

Where to Obtain

William M. Reynolds, PhD, Department of Psychology, Humboldt State University, Arcatta, CA 95521

Suicide Attitude Vignette Experience

Description

The Suicide Attitude Vignette Experience (SAVE; Stillion, McDowell, & Shamblin, 1984) is a method for evaluating attitudes toward suicide. The SAVE technique has now been used not only with adolescents (Stillion et al., 1984) but also with samples of college students (Lester, Guerriero, & Wachter, 1991) and elderly adults (Stillion, White, Edwards, & McDowell, 1989). The scale consists of 10 different vignettes (with the gender of the central character alternating across stories) describing situations that precipitate an attempted suicide. Vignette themes include areas such as academic problems, relationship problems, difficulties with parents, parental disapproval, rejection because of physical appearance, parental death, guilt over an accident, terminal illness associated with pain, and difficulties associated with substance abuse. Respondents are asked to rate the degree they empathize with the central character in each vignette, sympathize with the central character, and agree with his or her actions. In one study of high school students, youths who agreed more with suicidal behaviors had higher depression scores and lower self-esteem (Stillion et al., 1984). Youths more sympathetic with suicidal actions also were more depressed compared with peers (Stillion et al., 1984). Factor analysis of the scale revealed three factors accounting for the great majority of the variance in the SAVE scale (Stillion et al., 1984). Four-week test–retest reliability of these factor-derived scales ranged from $r = .52$ to $r = .65$ (Stillion et al., 1984).

Where to Obtain

The SAVE vignettes are presented in Stillion et al. (1984).

Suicidal Circumstances Schedule

Description

The semistructured Suicidal Circumstances Schedule (SCS) is a compilation of instruments by Brent et al. (1988, 1992) for use in research with adolescents. The SCS includes the previously reviewed Beck's Suicidal Intent Scale (Beck, Schuyler, & Herman, 1974) and the Risk–Rescue Rating Scale (Weisman & Worden, 1972), in addition to sections assessing the motivation and precipitants of suicidal behavior, previous exposure to suicidal behavior, and accessibility to firearms and medications.

Where to Obtain

David A. Brent, MD, University of Pittsburgh School of Medicine, Western Psychiatric Institute and Clinic, 3811 O'Hara Street, Pittsburgh, PA 15213

Part IV

Conclusion

Summary, Recommendations, and Future Directions

The purpose of this book was to update the critical overview of instruments for assessing suicidality in youths written by Lewinsohn et al. (Garrison, Lewinsohn, et al., 1991; Lewinsohn et al., 1989) a decade ago. There has been tremendous growth in interest in the assessment of youths thought to be at risk since Lewinsohn et al.'s review was published. The increase in interest focused on troubled youths is welcome. The National Institute of Mental Health (2000) has pointed out that there is a paucity of careful research systematically evaluating the efficacy or effectiveness of interventions with suicidal youths. A Suicide Consensus Workshop (Caine, 2001) sponsored by the University of Rochester and the National Institute of Mental Health (NIMH) has gone one step further by noting that the lack of systematic evaluation of suicide prevention efforts has made it difficult to recommend evidence-based "best practices" in the area. Hence, careful and objective evaluation of prevention and treatment efforts has been strongly encouraged. To assess the impact of programs, one needs psychometrically sound measures for evaluating suicidal behaviors and related constructs. The instruments reviewed in the book provide needed assistance in evaluating outcomes of interventions, as well as identifying at-risk youths and monitoring suicidal behavior and risk.

The objective of this book was not to offer specific recommendations about which instruments might or might not be useful in clinical work and research. As should be obvious from the individual reviews, virtually all of the instruments have their strengths as well as their weaknesses. The choice of instruments should depend primarily on the specific needs of the clinician or researcher, the intended use of the instruments, and an assessment of how an instrument compares with other similar instruments in meeting needs. Moreover, it is worth repeating the obvious fact that most of these instruments are not static entities. They are in constant development, and therefore, it behooves the clinician and researcher interested in a particular instrument to contact the author(s) of the instruments to obtain the most up-to-date information about the instrument before using it.

Despite the potential usefulness of the instruments described in this book in screening or detecting suicidal behaviors or risk, monitoring suicidal behaviors, and evaluating the impact of intervention efforts, there are a number of gaps in our knowledge about these instruments. These gaps are not always obvious to the uninformed because of unsubstantiated claims that may give the impression that we know more than we do. This is particularly troublesome in those instances in which instruments have been described or marketed as being useful for evaluating the propensity or probability or risk of suicide itself in the absence of prospective evaluation of this claim. For that reason, users of suicide assessment instruments are urged to be careful consumers and to examine all available information about instruments themselves rather than relying solely on claims about instruments' use (in the same way they would go about carefully choosing other products).

Clinical Considerations in Choice of Instruments

Although instruments may be in constant development, and there may be no single "best" instrument for all purposes, the practitioner can ask three central questions that help guide his or her choice of appropriate instrumentation.

1. *For what purpose is the instrument to be used?* The question about the ultimate need or use of the instrument should be at the top of the list when making decisions about which assessment device to choose. As has been described in this book, there are a number of different types of suicide assessment instruments: detection instruments, risk assessment instruments, and instruments for assessing clinical characteristics of suicidal behavior, among others. Each of these groups of instruments is ideal for answering certain types of questions, and use of the wrong instrument may yield insufficient or even misleading information. For example, a clinician should not rely exclusively on a risk assessment instrument if what he or she is really interested in knowing is whether a youngster is currently suicidal (an issue of detection). A youth may score low on a risk assessment instrument assessing a particular domain (e.g., hopelessness) while still experiencing current suicidal ideation or despite making a recent attempt. Likewise, in

assessing future risk, a clinician should not rely heavily on information about the clinical characteristics of recent or past suicidal behavior (suicide intent or medical lethality)—these latter characteristics have not yet been shown to be predictive of suicidal behavior.

In this context, it is worth noting that suicide assessment instruments may aid in decision making, but they should not supplant clinical judgment. Clinicians often have much more information at hand than can be captured in a single instrument, and they have the added benefit of being able to observe the individual being evaluated. Therein, suicide instruments are best considered tools in the armamentarium of the clinician, tools that can supplement or bolster the ability of the clinician to make an informed decision rather than devices to be used in lieu of clinical judgment.

2. *What is the outcome I really want to measure?* Practitioners often give suicide assessment instruments because they want to know who is at highest risk of completed suicide so they can intervene promptly and appropriately. Although a laudable goal, *none* of the suicide assessment instruments reviewed have been demonstrated to be predictive of completed suicide among youths. Suicide attempts are a much higher base-rate phenomena and are associated with significant costs and distress, as well as increased risk for eventual completed suicide. With these considerations, the practitioners should ask whether it might make more sense to screen or assess for higher base-rate phenomena such as suicidal ideation and history of attempts.

3. *Has the instrument been used in the way I want to use it, or with a group of youths similar to those I want to assess?* If an instrument is to be used for clinical purposes, it should have been demonstrated to be of use with that population. The prevalence of risk factors for suicidal behaviors differs in different samples or population groups, just as the base rates of suicidal ideation and suicide attempts differ. Moreover, some instruments may be more appropriate than others for certain age groups, and some instruments may be more "culturally sensitive" than others. For these and other reasons, an instrument that has been demonstrated to be of use in one population may not be as useful with other groups.

Research Issues in Suicide Assessment Instruments

In the process of critically evaluating the literature for the suicide assessment instruments, it is impossible to ignore the needs for further research. References have been made already to a number of research gaps in the preceding section on the clinical use of instruments, and elsewhere in this book. Eight areas in particular emerged as especially deserving of further research attention.

1. *Especially for assessment/detection instruments, there is a need for clinicians and researchers to use a common language to describe suicidal ideation and behaviors.* Thirty years ago, a special NIMH Task Force recommended a consistent system for defining and communicating about suicidal behaviors (Beck et al., 1973). It was pointedly stated that "much of the energy directed towards research, training, and prevention will be wasted unless uniform, reliable, and valid systems for defining, coding, and reporting suicidal behaviors are established" (Beck et al., 1973, p. 10). As a result of this Task Force's work, operational definitions for basic terms such as *suicidal ideation, suicide attempts,* and *completed suicide* were proposed.

Definitional issues were revisited with the 1996 Tower of Babel article in the journal *Suicide and Life-Threatening Behavior* (O'Carroll et al., 1996). Once again, the difficulties caused by lack of efficient communication and cross-talk were described, and a nomenclature with objective definitions of suicidal behaviors was proposed. It is interesting that some of the definitions proposed in O'Carroll et al's article are not appreciably different from those proposed for researchers three decades ago by the NIMH Task Force. During this same period, operational diagnostic criteria (such as the Research Diagnostic Criteria and *DSM* system) have improved our ability to communicate about psychiatric diagnoses and helped usher in increasingly more sophisticated and complex research about the etiology and course of psychopathology. Research in suicidology has obviously progressed as well, but for the field to continue to make progress, there is a striking need for researchers and clinicians in suicidology to use a common language or set of terms in describing suicidal phenomena.

2. *The paucity of prospective studies evaluating the usefulness of measures in predicting suicidal behavior is a major concern.* There are a number of instruments that have been developed for identifying youths thought to be at risk for suicidal behavior. Indeed, several instruments are explicitly marketed as being useful for identifying individuals at risk for suicide. Very few of these instruments, however, have been demonstrated to be predictive of attempted suicide, much less completed suicide in juvenile populations. Instruments without demonstrated predictive validity that are marketed as being able to identify individuals at future risk for suicide are falsely advertised; claims about identifying risk are speculation, or perhaps wishful thinking, but not conclusions grounded in empirical data.

When a researcher or clinician aspires to identify populations at risk, he or she is typically not concerned with predicting what has already happened. And yet that is the primary validation strategy used by most instruments for examining "risk." Individuals with different histories of suicidal and nonsuicidal behavior are contrasted with a particular measure, and if the average scores on the measure are sufficiently different for different groups, the measure is said to be able to "predict" suicide status. This is certainly an expedient strategy; longitudinal studies are methodologically difficult, and in the case of low base-rate behaviors such as suicidal behavior, they can be quite expensive. But when all is said and done, the reality is that it is much simpler just to ask individuals if they have attempted suicide in the past rather than using some probabilistic system for guessing at these facts. What clinicians and researchers alike really need to know is not what has already happened, but who is going to make the suicide attempt or complete suicide in the future. There is no short cut: The only way to discover who is at risk in the future is to follow individuals thought to be at risk over some significant period of time.

3. *There has been insufficient attention paid to discriminant validity, or the degree to which suicidal behavior does not correlate with constructs with which it should not. There also has been insufficient attention paid to issues of incremental validity, or the degree to which a test provides information not available elsewhere.* As part of the validation procedures for measures of suicidal behavior, it is common to demonstrate that the suicidal behavior instrument correlates in a predicted way with other related constructs such as depression and hopelessness (convergent validity). However, if a test developer designs a suicidality instrument that correlates highly with related measures of depression or hopelessness, all the test developer has succeeded in doing is developing a redundant measure of depression or perhaps psychological distress. Demonstrating relationships with theoretically related variables (i.e., the "nomological net") is an important part of establishing construct validity (Chronbach & Meehl, 1955) in establishing construct validity; however, a new test will be useful only to the extent that it also measures something important that is different from existing measures. If there is a need for a new test, there is also a need for the test to be different from what currently exists.

4. *Most of the risk assessment instruments reviewed in this book have a stated goal of predicting completed suicide (or identifying individuals thought to be at risk for completed suicide). However, no studies of youths have actually been undertaken that have demonstrated that we can accurately predict who will kill him- or herself.* It is a daunting task (both psychometrically and in terms of costs) to screen for risk of completed suicide in the general population (an outcome with a 1-year base rate of approximately 10 per 100,000 young people; Centers

for Disease Control and Prevention, 2000a). However, suicide attempts and suicidal ideation have considerably higher base rates (approximately 8 per 100 young people, and 19 per 100 young people per year, respectively; Centers for Disease Control and Prevention, 2000b). Moreover, suicide attempts are a primary reason for referral for child psychiatric emergency services and psychiatric hospitalization. Suicide attempts and suicide ideation are both markers for a variety of psychiatric problems and difficulties with coping, and they provide important clues regarding which youths are distressed and may be at risk for continuing suicidal (and other high-risk) behaviors.

Suicidal ideation and suicide attempts may not be an adequate proxy for completed suicide (because of their nonidentical base rates and nonidentical correlates; Shaffer, 1996), but they may in some cases precede or be a precursor for completed suicide. Given the low base rate of completed suicide among young people (Shaffer, 1996), and the importance of suicidal ideation and attempts in and of themselves, it may be time for researchers who develop risk assessment instruments to widen their focus beyond the single end point of completed suicide.

5. *Researchers and clinicians need to consider carefully the populations within which test instruments were developed and have demonstrated use (Meehl & Rosen, 1955).* Instruments developed with school-based or community samples may not have the same predictive *use* in high-risk or clinically ascertained samples, and vice versa. In samples selected because of their presumed high risk, the base rates of both the outcome of interest (e.g., suicide attempts) and of various risk factors may be far different from what is typically found in the community. Said differently, factors in a community sample that may be associated with a statistically significant increase in the outcome of interest may not be as useful as a predictor, or as specific in its relationship to suicidal behavior in samples in which the base rates of the risk factors are considerably higher. One cannot assume that different diagnostic and risk assessment instruments will always have the same usefulness in differing population groups, just as one cannot assume that research findings are always generalizable across different population groups.

Aside from base-rate issues, there are other reasons as well for careful consideration of the groups for which instruments have been developed and used. Certain risk factors may not have the same meaning or salience for one ethnic or cultural group as for another group, and some risk factors may be specific to a specific population.

6. *There is a need to better understand the relationship between vulnerability factors assessed with risk instruments (distal risk factors) and precipitating stresses*

(proximal risk factors). Using instruments focused on identifying groups based on various risk factors may tell us who is at risk but not when they are at risk. Specific life events may precipitate or provide the occasion for suicidal behavior, but they do not tell us who is likely to make those attempts. We need to know more about the course or persistence of vulnerability factors over time, what individuals' previous reactions to certain types of life events can tell us about their future behavior, "vulnerable" individual's roles in generating life stresses, and the differences in reactions between individuals who have and who have not already engaged in suicidal behavior. To accurately predict suicidal behavior, we ultimately will need a better understanding of the interplay between vulnerability factors and stresses.

7. *There is a need to address why it is important to assess the clinical characteristics of suicide attempts.* Our clinical instincts tell us that information about intent and medical lethality of suicide attempts is important to know, certainly important to describe, and perhaps important in differentiating various types or classes of suicidal behaviors. However, studying the clinical characteristics of juvenile suicide attempts has not been a particularly fruitful exercise to date. Empirical data about the clinical characteristics of suicide attempts have not been shown to be related to response in therapy, have not been used to demonstrate that certain types of therapy are any more or less effective with specific suicidal behaviors, and have not been found to be related to future suicidal behavior. Beyond simply using instruments that assess clinical characteristics of suicide attempts for descriptive purposes, psychologists need to better understand the significance of those clinical characteristics.

8. *The appropriateness of assessment measures for treatment research has not been fully examined.* An intervention for suicidal youths or potentially suicidal youths can potentially reduce risk factors associated with the increased risk, reduce suicidal behaviors or thinking directly, or combine the two strategies. A good outcome measure should ideally be directly related to the thrust or focus of the intervention, and may therefore focus on the risk factor(s) of interest, the measurement of suicidal behavior, or both. Outcome measures should ideally be sensitive to change, should not be subject to practice effects or attenuation with repeated administrations, and should have demonstrated use in intervention studies. Unfortunately, there are a limited number of prospective studies that have identified risk factors with predictive validity that might be candidates for potential intervention (it makes sense to intervene with variables that portend later risk rather than current or past risk). There are even fewer studies in which assessment measures have been administered on multiple occasions and that might yield data on the effects

of repeated test administrations. And it almost goes without saying that there is a paucity of controlled intervention studies with suicidal youths—studies that might yield clues about the usefulness of different measures related to suicidality. Therefore, despite an urgent need for development and comparison of interventions for suicidal youths, at this juncture, it is very difficult to make educated guesses about which assessment measures are the "best" candidates for use in controlled treatment outcome studies.

New Directions and Trends

As has been said several times already in this book, predicting the future is not easy. That said, after writing a book covering the last 10 years of an area, it is difficult to resist making at least some guesses as to the areas and trends that will be fruitful domain for suicide assessment instrument development over the next several years. Described below are seven such trends or areas in which progress is likely to occur.

1. As mentioned previously, there is considerable inconsistency in descriptions of suicidal behaviors in the suicide literature and in our clinical and research vernacular. Accompanying this inconsistency in the use of terms is a great deal of inconsistency in the measures used to assess suicidal behaviors and their correlates. The field is entering a new era with greater and renewed interest in evaluation of outcomes for prevention and intervention efforts. Along with this greater interest in evaluation of outcomes, it is anticipated that there will be a greater investment in using similar measures across studies so outcomes can be compared.

2. It also is anticipated that there will be greater interest in assessing behaviors that may be passively or indirectly associated with suicidal intent. For example, medically ill suicidal youths have been found to have a higher rate of serious noncompliance with their medical regimens (Goldston et al., 1996). Additionally, although the phenomenon of victim-precipitated homicide (instances in which the "victim" purposefully provokes others into trying to kill him- or herself) was described decades ago (e.g., Wolfgang, 1959), there recently has been increasing attention to the extent to which victim-precipitated homicides are actually proxies for or are a subset of suicidal behaviors, particularly among individuals in the inner-city areas with considerable gang-related activity.

3. It is now well-established that parents are often unaware of the suicidal behaviors of their children and adolescents (Breton et al., 2002;

Klimes-Dougan, 1998; Velez & Cohen, 1988; Walker et al., 1990), and therefore, it is essential that any screening for suicidal youths include a direct assessment with youths themselves. However, less attention has been paid to the optimal ways of assessing suicidal behaviors in the younger age groups. There have been suggestions that patients sometimes are more self-disclosing and prefer providing sensitive information (e.g., suicidal ideation) to a computer rather than a clinician (Kobak et al., 1996; Petrie & Abell, 1994). With increasing reliance of the populous on computer technology, it is anticipated that there will be increasing experimentation with computer-administered or computer-assisted suicidal behavior assessments.

4. With increasing awareness that all assessment instruments are not equally useful in every population group, one can anticipate that there might also be increasing attention to the risk factors specific to certain groups. For example, in this book, the relationship between suicidal behaviors and issues regarding sexual orientation was described (e.g., number of friends lost due to sexual orientation, telling parents about sexual orientation, sexual victimization) among lesbian, gay, and bisexual youths (D'Augelli & Hershberger, 1993; Hershberger & D'Augelli, 1995). Similarly, assessment instruments have been developed to examine correlates of suicidal behavior within substance-abusing youths (Reifman & Windle, 1995; Windle & Windle, 1997) and among homeless and runaway youths (Yoder, 1999; Yoder et al., 1998). Assessment instruments need to be developed for other high-risk populations as well, such as youths in juvenile justice settings and youths with serious or chronic physical illnesses.

5. Much of the research in the field of suicidology is not grounded in theory, despite the fact that the area is rich in theoretical speculation and proposed models. Frameworks that have been proposed to account for or describe suicidal behaviors include the social–cultural (e.g., Durkheim, 1897/1951), psychological (e.g., Beck, Kovacs, & Weissman, 1975; Menninger, 1938; Shneidman, 1996), behavioral (e.g., Lester, 1987; Linehan, 1993), and biological (e.g., Asberg, 1997; Roy, Rylander, & Sarchiapone, 1997). Integrative models have also been proposed in which multiple risk factors or processes (e.g., biochemical as well as temperamental or psychological) may interact to increase the chances of suicide (Fawcett, Busch, Jacobs, Kravitz, & Fogg, 1997). Several of the risk assessment instruments reviewed in this book tap psychological dimensions posited to be important in understanding suicidal behavior, but there is a notable absence of assessment instruments influenced by other perspectives. In particular, significant advances have been made in the last several years in our understanding of the biological underpinnings of suicidal behavior, but these advances have

yet to influence our methods of assessing risk for child and adolescent suicidal behaviors. The new generation of risk assessment instruments likely will be influenced increasingly by our growing knowledge of the biological correlates and processes culminating in suicidal and related behaviors.

6. When considering risk and the prediction of suicidal behavior, there often is a tendency to assume that all suicide attempts are equivalent. That is, in discussions about risk factors, there typically is no distinction made between what constitutes risk for an initial suicide attempt and what represents risk for recurrent suicidal behavior. Nonetheless, an emerging body of evidence suggests that repeat suicide attempters differ in significant ways from first-time attempters. Repeat attempters are more distressed and impaired (Goldston et al., 1996; Joiner et al., 2000; Walrath et al., 2001), are at increased risk for future suicide attempts (Goldston et al., 1999), and use more mental health services than first-time suicide attempters (Goldston et al., 2003). In a clinically ascertained sample, hopelessness, affective disorders, and severity of depression have been found to be better predictors of recurrent suicidal behavior than first-time attempts (Goldston et al., 1999, 2001). Cross-sectional analyses have indicated that there is a stronger association between life events and suicidal ideation among adult first-time suicide attempters than among repeat attempters (Joiner & Rudd, 2000). Individuals at risk for initial suicide attempts have not been exposed to the potentially reinforcing consequences (such as relief of distress, or attention and changes in the environment) that are often associated with suicidal behavior (Goldston et al., 1998, 1999). Repeat suicide attempters also may differ from first-time attempters in temperament and biological constitution. With increasing knowledge of the differences between first-time and repeat suicide attempters in presentation, course, and processes culminating in suicidal behavior, it is also anticipated that there will be increasing attention to whether suicide risk assessment instruments are equally predictive or useful in predicting first-time and repeat suicide attempts.

7. One last area that should prove fruitful domain for developers of suicide assessment instruments is that of individuals' own expectations about the likelihood of future suicidal behavior. Behavioral intentions or expectancies have been found to be predictive of subsequent behavior in a number of different areas, including contraceptive behavior, smoking, and alcohol use (Marcoux & Shope, 1997; Staunton et al., 1996; Sussman, Dent, Severson, Burton, & Flay, 1998). Several instruments (Beck Scale for Suicidal Ideation, Suicide Behaviors Questionnaire, Suicidal Behavior History Form) include questions about expectations of attempting suicide in the future, but the predictive validity of these particular questions has not been evaluated in

prospective studies. However, a question about expectations similar to those in existing instruments, "How likely is it that you will attempt suicide in the future (after your discharge)?," was found to be predictive of time until attempted suicide in a prospectively followed cohort of formerly psychiatrically hospitalized adolescents (Goldston et al., 2001). In many respects, individuals know themselves and are aware of the likelihood of their future actions more than outside observers. Individuals considering suicide also may assimilate information that is confirmatory of their negative expectations for the future, therein setting up self-fulfilling prophecies that are predictive of later behavior outcomes (e.g., Snyder & Stukas, 1999). For this reason, it is expected that future research regarding suicide assessment instruments will capitalize on this largely untapped area as a source of useful information. To the extent that youths' expectations are predictive of future suicidal behavior, it also is expected that there will be corresponding efforts to modify those expectations.

Summary

In conclusion, a great deal has been accomplished in the study of suicidal behaviors since Lewinsohn and his colleagues (Garrison, Lewinsohn, et al., 1991; Lewinsohn et al., 1989) wrote their review 10 years ago. A number of instruments have been developed that have been used in the detection and monitoring of suicidal behaviors and in the assessment of risk for suicidal behaviors. A number of other instruments have shown considerable promise. There are certainly areas that need further attention, but such identified needs simply provide a blueprint or roadmap for the work that still needs to be done rather than detracting from what has already been accomplished. The pace of research in this area seems to be accelerating, and it is expected that the next comprehensive review of this area will draw upon a much richer database regarding the predictive and clinical use of assessment instruments for suicidal behaviors and risk.

References

Achenbach, T. (1991a). *Integrative guide for the 1991 CBCL/4–18, YSR, & TRF profiles.* Burlington: University of Vermont, Department of Psychiatry.

Achenbach, T. (1991b). *Manual for the Child Behavior Checklist/4–18 & 1991 profile.* Burlington: University of Vermont, Department of Psychiatry.

Achenbach, T. (1991c). *Manual for the Teacher's Report Form and 1991 profile.* Burlington: University of Vermont, Department of Psychiatry.

Achenbach, T. (1991d). *Manual for the Youth Self-Report and 1991 profile.* Burlington: University of Vermont, Department of Psychiatry.

Achenbach, T. (1997a). *Guide for the Caregiver–Teacher Report Form for ages 2–5.* Burlington: University of Vermont, Department of Psychiatry.

Achenbach, T. (1997b). *Manual for the Young Adult Self-Report and Young Adult Behavior Checklist.* Burlington: University of Vermont, Department of Psychiatry.

Aish, A., & Wasserman, D. (2001). Does Beck's Hopelessness Scale really measure several components? *Psychological Medicine, 31,* 367–372.

Allan, W., Kashani, J., Dahlmeier, J., Taghizadeh, P., & Reid, J. (1997). Psychometric properties and clinical utility of the Scale for Suicidal Ideation with inpatient children. *Journal of Abnormal Child Psychology, 25,* 465–473.

Altman, D. (1991). *Practical statistics for medical research.* London: Chapman & Hall.

Ambrosini, P. (2000). The historical development and present status of the Schedule for Affective Disorders and Schizophrenia for School Aged Children (K–SADS). *Journal of the American Academy of Child and Adolescent Psychiatry, 39,* 49–58.

Ambrosini, P., & Dixon, J. (1996). *Schedule for Affective Disorders and Schizophrenia for School Aged Children—Present Version, Version IVR (K–SADS–IVR).* Unpublished instrument, Medical College of Pennsylvania, Eastern Pennsylvania Psychiatric Institute, Philadelphia, PA.

Ambrosini, P., Wagner, K., Biederman, J., Glick, I., Tan, C., Elia, J., Hebeler, J., Rabinovich, H., Lock, J., & Geller, D. (1999). Multicenter open-label sertraline study in adolescent outpatients with major depression. *Journal of the American Academy of Child and Adolescent Psychiatry, 38,* 566–572.

American Psychiatric Association. (1987). *Diagnostic and statistical manual of mental disorders* (3rd ed., rev.). Washington, DC: Author.

American Psychiatric Association. (1994). *Diagnostic and statistical manual of mental disorders* (4th ed.). Washington, DC: Author.

Anderson, J., & Larzelere, R. (1997). *Interim summary of the Child Suicide Assessment* (Residential Research Technical Report No. 972). Boys Town, NE: Boys Town.

Angold, A., & Costello, E. (1995). A test–retest reliability study of child-reported psychiatric symptoms and diagnoses using the Child and Adolescent Psychiatric Assessment (CAPA–C). *Psychological Medicine, 25,* 755–762.

Angold, A., & Costello, E. (2000). The Child and Adolescent Psychiatric Assessment (CAPA). *Journal of the American Academy of Child and Adolescent Psychiatry, 39,* 39–48.

Angold, A., Cox, A., Prendergast, M., Rutter, M., & Simonoff, E. (1995). *The Child and Adolescent Psychiatric Assessment (CAPA).* Unpublished instrument, Duke University School of Medicine, Durham, NC.

Angold, A., Patrick, K., Burns, B., & Costello, E. (1996). *The Child and Adolescent Impact Assessment (CAIA).* Unpublished instrument, Duke University School of Medicine, Durham, NC.

Angold, A., Prendergast, M., Cox, A., Harrington, R., Simonoff, E., & Rutter, M. (1995). The Child and Adolescent Psychiatric Assessment (CAPA). *Psychological Medicine, 25,* 739–753.

Appleton, P., Ellis, N., Minchom, P., Lawson, V., Boll, V., & Jones, P. (1997). Depressive symptoms and self-concept in young people with spina bifida. *Journal of Pediatric Psychology, 22,* 707–722.

Apter, A., Gothelf, D., Offer, R., Ratzoni, G., Orbach, I., Tyano, S., & Pfeffer, C. (1997). Suicidal adolescents and ego defense mechanisms. *Journal of the American Academy of Child and Adolescent Psychiatry, 36,* 1520–1527.

Apter, A., Gothelf, D., Orbach, I., Weizman, R., Ratzoni, G., Har-Even, D., & Tyano, S. (1995). Correlation of suicidal and violent behavior in different diagnostic categories in hospitalized adolescent patients. *Journal of the American Academy of Child and Adolescent Psychiatry, 34,* 912–918.

Apter, A., Orvaschel, H., Laseg, M., Moses, T., & Tyano, S. (1989). Psychometric properties of the K–SADS–P in an Israeli adolescent inpatient population. *Journal of the American Academy of Child and Adolescent Psychiatry, 28,* 61–65.

Asarnow, J., & Guthrie, D. (1989). Suicidal behavior, depression, and hopelessness in child psychiatric inpatients: A replication and extension. *Journal of Clinical Child Psychology, 18,* 129–136.

Asberg, M. (1997). Neurotransmitters and suicidal behavior: The evidence from cerebrospinal fluid studies. *Annals of the New York Academy of Sciences, 836,* 158–181.

Ascher, B., Farmer, E., Burns, B. J., & Angold, A. (1996). The Child and Adolescent Services Assessment (CASA): Description and psychometrics. *Journal of Emotional and Behavioral Disorders, 4,* 12–20.

Bancroft, J., Hawton, K., Simkin, S., Kingston, B., Cumming, C., & Whitwell, D. (1979). The reasons people give for taking overdoses: A further inquiry. *British Journal of Medical Psychology, 52,* 353–365.

Bancroft, J., Skrimshire, A., & Simkin, S. (1976). The reasons people give for taking overdoses. *British Journal of Psychiatry, 128,* 538–548.

Barbe, R., Bridge, J., Birmaher, B., Kolko, D., & Brent, D. (2001, November). *Outcome of a psychotherapy treatment in a population of suicidal depressed adolescents.* Paper presented at The Congress on Suicide and Suicide Prevention in Youth, Geneva, Switzerland.

Beck, A., Brown, G., Berchick, R., Stewart, B., & Steer, R. (1990). Relationship between hopelessness and ultimate suicide: A replication with psychiatric outpatients. *American Journal of Psychiatry, 147,* 190–195.

Beck, A., Brown, G., Steer, R., Dahlsgaard, K., & Grisham, J. (1999). Suicide ideation at its worst point: A predictor of eventual suicide in psychiatric outpatients. *Suicide and Life-Threatening Behavior, 29,* 1–9.

Beck, A., Davis, J., Frederick, C., Perlin, S., Pokorny, A., Schulman, R., Seiden, R., & Whittlin, B. (1973). Classification and nomenclature. In H. Resnik & B. Hathorne (Eds.), *Suicide prevention in the 70's* (pp. 7–12). Washington, DC: U.S. Government Printing Office.

Beck, A., Kovacs, M., & Weissman, A. (1975). Hopelessness and suicidal behavior: An overview. *Journal of the American Medical Association, 234,* 1146–1149.

Beck, A., Kovacs, M., & Weissman, A. (1979). Assessment of suicidal intention: The Scale for Suicidal Ideation. *Journal of Consulting and Clinical Psychology, 47,* 343–352.

Beck, A., Rush, A., Shaw, B., & Emery, G. (1979). *Cognitive therapy of depression.* New York: Guilford Press.

Beck, A., Schuyler, D., & Herman, I. (1974). Development of suicidal intent scales. In A. Beck, H. Resnik, & D. Lettieri (Eds.), *The prediction of suicide* (pp. 45–56). Bowie, MD: Charles Press.

Beck, A., & Steer, R. (1987). *Manual for the Beck Depression Inventory.* San Antonio, TX: Psychological Corporation.

Beck, A., & Steer, R. (1988). *Beck Hopelessness Scale manual.* San Antonio, TX: Psychological Corporation.

Beck, A., & Steer, R. (1991). *Manual for the Beck Scale for Suicidal Ideation.* San Antonio, TX: Psychological Corporation.

Beck, A., Steer, R., & Brown, G. (1996). *Manual for Beck Depression Inventory—II.* San Antonio, TX: Psychological Corporation.

Beck, A., Steer, R., Kovacs, M., & Garrison, B. (1985). Hopelessness and eventual suicide: A 10-year prospective study of patients hospitalized with suicidal ideation. *American Journal of Psychiatry, 142,* 559–563.

Beck, A., Steer, R., & Trexler, L. (1989). Alcohol abuse and eventual suicide: A 5- to 10-year prospective study of alcohol-abusing suicide attempters. *Journal of Studies of Alcohol, 50,* 202–209.

Beck, A., Weissman, A., Lester, D., & Trexler, L. (1974). The measurement of pessimism: The Hopelessness Scale. *Journal of Consulting and Clinical Psychology, 42,* 861–865.

Berman, A., & Jobes, D. (1991). *Adolescent suicide: Assessment and intervention.* Washington, DC: American Psychological Association.

Bernstein, G., Hektner, J., Borchardt, C., & McMillan, M. (2001). Treatment of school refusal: One-year follow-up. *Journal of the American Academy of Child and Adolescent Psychiatry, 40,* 206–213.

Bidaut-Russell, M., Valla, J., Thomas, J., Bergeron, L., & Lawson, E. (1998). Reliability of the Terry: A mental health cartoon-like screener for African-American children. *Child Psychiatry and Human Development, 28,* 249–263.

Blum, R., Harmon, B., Harris, L., Bergeisen, L., & Resnick, M. (1992). American Indian-Alaska native youth health. *Journal of the American Medical Association, 267,* 1637–1644.

Boergers, J., Spirito, A., & Donaldson, D. (1998). Reasons for adolescent suicide attempts: Associations with psychological functioning. *Journal of the American Academy of Child and Adolescent Psychiatry, 37,* 1287–1293.

Borowsky, I., Resnick, M., Ireland, M., & Blum, R. (1999). Suicide attempts among American Indian and Alaska native youth. *Archives of Pediatric Adolescent Medicine, 153,* 573–580.

Borst, S., Noam, G., & Bartok, J. (1991). Adolescent suicidality: A clinical-developmental approach. *Journal of the American Academy of Child and Adolescent Psychiatry, 30,* 796–803.

Bradley, J., & Rotheram-Borus, M. (1990). *Evaluation of imminent danger for suicide: A training manual.* Tulsa, OK: National Resource Center for Youth Services.

Brener, N., Collins, J., Kann, L., Warren, C., & Williams, B. (1995). Reliability of the Youth Risk Behavior Survey questionnaire. *American Journal of Epidemiology, 141,* 575–580.

Brent, D. (1987). Correlates of the medical lethality of suicide attempts in children and adolescents. *Journal of the American Academy of Child and Adolescent Psychiatry, 26,* 87–89.

Brent, D., Holder, D., Kolko, D., Birmaher, B., Baugher, M., Roth, C., Iyengar, S., & Johnson, B. (1997). A clinical psychotherapy trial for adolescent depression comparing cognitive, family, and supportive treatments. *Archives of General Psychiatry, 54,* 877–885.

Brent, D., Kalas, R., Edelbrock, C., Costello, A., Dulcan, M., & Conover, N. (1986). Psychopathology and its relationship to suicidal ideation in childhood and adolescence. *Journal of the American Academy of Child and Adolescent Psychiatry, 25*, 666–673.

Brent, D., Kolko, D., Allan, M., & Brown, R. (1990). Suicidality in affectively disordered adolescent inpatients. *Journal of the American Academy of Child and Adolescent Psychiatry, 29*, 586–593.

Brent, D., Kolko, D., Birmaher, B., Baugher, M., Bridge, J., Roth, C., & Holder, D. (1998). Predictors of treatment efficacy in a clinical trial of three psychosocial treatments for adolescent depression. *Journal of the American Academy of Child and Adolescent Psychiatry, 37*, 906–914.

Brent, D., Perper, J., Goldstein, C., Kolko, D., Allan, M., Allman, C., & Zelenak, J. (1988). Risk factors for adolescent suicide: A comparison of adolescent suicide victims with suicidal inpatients. *Archives of General Psychiatry, 45*, 581–588.

Brent, D., Perper, J., Moritz, G., Allman, C., Friend, A., Roth, C., Schweers, J., Balach, L., & Baugher, M. (1993). Psychiatric risk factors for adolescent suicide: A case-control study. *Journal of the American Academy of Child and Adolescent Psychiatry, 32*, 521–529.

Brent, D., Perper, J., Moritz, G., Allman, C., Friend, A., Schweers, J., Roth, C., Balach, L., & Harrington, K. (1992). Psychiatric effects of exposure to suicide among the friends and acquaintances of adolescent suicide victims. *Journal of the American Academy of Child and Adolescent Psychiatry, 31*, 629–640.

Brent, D., Perper, J., Moritz, G., Baugher, M., & Allman, C. (1993). Suicide in adolescents with no apparent psychopathology. *Journal of the American Academy of Child and Adolescent Psychiatry, 32*, 494–500.

Brent, D., Perper, J., Moritz, G., Baugher, M., Schweers, J., & Roth, C. (1994). Suicide in affectively ill adolescents: A case-control study. *Journal of Affective Disorders, 31*, 193–202.

Brent, D., Perper, J., Moritz, G., Liotus, L., Richardson, D., Canobbio, R., Schweers, J., & Roth, C. (1995). Posttraumatic stress disorder in peers of adolescent suicide victims: Predisposing factors and phenomenology. *Journal of the American Academy of Child and Adolescent Psychiatry, 34*, 209–215.

Brent, D., Perper, J., Moritz, G., Liotus, L., Schweers, J., & Canobbio, R. (1994). Major depression or uncomplicated bereavement? A follow-up of youth exposed to suicide. *Journal of the American Academy of Child and Adolescent Psychiatry, 33*, 231–239.

Brent, D., Perper, J., Moritz, G., Liotus, L., Schweers, J., Roth, C., Balach, L., & Allman, C. (1993). Psychiatric impact of the loss of an adolescent sibling to suicide. *Journal of Affective Disorders, 28*, 249–256.

Breton, J., Bergeron, L., Valla, J., Berthiaume, C., & St-Georges, M. (1998). Diagnostic Interview Schedule for Children (DISC–2.25) in Quebec: Reliability findings in light of the MECA study. *Journal of the American Academy of Child and Adolescent Psychiatry, 37*, 1167–1174.

Breton, J., Tousignant, M., Bergeron, L., & Berthiaume, C. (2002). Informant-specific correlates of suicidal behavior in a community survey of 12- to 14-year-olds. *Journal of the American Academy of Child and Adolescent Psychiatry, 41*, 723–730.

Brinkman-Sull, D., Overholser, J., & Silverman, E. (2000). Risk of future suicide attempts in adolescent psychiatric inpatients at 18-month follow-up. *Suicide and Life-Threatening Behavior, 30*, 327–340.

Brittlebank, A., Cole, A., Hassanyeah, F., Kenny, M, Simpson, D., & Scott, J. (1990). Hostility, hopelessness and deliberate self-harm: A prospective follow-up study. *Acta Psychiatrica Scandinavica, 81*, 280–283.

Brown, G. (2001). *A review of suicide assessment measures for intervention research with adults and older adults.* Technical report submitted to NIMH under Contract No. 263-MH-914950.

Brown, G., Beck, A., Steer, R., & Grisham, J. (2000). Risk factors for suicide in psychiatric outpatients: A 20-year prospective study. *Journal of Consulting and Clinical Psychology, 68,* 371–377.

Brown, L., Overholser, J., Spirito, A., & Fritz, G. (1991). The correlates of planning in adolescent suicide attempts. *Journal of the American Academy of Child and Adolescent Psychiatry, 30,* 95–99.

Burge, V., Felts, M., Chenier, T., & Parrillo, A. (1995). Drug use, sexual activity, and suicidal behavior in U.S. high school students. *Journal of School Health, 65,* 222–227.

Burns, B., Angold, A., Magruder-Habib, K., Costello, E., & Patrick, M. (1996). *The Child and Adolescent Services Assessment (CASA).* Unpublished instrument, Duke University School of Medicine, Durham, NC.

Butcher, J., Williams, C., Graham, J., Archer, R., Tellegen, A., Ben-Porath, Y., & Kaemmer, B. (1992). *MMPI–A (Minnesota Multiphasic Personality—Adolescent): Manual for administration, scoring, and interpretation.* Minneapolis: University of Minnesota Press.

Caine, E. (2001). Preventing suicide: A scientific consensus process [Executive summary]. Unpublished manuscript.

Campbell, N., Milling, L., Laughlin, A., & Bush, E. (1993). The psychosocial climate of families with suicidal pre-adolescent children. *American Journal of Orthopsychiatry, 63,* 142–145.

Cappelli, M., Clulow, M., Goodman, J., Davidson, S., Feder, S., Baron, P., Manion, I., & McGrath, P. (1995). Identifying depressed and suicidal adolescents in a teen health clinic. *Journal of Adolescent Health, 16,* 64–70.

Carlton, P., & Deane, F. (2000). Impact of attitudes and suicidal ideation on adolescents' intentions to seek professional psychological help. *Journal of Adolescence, 23,* 35–45.

Centers for Disease Control and Prevention. (2000a). *1997 United States deaths and rates per 100,000: Suicide.* Retrieved from http://www.cdc.gov/ncipc/osp/states/0014.htm

Centers for Disease Control and Prevention. (2000b). Youth risk behavior surveillance—United States, 1999. *Morbidity and Mortality Weekly Report, 49*(SS05), 1–96.

Cerel, J., Fristad, M., Weller, E., & Weller, R. (1999). Suicide-bereaved children and adolescents: A controlled longitudinal examination. *Journal of the American Academy of Child and Adolescent Psychiatry, 38,* 672–679.

Chan, D. (1995). Reasons for living among Chinese adolescents in Hong Kong. *Suicide and Life-Threatening Behavior, 25,* 347–357.

Chang, E. (2002). Predicting suicide ideation in an adolescent population: Examining the role of social problem solving as a moderator and a mediator. *Personality and Individual Differences, 32,* 1279–1291.

Chartier, G., & Lassen, M. (1994). Adolescent depression: Children's Depression Inventory norms, suicidal ideation, and (weak) gender effects. *Adolescence, 29,* 859–864.

Clark, D., Gibbons, R., Fawcett, J., & Scheftner, W. (1989). What is the mechanism by which suicide attempts predispose to later suicide attempts? A mathematical model. *Journal of Abnormal Psychology, 98,* 42–49.

Cole, D. (1989a). Psychopathology of adolescent suicide: Hopelessness, coping beliefs, and depression. *Journal of Abnormal Psychology, 9,* 248–255.

Cole, D. (1989b). Validation of the Reasons for Living Inventory in general and delinquent adolescent samples. *Journal of Abnormal Child Psychology, 17,* 13–27.

Colle, L., Belair, J., DiFeo, M., Weiss, J., & LaRoche, C. (1994). Extended open-label fluoxetine treatment of adolescents with major depression. *Journal of Child and Adolescent Psychopharmacology, 4,* 225–232.

Costello, E., Angold, A., Burns, B., Erkanli, A., Stangl, D., & Tweed, D. (1996b). The Great Smoky Mountains Study of Youth: Functional impairment and serious emotional disturbance. *Archives of General Psychiatry, 53,* 1137–1143.

Costello, E., Angold, A., Burns, B., Stangl, D., Tweed, D., Erkanli, A., & Worthman, C. (1996a). The Great Smoky Mountains Study of Youth: Goals, designs, methods, and the prevalence of *DSM–III–R* disorders. *Archives of General Psychiatry, 53,* 1129–1136.

Cotton, C., Peters, D., & Range, L. (1995). Psychometric properties of the Suicidal Behaviors Questionnaire. *Death Studies, 19,* 391–397.

Cotton, C., & Range, L. (1993). Suicidality, hopelessness, and attitudes toward life and death in children. *Death Studies, 17,* 185–191.

Cronbach, L., & Meehl, P. (1955). Construct validity in psychological tests. *Psychological Bulletin, 52,* 281–302.

Cull, J., & Gill, W. (1988). *Suicide Probability Scale (SPS) manual.* Los Angeles: Western Psychological Services.

D'Attilio, J., & Campbell, B. (1990). Relationship between death anxiety and suicide potential in an adolescent population. *Psychological Reports, 67,* 975–978.

D'Attilio, J., Campbell, B., Lubold, P., Jacobson, T., & Richard, J. (1992). Social support and suicide potential: Preliminary findings for adolescent populations. *Psychological Reports, 70,* 76–78.

Dahlsgaard, K., Beck, A., & Brown, G. (1998). Inadequate response to therapy as a predictor of suicide. *Suicide and Life-Threatening Behavior, 28,* 197–204.

D'Augelli, A., & Hershberger, S. (1993). Lesbian, gay, and bisexual youth in community settings: Personal challenges and mental health problems. *American Journal of Community Psychology, 21,* 421–448.

Dawes, R., Faust, D., & Meehl, P. (1989). Clinical versus actuarial judgment. *Science, 243,* 1668–1674.

De Man, A., Balkou, S., & Iglesias, R. (1987). A French-Canadian adaptation of the Scale for Suicidal Ideation. *Canadian Journal of Behavioral Science, 19,* 50–55.

De Man, A., & Leduc, C. (1994). Validity and reliability of a self-report Suicide Ideation Scale for use with adolescents. *Social Behavior and Personality, 22,* 261–266.

DeMan, A., Leduc, C., & Lebreche-Gauthier, L. (1993). A French-Canadian scale for suicidal ideation for use with adolescents. *Canadian Journal of Behavioral Science, 25,* 125–134.

DeMaso, D., Ross, L., & Beardslee, W. (1994). Depressive disorders and suicidal intent in adolescent suicide attempters. *Developmental and Behavioral Pediatrics, 15,* 74–77.

DeWilde, E., Kienhorst, I., Diekstra, R., & Wolters, W. (1992). The relationship between adolescent suicidal behavior and life events in childhood and adolescence. *American Journal of Psychiatry, 149,* 45–51.

DeWilde, E., Kienhorst, I., Diekstra, R., & Wolters, W. (1993). The specificity of psychological characteristics of adolescent suicide attempters. *Journal of the American Academy of Child and Adolescent Psychiatry, 32,* 51–59.

Dick, R., Beals, J., Manson, S., & Bechtold, D. (1994). *Psychometric properties of the suicidal ideation questionnaire in American Indian adolescents.* Unpublished manuscript, University of Colorado Health Sciences Center, Denver, CO.

Diekstra, R., & Kerkhof, A. (1989). Attitudes toward suicide: The development of a suicide-attitude-questionnaire (SUIATT). In R. Diekstra, R. Maris, S. Platt, A. Schmidtke, & G. Sonneck (Eds.), *Suicide and its prevention: The role of attitudes and imitations* (pp. 1–24). Leiden, The Netherlands: Brill.

Donaldson, D., Spirito, A., & Fawcett, E. (2000). The role of perfectionism and depressive cognitions in understanding the hopelessness experienced by adolescent suicide attempters. *Child Psychiatry and Human Development, 31,* 99–111.

Dori, G., & Overholser, J. (1999). Depression, hopelessness, and self-esteem: Accounting for suicidality in adolescent psychiatric inpatients. *Suicide and Life-Threatening Behavior, 29,* 309–318.

Durant, R., Krowchuk, D., Kreiter, S., Sinal, S., & Woods, C. (1999). Weapon carrying on school property among middle school students. *Archives of Pediatrics and Adolescent Medicine, 153,* 21–26.

Durant, R., Krowchuk, D., & Sinal, S. (1998). Victimization, use of violence, and drug use at school among male adolescents who engage in same-sex sexual behavior. *Journal of Pediatrics, 133,* 113–118.

Durkheim, D. (1951). *Suicide.* New York: Free Press. (Original work published 1897)

Eggert, L., Thompson, E., & Herting, J. (1994). A measure of adolescent potential for suicide (MAPS): Development and preliminary findings. *Suicide and Life-Threatening Behavior, 24,* 359–381.

Eggert, L., Thompson, E., Herting, J., & Nicholas, L. (1995). Reducing suicide potential among high-risk youth: Tests of a school-based prevention program. *Suicide and Life-Threatening Behavior, 25,* 276–296.

Emslie, G., Rush, A., Weinberg, W., Kowatch, R., Hughes, C., Carmady, J., & Rintelmann, J. (1997). A double-blind, randomized, placebo-controlled trial of fluoxetine in children and adolescents with depression. *Archives of General Psychiatry, 54,* 1031–1037.

Enns, M., Inayatulla, M., Cox, B., & Cheyne, L. (1997). Prediction of suicide intent in Aboriginal and non-Aboriginal adolescent inpatients: A research note. *Suicide and Life-Threatening Behavior, 27,* 218–224.

Ernst, M., Cookus, B., & Moravec, B. (2000). Pictorial Instrument for Children and Adolescents (PICA–III–R). *Journal of the American Association of Child and Adolescent Psychiatry, 39,* 94–99.

Esposito, C., & Clum, G. (1999). Specificity of depressive symptoms and suicidality in a juvenile delinquent population. *Journal of Psychopathology and Behavioral Assessment, 21,* 171–182.

Famularo, R., Fenton, T., Kinscherff, R., & Augustyn, M. (1996). Psychiatric comorbidity in childhood post traumatic stress disorder. *Child Abuse and Neglect, 20,* 953–961.

Fawcett, J., Busch, K., Jacobs, D., Kravitz, H., & Fogg, L. (1997). Suicide: A four-pathway clinical-biochemical model. *Annals of the New York Academy of Sciences, 836,* 288–301.

Fawcett, J., Scheftner, W., Fogg, L., Clark, D., Young, M., Hedeker, D., & Gibbons, R. (1990). Time-related predictors of suicide in major affective disorder. *American Journal of Psychiatry, 147,* 1189–1194.

Felts, W., Chenier, T., & Barnes, R. (1992). Drug use and suicide ideation and behavior among North Carolina public school students. *American Journal of Public Health, 82,* 870–872.

Firestone, R., & Firestone, L. (1998). Voices in suicide: The relationship between self-destructive thought processes, maladaptive behavior, and self-destructive manifestations. *Death Studies, 22,* 411–443.

Fristad, M., Cummins, J., Verducci, J., Teare, M., Weller, E., & Weller, R. (1998). Study IV: Concurrent validity of the *DSM–IV* Revised Children's Interview for Psychiatric Syndromes (ChIPS). *Journal of Child and Adolescent Psychopharmacology, 8,* 227–236.

Fristad, M., Glickman, A., Verducci, J., Teare, M., Weller, E., & Weller, R. (1998). Study V: Children's Interview for Psychiatric Syndromes (ChIPS): Psychometrics in two community samples. *Journal of Child and Adolescent Psychopharmacology, 8,* 237–245.

Fristad, M., Teare, M., Weller, E., Weller, R., & Salmon, P. (1998). Study III: Development and concurrent validity of the Children's Interview for Psychiatric Syndromes—Parent Version (P–ChIPS). *Journal of Child and Adolescent Psychopharmacology, 8,* 221–226.

Fritsch, S., Donaldson, D., Spirito, A., & Plummer, B. (2000). Personality characteristics of adolescent suicide attempters. *Child Psychiatry and Human Development, 30,* 219–235.

Garber, J. (1984). The developmental progression of depression in female children., *New Directions for Child Development, 26,* 29–58.

Garber, J., Little, S., Hilsman, R., & Weaver, K. (1998). Family predictors of suicidal symptoms in young adolescents. *Journal of Adolescence, 21,* 445–457.

Garofalo, R., Wolf, R., Wissow, L., Woods, E., & Goodman, E. (1999). Sexual orientation and risk of suicide attempts among a representative sample of youth. *Archives of Pediatrics and Adolescent Medicine, 153,* 487–493.

Garrison, C., Addy, C., Jackson, K., McKeown, R., & Waller, J. (1991). A longitudinal study of suicidal ideation in young adolescents. *Journal of the American Academy of Child and Adolescent Psychiatry, 30,* 597–603.

Garrison, C., Jackson, K., Addy, C., McKeown, R., & Waller, J. (1991). Suicidal behaviors in young adolescents. *American Journal of Epidemiology, 133,* 1005–1014.

Garrison, C., Lewinsohn, P., Marsteller, F., Langhinrichsen, J., & Lann, I. (1991). The assessment of suicidal behavior in adolescents. *Suicide and Life-Threatening Behavior, 21,* 217–230.

Garrison, C., McKeown, R., Valois, R., & Vincent, M. (1993). Aggression, substance use, and suicidal behaviors in high school students. *American Journal of Public Health, 83,* 179–184.

Goldsmith, S., Pellmar, T., Kleinman, A., Bunney, W. (2002). *Reducing suicide: A national imperative.* Washington, DC: National Academy Press.

Goldston, D. (2000). *Assessment of suicidal behaviors and risk among children and adolescents.* Technical report submitted to NIMH under Contract No. 263-MH-909995.

Goldston, D. (2001). [Unpublished data]. Winston-Salem, NC: Wake Forest University School of Medicine.

Goldston, D., Daniel, S., Reboussin, B., Reboussin, D., Frazier, P., & Harris, A. (2001). Cognitive risk factors and suicide attempts among formerly hospitalized adolescents: A prospective naturalistic study. *Journal of the American Academy of Child and Adolescent Psychiatry, 40,* 91–99.

Goldston, D., Daniel, S., Reboussin, B., Reboussin, D., Kelley, A., & Frazier, P. (1998). Psychiatric diagnoses of previous suicide attempters, first-time attempters, and repeat attempters on an adolescent inpatient psychiatry unit. *Journal of the American Academy of Child and Adolescent Psychiatry, 37,* 924–932.

Goldston, D., Daniel, S., Reboussin, D., Kelley, A., Ievers, C., & Brunstetter, R. (1996). First-time suicide attempters, repeat attempters, and previous attempters on an adolescent inpatient psychiatry unit. *Journal of the American Academy of Child and Adolescent Psychiatry, 35,* 631–639.

Goldston, D., Daniel, S., Reboussin, D., Reboussin, B., Frazier, P., & Kelley, A. (1999). Suicide attempts among formerly hospitalized adolescents: A prospective naturalistic study of risk during the first 5 years after discharge. *Journal of the American Academy of Child and Adolescent Psychiatry, 38,* 660–671.

Goldston, D., Kelley, A., Reboussin, D., Daniel, S., Smith, J., Schwartz, R., Lorentz, W., & Hill, C. (1997). Suicidal ideation and behavior and noncompliance with the medical regimen among diabetic adolescents. *Journal of the American Academy of Child and Adolescent Psychiatry, 36,* 1528–1536.

Goldston, D., Kovacs, M., Ho, V., Parrone, P., & Stiffler, L. (1994). Suicidal ideation and suicidal attempts among youth with insulin-dependent diabetes mellitus. *Journal of the American Academy of Child and Adolescent Psychiatry, 33,* 240–246.

Goldston, D., Reboussin, B., Kancler, C., Daniel, S., Frazier, P., Harris, A., Kelley, A., & Reboussin, D. (2003). Rates and predictors of aftercare services among formerly hospitalized adolescents: A prospective naturalistic study. *Journal of the American Academy of Child and Adolescent Psychiatry, 42,* 49–56.

Goodnick, P., Jorge, C., Hunter, T., & Kumar, A. (2000). Nefazodone treatment of adolescent depression: An open-label study of response and biochemistry. *Annals of Clinical Psychiatry, 12,* 97–100.

Gothelf, D., Apter, A., Brand-Gothelf, A., Offer, N., Ofek, H., Tyano, S., & Pfeffer, C. (1998). Death concepts in suicidal adolescents. *Journal of the American Academy of Child and Adolescent Psychiatry, 37,* 1279–1286.

Gould, M., King, R., Greenwald, S., Fisher, P., Schwab-Stone, M., Kramer, R., Flisher, A., Goodman, S., Canino, G., & Shaffer, D. (1998). Psychopathology associated with suicidal ideation and attempts among children and adolescents. *Journal of the American Academy of Child and Adolescent Psychiatry, 37,* 915–923.

Grilo, C., Sanislow, C., Fehon, D., Martino, S., & McGlashan, T. (1999). Psychological and behavioral functioning in adolescent psychiatric inpatients who report histories of childhood abuse. *American Journal of Psychiatry, 156,* 538–543.

Groholt, B., Ekeberg, O., & Haldorsen, T. (2000). Adolescents hospitalized with deliberate self-harm: The significance of an intention to die. *European Child & Adolescent Psychiatry, 9,* 244–254.

Grossman, D., Milligan, B., & Deyo, R. (1991). Risk factors for suicide attempts among Navajo adolescents. *American Journal of Public Health, 81,* 870–874.

Gutierrez, P. (1999). Suicidality in parentally bereaved adolescents. *Death Studies, 23,* 359–370.

Gutierrez, P., Osman, A., Kopper, B., & Barrios, F. (2000). Why young people do not kill themselves: The Reasons for Living Inventory for Adolescents. *Journal of Clinical Child Psychology, 29,* 177–187.

Gutierrez, P., Osman, A., Watkins, R., Konick, L., Muehlenkamp, J., & Brausch, M. (2002, October). *Development and validation of the Suicide Resilience Inventory—25 (SRI–25) in clinical and nonclinical samples.* Paper presented at the Kansas Conference in Clinical Child and Adolescent Psychology, Lawrence, KS.

Hamilton, M. (1960). A rating scale for depression. *Journal of Neurology, Neurosurgery, and Psychiatry, 23,* 56–62.

Hamilton, M. (1967). Development of a rating scale for primary depressive illness. *British Journal of Social and Clinical Psychology, 6,* 278–296.

Handwerk, M., Larzelere, R., Friman, P., & Mitchell, A. (1998). The relationship between lethality of attempted suicide and prior suicidal communications in a sample of residential youth. *Journal of Adolescence, 21,* 407–414.

Harkavy Friedman, J., & Asnis, G. (1989a). Assessment of suicidal behavior: A new instrument. *Psychiatric Annals, 19,* 382–387.

Harkavy Friedman, J., & Asnis, G. (1989b). Correction. *Psychiatric Annals, 19,* 438.

Harrington, R., Kerfoot, M., Dyer, E., McNiven, F., Gill, J., Harrington, V., Woodham, A., & Byford, S. (1998). Randomized trial of a home-based family intervention for children who have deliberately poisoned themselves. *Journal of the American Academy of Child and Adolescent Psychiatry, 37,* 512–518.

Harter, S., & Nowakowski, M. (1987). *Manual for the Dimensions of Depression Profile for Children and Adolescents.* Denver, CO: University of Denver Press.

Hawton, K., Cole, D., O'Grady, J., & Osborn, M. (1982). Motivational aspects of deliberate self-poisoning in adolescents. *British Journal of Psychiatry, 141,* 286–291.

Hawton, K., Kingsbury, S., Steinhardt, K., James, A., & Fagg, J. (1999). Repetition of deliberate self-harm by adolescents: The role of psychological factors. *Journal of Adolescence, 22,* 369–378.

Hershberger, S., & D'Augelli, A. (1995). The impact of victimization on the mental health and suicidality of lesbian, gay, and bisexual youths. *Developmental Psychology, 31,* 65–74.

Hershberger, S., Pilkington, N., & D'Augelli, A. (1997). Predictors of suicide attempts among gay, lesbian, and bisexual youth. *Journal of Adolescent Research, 12,* 477–497.

Hewitt, P., Newton, J., Flett, G., & Callander, L. (1997). Perfectionism and suicide ideation in adolescent psychiatric patients. *Journal of Abnormal Child Psychology, 25,* 95–101.

Hiatt, M., & Cornell, D. (1999). Concurrent validity of the Millon Adolescent Clinical Inventory as a measure of depression in hospitalized adolescents. *Journal of Personality Assessment, 73,* 64–79.

Horowitz, L., Wang, P., Koocher, G., Burr, B., Smith, M., Klavon, S., & Cleary, P. (2001). Detecting suicide risk in a pediatric emergency department: Development of a brief screening tool. *Pediatrics, 107,* 1133–1137.

Hovey, J., & King, C. (1996). Acculturative stress, depression, and suicidal ideation among immigrant and second-generation Latino adolescents. *Journal of the American Academy of Child and Adolescent Psychiatry, 35,* 1183–1192.

Ivanoff, A., Jang, S. J., Smyth, N. F., & Linehan, M. M. (1994). Fewer reasons for staying alive when you are thinking of killing yourself: The Brief Reasons for Living Inventory. *Journal of Psychopathology and Behavioral Assessment, 16,* 1–13.

Ivarsson, T., Gillberg, C., Arvidsson, T., & Broberg, A. (2002). The Youth Self-Report (YSR) and the Depression Self-Rating Scale (DSRS) as measures of depression and suicidality among adolescents. *European Child and Adolescent Psychiatry, 11,* 31–37.

Ivarsson, T., Larsson, B., Gillberg, C. (1998). A 2–4 year follow-up of depressive symptoms, suicidal ideation, and suicide attempts among adolescent psychiatric inpatients. *European Child & Adolescent Psychiatry, 7,* 96–104.

Jacobs, D. (1999). *The Harvard Medical School guide to suicide assessment and intervention.* San Francisco: Jossey-Bass.

Jobes, D., Eyman, J., & Yufit, R. (1995). How clinicians assess suicide risk in adolescents and adults. *Crisis Intervention and Time-Limited Treatment, 2,* 1–12.

Joffe, R., Offord, D., & Boyle, M. (1988). Ontario Child Health Study: Suicidal behavior in youth age 12–16 years. *American Journal of Psychiatry, 145,* 1420–1423.

Johnson, W., Lall, R., Bongar, B., & Nordlund, M. (1999). The role of objective personality inventories in suicide risk assessment: An evaluation and proposal. *Suicide and Life-Threatening Behavior, 29,* 165–185.

Joiner, T., & Rudd, M. (2000). Intensity and duration of crises vary as a function of previous suicide attempts and negative life events. *Journal of Consulting and Clinical Psychology, 68,* 909–916.

Joiner, T., Rudd, M., Rouleau, M., & Wagner, K. (2000). Parameters of suicidal crises vary as a function of previous suicide attempts in young inpatients. *Journal of the American Academy of Child and Adolescent Psychiatry, 39,* 876–880.

Juhnke, G. (1996). The adapted–SAD PERSONS: A suicide assessment scale designed for use with children. *Elementary School Guidance and Counseling, 30,* 252–258.

Kandell, D. (1988). Substance use, depressive mood, and suicidal ideation in adolescence and young adulthood. In A. Stiffman (Ed.), *Advances in adolescent mental health* (3rd ed., Vol. 3, pp. 127–143). Greenwich, CT: JAI Press.

Kann, L., Kinchen, S., Williams, B., Ross, J., Lowry, R., Hill, C., Grunbaum, J., Blumson, P., Collins, J., & Kolbe, L. (1998). Youth risk behavior surveillance: United States, 1997. *Morbidity and Mortality Weekly Report, CDC Surveillance Summaries, 47,* 1–89.

Kaplan, S., Pelcovitz, D., Salzinger, S., Mandel, F., & Weiner, M. (1997). Adolescent physical abuse and suicide attempts. *Journal of the American Academy of Child and Adolescent Psychiatry, 36,* 799–808.

Kashani, J., Nair, S., Rao, V., Nair, J., & Reid, J. (1996). Relationship of personality, environmental, and DICA variables to adolescent hopelessness: A neural network sensitivity approach. *Journal of the American Academy of Child and Adolescent Psychiatry, 35,* 640–645.

Kashani, J., Soltys, S., Dandoy, A., Vaidya, A., & Reid, J. (1991). Correlates of hopelessness in psychiatrically hospitalized children. *Comprehensive Psychiatry, 32,* 330–337.

Kashani, J., Suarez, L., Allan, W., & Reid, J. (1997). Hopelessness in inpatient youths: A closer look at behavior, emotional expression, and social support. *Journal of the American Academy of Child and Adolescent Psychiatry, 36,* 1625–1631.

Kashden, J., Fremouw, W., Callahan, T., & Franzen, M. (1993). Impulsivity in suicidal and nonsuicidal adolescents. *Journal of Abnormal Child Psychology, 21,* 339–353.

Kaufman, J., Birmaher, B., Brent, D., Rao, U., Flynn, C., Moreci, P., Williamson, D., & Ryan, N. (1997). Schedule for Affective Disorders and Schizophrenia for School-Aged Children—Present and Lifetime (K–SADS–PL): Initial reliability and validity data. *Journal of the American Academy of Child and Adolescent Psychiatry, 36,* 980–988.

Kaufman, J., Birmaher, B., Brent, D., Rao, U., & Ryan, N. (1996). *Kiddie SADS—Present and Lifetime Version (K–SADS–PL).* Unpublished instrument, University of Pittsburgh School of Medicine, Western Psychiatric Institute and Clinics, Pittsburgh, PA.

Kazdin, A., Rodgers, A., & Colbus, D. (1986). The Hopelessness Scale for Children: Psychometric characteristics and concurrent validity. *Journal of Consulting and Clinical Psychology, 54,* 241–245.

Keane, E., Dick, R., Bechtold, D., & Manson, S. (1996). Predictive and concurrent validity of the Suicidal Ideation Questionnaire among American Indian adolescents. *Journal of Abnormal Child Psychology, 24,* 735–747.

Keller, M. (1993). *Adolescent—Longitudinal Interval Follow-Up Evaluation (A–LIFE).* Unpublished instrument, Brown University School of Medicine, Providence, RI.

Keller, M., & Nielsen, E. (1988). *Kiddie—Longitudinal Interval Follow-Up Evaluation (K–LIFE).* Unpublished instrument, Massachusetts General Hospital, Boston, MA.

Keller, M., Warshaw, M., Dyck, I., Dolan, R., Shea, M., Riley, K., & Shapiro, R. (1997). *LIFE–IV: The Longitudinal Interval Follow-Up Evaluation for DSM–IV.* Unpublished instrument, Brown University School of Medicine, Providence, RI.

Kempton, T., & Forehand, R. (1992). Suicide attempts among juvenile delinquents: The contribution of mental health factors. *Behaviour Research and Therapy, 30,* 537–541.

Kienhorst, I., DeWilde, E., Diekstra, R., & Wolters, W. (1991). Construction of an index for predicting suicide attempts in depressed adolescents. *British Journal of Psychiatry, 159,* 676–682.

Kienhorst, I., DeWilde, E., Diekstra, R., & Wolters, W. (1995). Adolescents' image of their suicide attempt. *Journal of the American Academy of Child and Adolescent Psychiatry, 34,* 623–628.

King, C., Franzese, R., Gargan, S., McGovern, L., Ghaziuddin, N., & Naylor, M. (1995). Suicide contagion among adolescents during acute psychiatric hospitalization. *Psychiatric Services, 46,* 915–918.

King, C., Hill, E., Naylor, M., Evans, T., & Shain, B. (1993). Alcohol consumption in relation to other predictors of suicidality among adolescent inpatient girls. *Journal of the American Academy of Child and Adolescent Psychiatry, 32,* 82–88.

King, C., Hovey, J., Brand, E., & Ghaziuddin, N. (1997). Prediction of positive outcomes for adolescent psychiatric inpatients. *Journal of the American Academy of Child and Adolescent Psychiatry, 36,* 1434–1442.

King, C., Katz, S., Ghaziuddin, N., Brand, E., Hill, E., & McGovern, L. (1997). Diagnosis and assessment of depression and suicidality using the NIMH Diagnostic Interview Schedule for Children (DISC–2.3). *Journal of Abnormal Child Psychology, 25,* 173–181.

King, C., Raskin, A., Gdowski, C., Butkus, M., & Opipari, L. (1990). Psychosocial factors associated with urban adolescent female suicide attempts. *Journal of the American Academy of Child and Adolescent Psychiatry, 29,* 289–294.

King, C., Segal, H., Kaminski, K., Naylor, M., Ghaziuddin, N., & Radpour, L. (1995). A prospective study of adolescent suicidal behavior following hospitalization. *Suicide and Life-Threatening Behavior, 25,* 327–338.

King, C., Segal, H., Naylor, M., & Evans, T. (1993). Family functioning and suicidal behavior in adolescent inpatients with mood disorders. *Journal of the American Academy of Child and Adolescent Psychiatry, 32,* 1198–1206.

King, J., & Kowalchuk, B. (1994). *Manual for ISO–30 Adolescent: Inventory of Suicide Orientation— 30.* Minneapolis, MN: National Computer Systems.

Kingsbury, S. (1993). Clinical components of suicidal intent in adolescent overdose. *Journal of the American Academy of Child and Adolescent Psychiatry, 32,* 518–520.

Kingsbury, S. (1996). PATHOS: A screening instrument for adolescent overdose: A research note. *Journal of Child Psychology and Psychiatry, 37,* 609–611.

Klein, R. (1994). *Kiddie SADS—Lifetime (K–SADS–L).* Unpublished instrument, Columbia University, New York State Psychiatric Institute, New York.

Klimes-Dougan, B. (1998). Screening for suicidal ideation in children and adolescents: Methodological considerations. *Journal of Adolescence, 21,* 435–444.

Klimes-Dougan, B., Free, K., Ronsaville, D., Stilwell, J., Welsh, J., & Radke-Yarrow, M. (1999). Suicidal ideation and attempts: A longitudinal investigation of children of depressed and well mothers. *Journal of the American Academy of Child and Adolescent Psychiatry, 38,* 651–659.

Kobak, K., Greist, J., Jefferson, J., & Katzelnick, D. (1996). Computer-administered clinical rating scales: A review. *Psychopharmacology, 127,* 291–301.

Kobak, K., Reynolds, W., Rosenfeld, R., & Greist, J. (1990). Development and validation of a computer-administered version of the Hamilton Depression Rating Scale. *Psychological Assessment, 2,* 56–63.

Kovacs, M. (1981). *The Interview Schedule for Children (ISC): Interrater and parent–child agreement.* Unpublished manuscript, University of Pittsburgh School of Medicine, Western Psychiatric Institute and Clinics, Pittsburgh, PA.

Kovacs, M. (1985). The Children's Depression Inventory (CDI). *Psychopharmacology Bulletin, 21,* 995–998.

Kovacs, M. (1992). *Children's Depression Inventory manual.* North Tonawanda, NY: Multi-Health Systems.

Kovacs, M. (1997). *The Interview Schedule for Children and Adolescents (ISCA): Current and Lifetime (ISCA–C & L) and Current and Interim (ISCA–C & I) versions.* Unpublished instruments, University of Pittsburgh School of Medicine, Western Psychiatric Institute and Clinics, Pittsburgh, PA.

Kovacs, M., Goldston, D., & Gatsonis, C. (1993). Suicidal behaviors and childhood-onset depressive disorders: A longitudinal investigation. *Journal of the American Academy of Child and Adolescent Psychiatry, 32,* 8–20.

Kresnow, M., Ikeda, R., Mercy, J., Powell, K., Potter, L., Simon, T., Lee, R., & Frankowski, R. (2001). An unmatched case-control study of nearly lethal suicide attempts in Houston, Texas: Research methods and measurements. *Suicide and Life-Threatening Behavior, 32,* 7–20.

Kumar, G., & Steer, R. (1995). Psychosocial correlates of suicidal ideation in adolescent psychiatric inpatients. *Suicide and Life-Threatening Behavior, 25,* 339–346.

Kye, C., Waterman, S., Ryan, N., Birmaher, B., Williamson, D., Iyengar, S., & Dachille, S. (1996). A randomized, controlled trial of Amitriptyline in the acute treatment of adolescent major depression. *Journal of the American Academy of Child and Adolescent Psychiatry, 35,* 1139–1144.

Lamb, J., & Pusker, K. (1991). School-based adolescent mental health project survey of depression, suicidal ideation, and anger. *Journal of Child and Adolescent Psychiatric and Mental Health Nursing, 4,* 101–104.

Larsson, B., & Ivarsson, T. (1998). Clinical characteristics of adolescent psychiatric inpatients who have attempted suicide. *European Child and Adolescent Psychiatry, 7,* 201–208.

Larsson, B., & Melin, L. (1992). Prevalence and short-term stability of depressive symptoms in schoolchildren. *Acta Psychiatrica Scandinavica, 85,* 17–22.

Larsson, B., Melin, L., Breitholtz, E., & Andersson, G. (1991). Short-term stability of depressive symptoms and suicide attempts in Swedish adolescents. *Acta Psychiatrica Scandinavica, 83,* 385–390.

Larzelere, R., Jorgensen, D., & Anderson, J. (2001). *Child Suicide Risk Assessment manual.* Boys Town, NE: Father Flanagan's Boys Home.

Larzelere, R., Smith, G., Batenhorst, L., & Kelly, D. (1996). Predictive validity of the Suicide Probability Scale among adolescents in group home treatment. *Journal of the American Academy of Child and Adolescent Psychiatry, 35,* 166–172.

Leon, A., Friedman, R., Sweeney, J., Brown, R., & Mann, J. (1990). Statistical issues in the identification of risk factors for suicidal behavior: The application of survival analysis. *Psychiatry Research, 31,* 99–108.

Lessard, J., & Moretti, M. (1998). Suicidal ideation in an adolescent clinical sample: Attachment patterns and clinical implications. *Journal of Adolescence, 21,* 383–95.

Lester, D. (1987). *Suicide as a learned behavior.* Springfield, IL: Charles C Thomas.

Lester, D., Guerriero, J., & Wachter, S. (1991). The Suicide Attitude Vignette Experience (SAVE): A search for sexual stereotypes in the perception of suicidal behavior. *Death Studies, 15,* 435–441.

Lewinsohn, P., Garrison, C., Langhinrichsen, J., & Marsteller, F. (1989). *The assessment of suicidal behavior in adolescents: A review of scales suitable for epidemiologic and clinical research.* Washington, DC: U.S. Government Printing Office.

Lewinsohn, P., Langhinrichsen-Rohling, J., Langford, R., Rohde, P., Seeley, J., & Chapman, J. (1995). The Life Attitudes Schedule: A scale to assess adolescent life-enhancing and life-threatening behaviors. *Suicide and Life-Threatening Behavior, 25,* 458–474.

Lewinsohn, P., Rohde, P., & Seeley, J. (1993). Psychosocial characteristics of adolescents with a history of suicide attempt. *Journal of the American Academy of Child and Adolescent Psychiatry, 32,* 60–68.

Lewinsohn, P., Rohde, P., & Seeley, J. (1994). Psychosocial risk factors for future adolescent suicide attempts. *Journal of Consulting and Clinical Psychology, 62,* 297–305.

Lewinsohn, P., Rohde, P., & Seeley, J. (1996). Adolescent suicidal ideation and attempts: Prevalence, risk factors, and clinical implications. *Clinical Psychology: Science and Practice, 3,* 25–46.

Linehan, M. (1993). *Cognitive–behavioral treatment of borderline personality disorder.* New York: Guilford Press.

Linehan, M. (1996). *Suicidal Behaviors Questionnaire (SBQ).* Unpublished instrument, University of Washington, Seattle.

Linehan, M., Armstrong, H., Suarez, A., Allmon, D., & Heard, H. (1991). Cognitive–behavioral treatment of chronically parasuicidal borderline patients. *Archives of General Psychiatry, 48,* 1060–1064.

Linehan, M., & Comtois, K. (1997). *Lifetime Parasuicide Count.* Unpublished instrument, University of Washington, Seattle.

Linehan, M., Goodstein, J., Nielsen, S., & Chiles, J. (1983). Reasons for staying alive when you are thinking of killing yourself: The Reasons for Living Inventory. *Journal of Consulting and Clinical Psychology, 51,* 276–286.

Linehan, M., & Nielsen, S. (1981). *Suicidal Behaviors Questionnaire (SBQ).* Unpublished instrument, University of Washington, Seattle.

Lonnqvist, J., & Ostano, A. (1991). Suicide following the first suicide attempt: A five-year follow-up using a survival analysis. *Psychiatria Fennica, 22,* 171–179.

Lucas, C. (1997). *The Multimedia Adolescent Suicide Interview (MASI).* Unpublished instrument, Columbia University, New York State Psychiatric Institute, New York.

Lucas, C., & Fisher, P. (1999, June). *New DISC developments.* Paper presented at the meeting of the International Society of Research in Child and Adolescent Psychopathology, Barcelona, Spain.

Lucas, C., Zhang, H., Xu, L., Shaffer, D., Friman, P., Handwerk, M., Jordan, C., & Giaime, A. (1999b). *Assessment of adolescent suicidal ideation & behavior using Audio-CASI.* In "Treatment Research With Suicidal Patients" workshop sponsored by NIMH, NIHORD, and AFSP, Washington, DC.

Malone, K., Szanto, K., Corbitt, E., & Mann, J. (1995). Clinical assessment versus research methods in the assessment of suicidal behavior. *American Journal of Psychiatry, 152,* 1601–1607.

Marciano, P., & Kazdin, A. (1994). Self-esteem, depression, hopelessness, and suicidal intent among psychiatrically disturbed inpatient children. *Journal of Clinical Child Psychology, 23,* 151–160.

Marcoux, B., & Shope, J. (1997). Application of the theory of planned behavior to adolescent use and misuse of alcohol. *Health Education Research,* 12, 323–331.

Martin, G., Clarke, M., & Pearce, C. (1993). Adolescent suicide: Music preference as an indicator of vulnerability. *Journal of the American Academy of Child and Adolescent Psychiatry, 32,* 530–535.

Martin, G., & Waite, S. (1994). Parental bonding and vulnerability to adolescent suicide. *Acta Psychiatrica Scandinavica, 89,* 246–254.

Mazza, J. (2000). The relationship between posttraumatic stress symptomatology and suicidal behavior in school-based adolescents. *Suicide and Life-Threatening Behavior, 30,* 91–103.

Mazza, J., & Eggert, L. (2001). Activity involvement among suicidal and nonsuicidal high-risk and typical adolescents. *Suicide and Life-Threatening Behavior, 31,* 265–281.

Mazza, J., & Reynolds, W. (1998). A longitudinal investigation of depression, hopelessness, social support, and major and minor life events and their relation to suicidal ideation in adolescents. *Suicide and Life-Threatening Behavior, 28,* 358–374.

McKeown, R., Garrison, C., Cuffe, S., Waller, J., Jackson, K., & Addy, C. (1998). Incidence and predictors of suicidal behaviors in a longitudinal sample of young adolescents. *Journal of the American Academy of Child and Adolescent Psychiatry, 37,* 612–619.

McLaughlin, J., Miller, P., & Warwick, H. (1996). Deliberate self-harm in adolescents: Hopelessness, depression, problems and problem-solving. *Journal of Adolescence, 19,* 523–532.

Meehan, P., Lamb, J., Saltzman, L., & O'Carroll, P. (1992). Attempted suicide among young adults: Progress toward a meaningful estimate of prevalence. *American Journal of Psychiatry, 149,* 41–44.

Meehl, P., & Rosen, A. (1955). Antecedent probability and the efficiency of psychometric signs, patterns, or cutting scores. *Psychological Bulletin, 52,* 194–216.

Menninger, K. (1938). *Man against himself.* New York: Harcourt, Brace.

Middleman, A., Faulkner, A., Woods, E., Emans, S., & Durant, R. (1995). High-risk behaviors among high school students in Massachusetts who use anabolic steroids. *Pediatrics, 96,* 268–272.

Miller, I., Norman, W., Bishop, S., & Dow, M. (1986). The modified scale for suicidal ideation: Reliability and validity. *Journal of Consulting and Clinical Psychology, 54,* 724–725.

Miller, K., King, C., Shain, B., & Naylor, M. (1992). Suicidal adolescents' perceptions of their family environment. *Suicide and Life-Threatening Behavior, 22,* 226–239.

Milling, L., Campbell, N., Bush, E., & Laughlin, A. (1992). The relationship of suicidality and psychiatric diagnosis in hospitalized pre-adolescent children. *Child Psychiatry and Human Development, 23,* 41–49.

Millon, T. (1993). *Millon Adolescent Clinical Inventory: Manual.* Minneapolis, MN: National Computer Systems.

Miniño, A., Arias, E., Kochanek, K., Murphy, S., & Smith, B. (2002). Deaths: Final data for 2000. *National Vital Statistics Report, 50* (15), 1–120.

Morano, C., Cisler, R., & Lemerond, J. (1993). Risk factors for adolescent suicidal behavior: Loss, insufficient familial support, and hopelessness. *Adolescence, 28,* 851–865.

Myers, K., Burke, P., & McCauley, E. (1985). Suicidal behavior by hospitalized preadolescent children on a psychiatric unit. *Journal of the American Academy of Child and Adolescent Psychiatry, 24,* 474–480.

Myers, K., McCauley, E., Calderon, R., Mitchell, J., Burke, P., & Schloredt, K. (1991). Risks for suicidality in major depressive disorder. *Journal of the American Academy of Child and Adolescent Psychiatry, 30,* 86–94.

Myers, K., McCauley, E., Calderon, R., & Treder, R. (1991). The 3-year longitudinal course of suicidality and predictive factors for subsequent suicidality in youths with major depressive disorder. *Journal of the American Academy of Child and Adolescent Psychiatry, 30,* 804–810.

Nasser, E., & Overholser, J. (1999). Assessing varying degrees of lethality in depressed adolescent suicide attempters. *Acta Psychiatrica Scandinavica, 99,* 423–431.

National Center for Health Statistics. (2000). *Health, United States 2000: With adolescent health chartbook.* Hyattsville, MD: U.S. Government Printing Office.

National Institute of Mental Health. (2000). *Interventions for suicidal youth* [Program announcement]. Washington, DC: U.S. Government Printing Office.

Nelson, D., Higginson, G., & Grant-Worley, J. (1994). Using the youth risk behavior survey to estimate prevalence of sexual abuse among Oregon high school students. *Journal of School Health, 64,* 413–416.

Neumark-Sztainer, D., Story, M., Dixon, L., & Murray, D. (1998). Adolescents engaging in unhealthy weight control behaviors: Are they at risk for other health-compromising behaviors? *American Journal of Public Health, 88,* 952–955.

Ng, B. (1996). Characteristics of 61 Mexican American adolescents who attempted suicide. *Hispanic Journal of Behavioral Sciences, 18,* 3–12.

Nock, M., & Kazdin, A. (2002). Examination of affective, cognitive, and behavioral factors and suicide-related outcomes in children and young adolescents. *Journal of Clinical Child and Adolescent Psychology, 31,* 48–58.

Novins, D., Beals, J., Roberts, R., & Manson, S. (1999). Factors associated with suicidal ideation among American Indian adolescents: Does culture matter? *Suicide and Life-Threatening Behavior, 29,* 332–346.

O'Carroll, P., Berman, A., Maris, R., Moscicki, E., Tanney, B., & Silverman, M. (1996). Beyond the Tower of Babel: A nomenclature for suicidology. *Suicide and Life-Threatening Behavior, 26,* 237–252.

Ofek, H., Weizman, T., & Apter, A. (1998). The Child Suicide Potential Scale: Inter-rater reliability and validity in Israeli in-patient adolescents. *Israeli Journal of Psychiatry and Related Sciences, 35,* 253–261.

Olsson, G., & von Knorring, A. (1997). Beck's Depression Inventory as a screening instrument for adolescent depression in Sweden: Gender differences. *Acta Psychiatrica Scandinavica, 95,* 277–282.

Olsson, G., & von Knorring, A. (1999). Adolescent depression: Prevalence in Swedish high school students. *Acta Psychiatrica Scandinavica, 99,* 324–331.

Olvera, R. (2001). Suicide ideation in Hispanic and mixed-ancestry adolescents. *Suicide and Life-Threatening Behavior, 31,* 416–427.

Orbach, I., & Bar-Joseph, H. (1993). The impact of a suicide prevention program for adolescents on suicidal tendencies, hopelessness, ego identity, and coping. *Suicide and Life-Threatening Behavior, 23,* 120–129.

Orbach, I., Feshbach, S., Carlson, G., & Ellensberger, I. (1984). Attitudes toward life and death in suicidal, normal and chronically ill children: An extended replication. *Journal of Consulting and Clinical Psychology, 52,* 1020–1027.

Orbach, I., Feshbach, S., Carlson, G., Glaubman, H., & Gross, Y. (1983). Attraction and repulsion by life and death in suicidal and in normal children. *Journal of Consulting and Clinical Psychology, 51,* 661–670.

Orbach, I., Kedem, P., Gorchover, O., Apter, A., & Tyano, S. (1993). Fears of death in suicidal and nonsuicidal adolescents. *Journal of Abnormal Psychology, 102,* 553–558.

Orbach, I., Lotem-Peleg, M., & Kedem, P. (1995). Attitudes toward the body in suicidal, depressed and normal adolescents. *Suicide and Life-Threatening Behavior, 25,* 211–221.

Orbach, I., & Mikulincer, M. (1998). The Body Investment Scale: Construction and validation of a body experience scale. *Psychological Assessment, 10,* 415–425.

Orbach, I., Mikulincer, M., Blumenson, R., Mester, R., & Stein, D. (1999). The subjective experience of problem irresolvability and suicidal behavior: Dynamics and measurement. *Suicide and Life-Threatening Behavior, 29,* 150–164.

Orbach, I., Milstein., I., Har-Even., D., Apter, A., Tiano, S., & Elizur, A. (1991). A Multi-Attitude Suicide Tendency Scale for adolescents. *Psychological Assessment, 3,* 398–404.

Orpinas, P., Basen-Engquist, K., Grunbaum, J., & Parcel, G. (1995). The co-morbidity of violence-related behaviors in a population of high school students. *Journal of Adolescent Health, 16,* 216–225.

Orvaschel, H. (1994). *Schedule for Affective Disorders and Schizophrenia for School-Aged Children— Epidemiologic Version 5 (K–SADS–E).* Unpublished instrument, Nova Southeastern University, Ft. Lauderdale, FL.

Osman, A., Barrios, F., Gutierrez, P., Wrangham, J., Kopper, B., Truelove, R., & Linden, S. (2002). The Positive and Negative Suicide Ideation (PANSI) Inventory: Psychometric evaluation with adolescent psychiatric inpatient samples. *Journal of Personality Assessment, 79,* 522–540.

Osman, A., Barrios, F., Panak, W., Osman, J., Hoffman, J., & Hammer, R. (1994). Validation of the Multi-Attitude Suicide Tendency Scale in adolescent samples. *Journal of Clinical Psychology, 50,* 847–855.

Osman, A., Downs, W., Kopper, B., Barrios, F., Baker, M., Osman, J., Besett, T., & Linehan, M. (1998). The Reasons for Living Inventory for Adolescents (RFL–A): Development and psychometric properties. *Journal of Clinical Psychology, 54,* 1063–1078.

Osman, A., Kopper, B., Barrios, F., Osman, J., Besett, T., & Linehan, M. (1996). The Brief Reasons for Living Inventory for Adolescents (BRFL–A). *Journal of Abnormal Child Psychology, 24,* 433–443.

Osman, A., Gutierrez, P., Jiandani, J., Kopper, B., Barrios, F., Linden, S., & Truelove, R. (in press). A preliminary validation of the Positive and Negative Suicide Ideation (PANSI) Inventory with normal adolescent samples. *Journal of Clinical Psychology.*

Overholser, J., Adams, D., Lehnert, K., & Brinkman, D. (1995). Self-esteem deficits and suicidal tendencies among adolescents. *Journal of the American Academy of Child and Adolescent Psychiatry, 34,* 919–928.

Overholser, J., Freiheit, S., & DiFilippo, J. (1997). Emotional distress and substance abuse as risk factors for suicide attempts. *Canadian Journal of Psychiatry, 42,* 402–408.

Payne, B., & Billie, S. (1996, March). *Reliability and validity of the Suicidal Behaviors Questionnaire for Children.* Paper presented at the meeting of the Southeastern Psychological Association, Norfolk, VA.

Peruzzi, N., & Bongar, B. (1999). Assessing risk for completed suicide in patients with major depression: Psychologists' view of critical factors. *Professional Psychology, Research and Practice, 30,* 576–580.

Peterson, B., Zhang, H., Santa Lucia, R., King, R., & Lewis, M. (1996). Risk factors for presenting problems in child psychiatric emergencies. *Journal of the American Academy of Child and Adolescent Psychiatry, 35,* 1162–1173.

Petrie, K., & Abell, W. (1994). Responses of parasuicides to a computerized interview. *Computers in Human Behavior, 10,* 415–418.

Pfeffer, C., Conte, H., Plutchik, R., & Jerrett, I. (1979). Suicidal behavior in latency age children: An empirical study. *Journal of the American Academy of Child Psychiatry, 18,* 679–692.

Pfeffer, C., Conte, H., Plutchik, R., & Jerrett, I. (1980). Suicidal behavior in latency age children: An outpatient population. *Journal of the American Academy of Child Psychiatry, 19,* 703–710.

Pfeffer, C., Jiang, H., & Kakuma, T. (2000). Child–Adolescent Suicidal Potential Index (CASPI): A screen for risk for early onset suicidal behavior. *Psychological Assessment, 12,* 304–318.

Pfeffer, C., Karus, D., Siegel, K., & Jiang, H. (2000). Child survivors of parental death from cancer or suicide: Depressive and behavioral outcomes. *Psycho-Oncology, 9,* 1–10.

Pfeffer, C., Klerman, G., Hurt, S., Kakuma, T., Peskin, J., & Siefker, C. (1993). Suicidal children grow up: Rates and psychosocial risk factors for suicide attempts during follow-up. *Journal of the American of Child and Adolescent Psychiatry, 32,* 106–113.

Pfeffer, C., Klerman, G., Hurt, S., Lesser, M., Peskin, J., & Siefker, C. (1991). Suicidal children grow up: Demographic and clinical risk factors for adolescent suicide attempts. *Journal of the American Academy of Child and Adolescent Psychiatry, 30,* 609–616.

Pfeffer, C. R., Plutchik, R., Mizruchi, M. S., Faughnan, L., Mintz, M., & Shindledecker, R. (1989). Changes in suicidal behavior in child psychiatric inpatients. *Acta Psychiatrica Scandinavica, 79,* 431–435.

Pfeffer, C., Solomon, G., Plutchik, R., Mizruchi, M., & Weiner, A. (1982). Suicidal behavior in latency-age psychiatric inpatients: A replication and cross-validation. *Journal of the American Academy of Child Psychiatry, 21,* 564–569.

Pfeffer, C., Zuckerman, S., Plutchik, R., & Mizruchi, M. (1984). Suicidal behavior in normal school children: A comparison with child psychiatric inpatients. *Journal of the American Academy of Child Psychiatry, 23,* 416–423.

Pharris, M., Resnick, M., & Blum, R. (1997). Protecting against hopelessness and suicidality in sexually abused American Indian Adolescents. *Journal of Adolescent Health, 21,* 400–406.

Pierce, D. (1977). Suicidal intent in self-injury. *British Journal of Psychiatry, 130,* 377–385.

Piersma, H., & Boes, J. (1997). Utility of the Inventory of Suicide Orientation—30 (ISO–30) for adolescent psychiatric inpatients: Linking clinical decision making with outcome evaluation. *Journal of Clinical Psychology, 53,* 65–72.

Pillay, A., & Wassenaar, D. (1995). Psychological intervention, spontaneous remission, hopelessness, and psychiatric disturbance in adolescent parasuicides. *Suicide and Life-Threatening Behavior, 25,* 386–392.

Pinto, A., & Whisman, M. (1996). Negative affect and cognitive biases in suicidal and nonsuicidal hospitalized adolescents. *Journal of the American Academy of Child and Adolescent Psychiatry, 35,* 158–165.

Pinto, A., Whisman, M., & Conwell, Y. (1998). Reasons for living in a clinical sample of adolescents. *Journal of Adolescence, 21,* 397–405.

Pinto, A., Whisman, M., & McCoy, K. (1997). Suicidal ideation in adolescents: Psychometric properties of the Suicidal Ideation Questionnaire in a clinical sample. *Psychological Assessment, 9,* 63–66.

Plutchik, R. (1997). Expanding our conceptual horizons on the future of suicide research. In A. Botsis, C. Soldatos, & C. Stafanis (Eds.), *Suicide: Biopsychosocial Approaches* (pp. 271–274). New York: Elsevier Science.

Plutchik, R., Botsis, A., Weiner, M., & Kennedy, G. (1996). Clinical measurement of suicidality and coping in late life: A theory of countervailing forces. In G. Kennedy (Ed.), *Suicide and depression in late life: Critical issues in treatment* (pp. 83–101). New York: John Wiley & Sons.

Plutchik, R., & Van Praag, H. (1989). The measurement of suicidality, aggressivity, and impulsivity. *Progress in Neuro-Psychopharmacology and Biological Psychiatry, 13,* S23–S34.

Plutchik, R., & Van Praag, H. (1990). A self-report measure of violence risk: II. *Comprehensive Psychiatry, 31,* 450–456.

Plutchik, R., Van Praag, H., & Conte, H. (1989). Correlates of suicide and violence risk: III. A two-stage model of countervailing forces. *Psychiatric Research, 28,* 215–225.

Plutchik, R., Van Praag, H., Conte, H., & Picard, S. (1989). Correlates of suicide and violence risk: I. The Suicide Risk Measure. *Comprehensive Psychiatry, 30,* 296–302.

Plutchik, R., Van Praag, H., Picard, S., Conte, H., & Korn, M. (1989). Is there a relationship between the seriousness of suicidal intent and the lethality of the suicide attempt? *Psychiatry Research, 27,* 71–79.

Potter, L., Kresnow, M., Powell, K., O'Carroll, P., Lee, R., Frankowski, R., Swann, A., Bayer, T., Bautista, M., & Briscoe, M. (1998). Identification of nearly fatal suicide attempts: Self-Inflicted Injury Severity Form. *Suicide and Life-Threatening Behavior, 28,* 174–186.

Potts, M., Daniels, M., Burnam, M., & Wells, K. (1990). A structured interview version of the Hamilton Depression Rating Scale: Evidence of reliability and versatility of administration. *Journal of Psychiatric Research, 24,* 335–350.

Powell, K., Kresnow, M., Mercy, J., Potter, L., Swann, A., Frankowski, R., Lee, R., & Bayer, T. (2001). Alcohol consumption and nearly lethal suicide attempts. *Suicide and Life-Threatening Behavior, 32,* 30–41.

Poznanski, E., & Mokros, H. (1999). *Children's Depression Rating Scale Revised (CDRS–R)—Manual.* Western Psychological Services: Los Angeles.

Prinstein, M., Nock, M., Spirito, A., & Grapentine, W. (2001). Multimethod assessment of suicidality in adolescent psychiatric inpatients: Preliminary results. *Journal of the American Academy of Child and Adolescent Psychiatry, 40,* 1053–1061.

Radloff, L. (1977). The CES-D Scale: A self-report depression scale for research in the general population. *Applied Psychological Measurement, 1,* 385–401.

Radloff, L. (1991). The use of the Center for Epidemiologic Studies Depression Scale in adolescents and young adults. *Journal of Youth and Adolescence, 20,* 149–166.

Rathus, J., & Miller, A. (2002). Dialectical behavior therapy adapted for suicidal adolescents. *Suicide and Life-Threatening Behavior, 32,* 146–157.

Reich, W. (2000). Diagnostic Interview for Children and Adolescents (DICA). *Journal of the American Academy of Child and Adolescent Psychiatry, 39,* 59–66.

Reifman, A., & Windle, M. (1995). Adolescent suicidal behaviors as a function of depression, hopelessness, alcohol use, and social support: A longitudinal investigation. *American Journal of Community Psychology, 23,* 329–354.

Reinecke, M., DuBois, D., & Schultz, T. (2001). Social problem solving, mood, and suicidality among inpatient adolescents. *Cognitive Therapy and Research, 25,* 743–756.

Reinherz, H., Giaconia, R., Silverman, A., Friedman, A., Pakiz, B., Frost, A., & Cohen, E. (1995). Early psychosocial risks for adolescent suicidal ideation and attempts. *Journal of the American Academy of Child and Adolescent Psychiatry, 34,* 599–611.

Renaud, J., Brent, D., Birmaher, B., Chiappeta, L., & Bridge, J. (1999). Suicide in adolescents with disruptive disorders. *Journal of the American Academy of Child and Adolescent Psychiatry, 38,* 846–851.

Resnik, H., & Hathorne, B. (1973). *Suicide prevention in the 70's.* Washington, DC: U.S. Government Printing Office.

Rey, J., & Bird, K. (1991). Sex differences in suicidal behavior of referred adolescents. *British Journal of Psychiatry, 158,* 776–781.

Reynolds, W. (1988). *Suicidal Ideation Questionnaire: Professional manual.* Odessa, FL: Psychological Assessment Resources.

Reynolds, W. (1989). *Suicidal Behaviors Inventory (SBI).* Unpublished instrument, University of Wisconsin, Madison, WI. (Copyright for this instrument is currently held by Psychological Assessment Resources)

Reynolds, W. (1990). Development of a semistructured clinical interview for suicidal behaviors in adolescents. *Psychological Assessment, 2,* 382–393.

Reynolds, W. (1991). A school-based procedure for the identification of adolescents at risk for suicidal behaviors. *Family and Community Health, 14,* 64–75.

Reynolds, W. (1992, April). *Measurement of suicidal ideation in adolescents.* Paper presented at the meeting of the American Association of Suicidology, Chicago.

Reynolds, W. (1998). *Adolescent Psychopathology Scale: Psychometric and Technical Manual.* Odessa, FL: Psychological Assessment Resources.

Reynolds, W. (2000). *Adolescent Psychopathology Scale—Short Form: Professional Manual.* Odessa, FL: Psychological Assessment Resources.

Reynolds, W., & Kobak, K. (1995). Reliability and validity of the Hamilton Depression Inventory: A paper-and-pencil version of the Hamilton Depression Rating Scale clinical interview. *Psychological Assessment, 7,* 472–483.

Reynolds, W., & Mazza, J. (1992a). *Suicidal Behavior History Form.* Odessa, FL: Psychological Assessment Resources.

Reynolds, W., & Mazza, J. (1992b). *Suicidal Behavior History Form—Clinician's Guide.* Odessa, FL: Psychological Assessment Resources.

Reynolds, W., & Mazza, J. (1993). *Evaluation of suicidal behavior in adolescents: Reliability of the Suicidal Behaviors Interview.* Unpublished manuscript, University of British Columbia, Vancouver, British Columbia, Canada.

Reynolds, W., & Mazza, J. (1994, June). *Use of the Suicidal Behaviors Interview for screening of school-based adolescents for risk of suicidal behaviors.* Paper presented at the meeting of the National Conference on Risk-Taking Behaviors Among Children and Adolescents, Arlington, VA.

Reynolds, W., & Mazza, J. (1999). Assessment of suicidal ideation in inner-city children and young adolescents: Reliability and validity of the Suicidal Ideation Questionnaire—JR. *School Psychology Review, 28,* 17–30.

Ribera, J., Canino, G., Rubio-Stipec, M., Bravo, M., Bauermeister, J., Alegria, M., Woodbury, M., Huertas, S., Guevara, L., Bird, H., Freeman, D., & Shrout, P. (1996). The Diagnostic Interview Schedule for Children (DISC–2.1) in Spanish: Reliability in a Hispanic population. *Journal of Child Psychology & Psychiatry and Allied Disciplines, 37,* 195–204.

Ritter, D. (1990). Adolescent suicide: Social competence and problem behavior of youth at high risk and low risk of suicide. *School Psychology Review, 19,* 83–95.

Roberts, R., & Chen, Y. (1995). Depressive symptoms and suicidal ideation among Mexican-origin and Anglo adolescents. *Journal of the American Academy of Child and Adolescent Psychiatry, 34,* 81–90.

Roberts, R., Chen, Y., & Roberts, C. (1997). Ethnocultural differences in prevalence of adolescent suicidal behaviors. *Suicide and Life-Threatening Behavior, 27,* 208–217.

Roberts, R., Roberts, C., & Chen, Y. (1998). Suicidal thinking among adolescents with a history of attempted suicide. *Journal of the American Academy of Child and Adolescent Psychiatry, 37,* 1294–1300.

Robertson, B., Ensink, K., Parry, C., & Chalton, D. (1999). Performance of the Diagnostic Interview Schedule for Children Version 2. 3 (DISC–2.3) in an informal settlement area in South Africa. *Journal of the American Academy of Child and Adolescent Psychiatry, 38,* 1156–1164.

Rohde, P., Lewinsohn, P., Seeley, J., & Langhinrichsen, J. (1996). The Life Attitudes Schedule short form: An abbreviated measure of life-enhancing and life-threatening behaviors in adolescents. *Suicide and Life-Threatening Behavior, 26,* 272–281.

Rohde, P., Mace, D., & Seeley, J. (1997). The association of psychiatric disorders with suicide attempts in a juvenile delinquent sample. *Criminal Behaviour and Mental Health, 7,* 187–200.

Rohde, P., Noell, J., Ochs, L., & Seeley, J. (2001). Depression, suicidal ideation and STD-related risk in homeless older adolescents. *Journal of Adolescence, 24,* 447–460.

Rohde, P., Seeley, J., & Mace, D. (1997). Correlates of suicidal behavior in a juvenile detention population. *Suicide and Life-Threatening Behavior, 27,* 164–175.

Rooney, M., Fristad, M., Weller, E., & Weller, R. (1999). *Administration manual for the ChIPS.* Washington, DC: American Psychiatric Press.

Rotheram-Borus, M. (1987). Evaluation of imminent danger for suicide among youth. *American Journal of Orthopsychiatry, 57,* 102–110.

Rotheram-Borus, M. (1989). Evaluation of suicide risk among youths in community settings. *Suicide and Life-Threatening Behavior, 19,* 108–119.

Rotheram-Borus, M., & Bradley, J. (1991). Triage model for suicidal runaways. *American Journal of Orthopsychiatry, 61,* 122–127.

Rotheram-Borus, M., Hunter, J., & Rosario, M. (1994). Suicidal behavior and gay-related stress among gay and bisexual male adolescents. *Journal of Adolescent Research, 9,* 498–508.

Rotheram-Borus, M., & Trautman, P. (1988). Hopelessness, depression, and suicidal intent among adolescent suicide attempters. *Journal of the American Academy of Child and Adolescent Psychiatry, 27,* 700–704.

Rotheram-Borus, M., & Trautman, P. (1990). Cognitive style and pleasant activities among female adolescent suicide attempters. *Journal of Consulting and Clinical Psychology, 58,* 554–561.

Rotheram-Borus, M., Walker, J., & Ferns, W. (1996). Suicidal behavior among middle-class adolescents who seek crisis services. *Journal of Clinical Psychology, 52,* 137–143.

Roy, A., Rylander, G., & Sarchiapone, M. (1997). Suicide: Family studies and molecular genetics. *Annals of the New York Academy of Sciences, 836,* 135–157.

Rush, A., Beck, A., Kovacs, M., Weissenburger, J., & Hollon, S. (1982). Comparison of the effects of cognitive therapy and pharmacotherapy on hopelessness and self-concept. *American Journal of Psychiatry, 139,* 862–866.

Sadowski, C., & Kelley, M. (1993). Social problem solving in suicidal adolescents. *Journal of Consulting and Clinical Psychology, 61,* 121–127.

Schwab-Stone, M., Shaffer, D., Dulcan, M., Jenson, P., Fisher, P., Bird, H., Goodman, S., Lahey, B., Lichtman, J., Canino, G., Rubio-Stipec, M., & Rae, D. (1996). Criterion validity of the NIMH Diagnostic Interview Schedule for Children Version 2.3 (DISC–2.3). *Journal of the American Academy of Child and Adolescent Psychiatry, 35,* 878–888.

Scott, J., House, R., Yates, M., & Harrington, J. (1997). Individual risk factors for early repetition of deliberate self-harm. *British Journal of Medical Psychology, 70,* 387–393.

Shaffer, D. (1996). Discussion of "Predictive validity of the Suicide Probability Scale among adolescents in group home treatment." *Journal of the Academy of Child and Adolescent Psychiatry, 35,* 172–174.

Shaffer, D., & Craft, L. (1999). Methods of adolescent suicide prevention. *Journal of Clinical Psychiatry, 60,* 70–74.

Shaffer, D., Fisher, P., Dulcan, M., Davies, M., Piacentini, J., Schwab-Stone, M., Lahey, B., Bourdon, K., Jensen, P., Bird, H., Canino, G., & Regier, D. (1996). The NIMH Diagnostic Interview Schedule for Children Version 2.3 (DISC–2.3): Description, acceptability, prevalence rates, and performance in the MECA study. *Journal of the American Academy of Child and Adolescent Psychiatry, 35,* 865–877.

Shaffer, D., Fisher, P., Lucas, C., Dulcan, M., & Schwab-Stone, M. (2000). NIMH Diagnostic Interview Schedule for Children, Version IV (NIMH DISC–IV): Description, differences from previous versions, and reliability of some common diagnoses. *Journal of the American Academy of Child and Adolescent Psychiatry, 39,* 28–38.

Shaffer, D., Garland A., Vieland, V., Underwood, M., & Busner, C. (1991). The impact of curriculum-based suicide prevention programs for teenagers. *Journal of the American Academy of Child and Adolescent Psychiatry, 30,* 588–596.

Shaffer, D., Gould, M., Fisher, P., Trautman, P., Moreau, D., Kleinman, M., & Flory, M. (1996). Psychiatric diagnosis in child and adolescent suicide. *Archives of General Psychiatry, 53,* 339–348.

Shaffer, D., Trautman, Mufson, L., Piacentini, J., & Grae, F. (1997). *Columbia/Ruane Initial Evaluation Form for Child and Adolescent Suicide Attempters/Ideators.* Unpublished instrument, Columbia University—New York State Psychiatric Institute, New York.

Shaffer, D., Wilcox, H., Lucas, C., Hicks, R., Busner, C., & Parides, M. (1996, October). *The development of a screening instrument for teens at risk for suicide.* Poster presented at the meeting of the Academy of Child and Adolescent Psychiatry, New York.

Shaffii, M., Steltz-Lenarsky, J., Derrick, A., Beckner, C., Whittinghill, J. (1988). Comorbidity of mental disorders in the post-mortem diagnosis of completed suicide in children and adolescents. *Journal of Affective Disorders, 15,* 227–233.

Shaunesey, K., Cohen, J., Plummer, B., & Berman, A. (1993). Suicidality in hospitalized adolescents: Relationship to prior abuse. *American Journal of Orthopsychiatry, 63,* 113–119.

Shea, S. (1999). *The practical art of suicide assessment: A guide for mental health professionals and substance abuse counselors.* New York: John Wiley and Sons.

Sherrill, J., & Kovacs, M. (2000). The Interview Schedule for Children and Adolescents (ISCA). *Journal of the American Academy of Child and Adolescent Psychiatry, 39,* 67–75.

Shneidman, E. (1986). Ten commonalities of suicide and their implications for response. *Crisis, 7,* 88–93.

Shneidman, E. (1996). *The suicidal mind.* New York: Oxford University Press.

Shneidman, E. (1999). The Psychological Pain Assessment Scale. *Suicide and Life-Threatening Behavior, 29,* 287–294.

Shrout, P. (1995). Assessment: Part III. Reliability. In M. Tsuang, M. Tohen, & G. Zahner (Eds.), *Textbook in psychiatric epidemiology* (pp. 213–228). New York: Wiley-Liss.

Siemen, J., Warrington, C., & Mangano, E. (1994). Comparison of the Millon Adolescent Personality Inventory and the Suicide Ideation Questionnaire—Junior with an adolescent inpatient sample. *Psychological Reports, 75,* 947–950.

Smith, K., Conroy, R., & Ehler, B. (1984). Lethality of Suicide Attempt Rating Scale. *Suicide and Life-Threatening Behavior, 14,* 215–242.

Snyder, M., & Stukas, A. (1999). The interplay of cognitive, motivational, and behavioral activities in social interaction. *Annual Review of Psychology, 50,* 273–303.

Sourander, A., Helstela, L., Haavisto, A., & Bergroth, L. (2001). Suicidal thoughts and attempts among adolescents: A longitudinal 8-year follow-up study. *Journal of Affective Disorders, 63,* 59–66.

Spirito, A., Boergers, J., Donaldson, D., Bishop, D., & Lewander, W. (2002). An intervention trial to improve adherence to community treatment by adolescents after a suicide attempt. *Journal of the American Academy of Child and Adolescent Psychiatry, 41,* 435–442.

Spirito, A., Brown, L., Overholser, J., Fritz, G., & Bond, A. (1991). Use of the Risk-Rescue Rating Scale with adolescent suicide attempters: A cautionary note. *Death Studies, 15,* 269–280.

Spirito, A., Lewander, W., Levy, S., Kurkjian, J., & Fritz, G. (1994). Emergency department assessment of adolescent suicide attempters: Factors related to short-term follow-up outcome. *Pediatric Emergency Care, 10,* 6–12.

Spirito, A., Stark, L., Fristad, M., Hart, K., & Owens-Stively, J. (1987). Adolescent suicide attempters hospitalized on a pediatric unit. *Journal of Pediatric Psychology, 12,* 171–189.

Spirito, A., Sterling, C., Donaldson, D., & Arrigan, M. (1996). Factor analysis of the Suicide Intent Scale with adolescent suicide attempters. *Journal of Personality Assessment, 67,* 90–101.

Spirito, A., Williams, C., Stark, L., & Hart, K. (1988). The Hopelessness Scale for Children: Psychometric properties with normal and emotionally disturbed adolescents. *Journal of Abnormal Child Psychology, 16,* 445–458.

Stanger, C., Achenbach, T., & McConaughy, S. (1993). Three-year course of behavioral/ emotional problems in a national sample of 4- to 16-year-olds: 3. Predictors of signs of disturbance. *Journal of Consulting and Clinical Psychology, 61,* 839–848.

Stanton, B., Li, X., Black, M., Ricardo, I., Galbraith, J., Feigelman, S., & Kaljee, L. (1996). Longitudinal stability and predictability of sexual perceptions, intentions, and behaviors among early adolescent African-Americans. *Journal of Adolescent Health, 18,* 10–19

Steer, R., & Beck, A. (1988). Use of the Beck Depression Inventory, Hopelessness Scale, Scale for Suicidal Ideation, and Suicidal Intent Scale with adolescents. *Advances in Adolescent Mental Health, 3,* 219–231.

Steer, R., Beck, A., & Brown, G. (1997). Factors of the Beck Hopelessness Scale: Fact or artifact? *Multivariate Experimental Clinical Research, 11,* 131–144.

Steer, R., Kumar, G., & Beck, A. (1993a). Hopelessness in adolescent psychiatric inpatients. *Psychological Reports, 72,* 559–564.

Steer, R., Kumar, G., & Beck, A. (1993b). Self-reported suicidal ideation in adolescent psychiatric inpatients. *Journal of Consulting and Clinical Psychology, 61,* 1096–1099.

Steer, R., Kumar, G., Ranieri, W., & Beck, A. (1998). Use of the Beck Depression Inventory— II with adolescent psychiatric outpatients. *Journal of Psychopathology and Behavioral Assessment, 20,* 127–137.

Stein, D., Apter, A., Ratzoni, G., Har-Even, D., & Avidan, G. (1998). Association between multiple suicide attempts and negative affects in adolescents. *Journal of the American Academy of Child and Adolescent Psychiatry, 37,* 488–494.

Stein, D., Brom, D., Elizur, A., & Witztum, E. (1998). The association between attitudes toward suicide and suicidal ideation in adolescents. *Acta Psychiatrica Scandinavica, 97,* 195–201.

Stewart, S., Lam, T., Betson, C., & Chung, S. (1999). Suicide ideation and its relationship to depressed mood in a community sample of adolescents in Hong Kong. *Suicide and Life-Threatening Behavior, 29,* 227–240.

Stillion, J. McDowell, E., & Shamblin, J. (1984). The Suicide Attitude Vignette Experience: A method for measuring adolescent attitudes toward suicide. *Death Education, 8,* 65–79.

Stillion, J., White, H., Edwards, P., & McDowell, E. (1989). Ageism and sexism and suicide attitudes. *Death Studies, 13,* 247–261.

Strauss, J., Birmaher, B., Bridge, J., Axelson, D., Chiappetta, L., Brent, D., & Ryan, D. (2000). Anxiety disorders in suicidal youth. *Canadian Journal of Psychiatry, 45,* 739–745.

Substance Abuse and Mental Health Services Administration (SAMHSA). (2002). *SAMHSA unveils data on youths contemplating suicide* [News release]. Retrieved from http:// www.samhsa.gov/news/news.html

Sussman, S., Dent, C., Severson, H., Burton, D., & Flay, B. (1998). Self-initiated quitting among adolescent smokers. *Preventive Medicine: An International Journal Devoted to Practice and Theory, 27,* A19-A28.

Swahn, M., & Potter, L. (2001). Factors associated with the medical severity of suicide attempts in youths and young adults. *Suicide and Life-Threatening Behavior, 32,* 21–29.

Swedo, S., Albert, J., Glod, C., Clark, C., Teicher, M., Richter, D., Hoffman, C., Hamburger, S., Dow, S., Brown, C., & Rosenthal, N. (1997). A controlled trial of light therapy for the treatment of pediatric Seasonal Affective Disorder. *Journal of the American Academy of Child and Adolescent Psychiatry, 36,* 816–821.

Swedo, S., Rettew, D., Kuppenheimer, M., Lum, D., Dolan, S., & Goldberger, E. (1991). Can adolescent suicide attempters be distinguished from at-risk adolescents? *Pediatrics, 88,* 620–629.

Tatman, S., Greene, A., & Karr, L. (1993). Use of the Suicide Probability Scale (SPS) with adolescents. *Suicide and Life-Threatening Behavior, 23,* 188–203.

Teare, M., Fristad, M., Weller, E., Weller, R., & Salmon, P. (1998a). Study I: Development and criterion validity of the Children's Interview for Psychiatric Syndromes (ChIPS). *Journal of Child and Adolescent Psychopharmacology, 8,* 205–211.

Teare, M., Fristad, M., Weller, E., Weller, R., & Salmon, P. (1998b). Study II: Concurrent validity of the *DSM–III–R* Children's Interview for Psychiatric Syndromes (ChIPS). *Journal of Child and Adolescent Psychopharmacology, 8,* 213–219

Tejedor, M., Diaz, A., Castillon, J., & Pericay, J. (1999). Attempted suicide: Repetition and survival. Findings of a follow-up study. *Acta Psychiatrica Scandinavica, 100,* 205–211.

Teri, L. (1982). The use of the Beck Depression Inventory with adolescents. *Journal of Abnormal Child Psychology, 10,* 277–284.

Thompson, E., & Eggert, E. (1999). Using the Suicide Risk Screen to identify suicidal adolescents among potential high school dropouts. *Journal of the American Academy of Child and Adolescent Psychiatry, 36,* 1506–1514.

Thompson, E., Eggert, L., & Herting, J. (2000). Mediating effects of an indicated prevention program for reducing youth depression and suicide risk behaviors. *Suicide and Life-Threatening Behaviors, 30,* 252–271.

Thompson, E., Eggert, L., Randell, P., & Pike, K. (2001). Evaluation of indicated suicide risk prevention approaches for potential high school dropouts. *American Journal of Public Health, 91,* 742–752.

Topol, P., & Reznikoff, M. (1982). Perceived peer and family relationships, hopelessness and locus of control as factors in adolescent suicide attempts. *Suicide and Life-Threatening Behavior, 12,* 141–150.

Tortolero, S., & Roberts, R. (2001). Differences in nonfatal suicide behaviors among Mexican and European American middle school children. *Suicide and Life-Threatening Behavior, 31,* 214–223.

Trautman, P., Rotheram-Borus, M., Dopkins, S., & Lewin, N. (1991). Psychiatric diagnoses in minority female adolescent suicide attempters. *Journal of the American Academy of Child and Adolescent Psychiatry, 30,* 617–622.

U.S. Department of Health and Human Services. (1998). *Leading indicators for Healthy People 2010: A report from the HHS working group on sentinel objectives.* Washington, DC: U.S. Government Printing Office.

U.S. Public Health Service. (2000). *Report of the Surgeon General's Conference on Children's Mental Health: A national action agenda.* Washington, DC: U.S. Government Printing Office.

U.S. Public Health Service. (2001). *National strategy for suicide prevention: Goals and objectives for action.* Washington, DC: U.S. Government Printing Office.

Valla, J. (2002). *The Dominic Interactive instruction manual.* Montreal, Quebec, Canada: DIMAT Inc.

Valla, J., Bergeron, L., Bidaut-Russell, M., St-Georges, M., & Gaudet, N. (1997). Reliability of the Dominic–R: A young child mental health questionnaire combining visual and auditory stimuli. *Journal of Child Psychology and Psychiatry and Allied Disciplines, 38,* 717–724.

Valla, J., Bergeron, L., & Smolla, N. (2000). The Dominic–R: A pictorial interview for 6- to 11-year-old children. *Journal of the American Association of Child and Adolescent Psychiatry, 39*, 85–93.

Velez, C., & Cohen, P. (1988). Suicidal behavior and ideation in a community sample of children: Maternal and youth reports. *Journal of the American Academy of Child and Adolescent Psychiatry, 27*, 349–356.

Velting, D., & Miller, A. (1998, November). Diagnostic risk factors for adolescent parasuicidal behavior. In Jane Pearson (Organizer), *Suicidality in youth: Developing the knowledge base for youth at risk.* Symposium conducted at the meeting of the National Institute of Mental Health, Bethesda, MD.

Velting, D., Rathus, J., & Asnis, G. (1998). Asking adolescents to explain discrepancies in self-reported suicidality. *Suicide and Life-Threatening Behavior, 28*, 187–196.

Velting, D., Rathus, J., & Miller, A. (2000). MACI Personality Scale profiles of depressed adolescent suicide attempters: A pilot study. *Journal of Clinical Psychology, 56*, 1381–1385.

Walker, M., Moreau, D., & Weissman, M. (1990). Parents' awareness of children's suicide attempts. *American Journal of Psychiatry, 147*, 1364–1366.

Walrath, C., Mandell, D., Liao, Q., Holden, E. W., DeCarolis, G., Santiago, R., & Leaf, P. (2001). Suicidal behaviors among children in the Comprehensive Community Mental Health Services for Children and Their Families program. *Journal of the American Academy of Child and Adolescent Psychiatry, 40*, 1197–1205

Warren, W. (1998). *Revised Hamilton Rating Scale for Depression (RHRSD).* Los Angeles: Western Psychological Services.

Weisman, A., & Worden, J. (1972). Risk-rescue rating in suicide assessment. *Archives of General Psychiatry, 26*, 737–746.

Weisz, J., Thurber, C., Sweeney, L., Proffitt, V., & LeGagnoux, G. (1997). Brief treatment of mild-to-moderate child depression using primary and secondary control enhancement training. *Journal of Consulting and Clinical Psychology, 65*, 703–707.

Weller, E., Weller, R., Fristad, M., Rooney, M., & Schecter, J. (2000). Children's Interview for Psychiatric Syndromes (ChIPS). *Journal of the American Academy of Child and Adolescent Psychiatry, 39*, 76–84.

Weller, E., Weller, R., Rooney, M., & Fristad, M. (1999a). *ChIPS—Children's Interview for Psychiatric Syndromes.* Washington, DC: American Psychiatric Press.

Weller, E., Weller, R., Rooney, M., & Fristad, M. (1999b). *Children's Interview for Psychiatric Syndromes—Parent Version (P–ChIPS).* Washington, DC: American Psychiatric Press.

West, S., Keck, P., McElroy, S., Strakowski, S., Minnery, K., McConville, B., & Sorter, M. (1994). Open trial of valproate in the treatment of adolescent mania. *Journal of Child and Adolescent Psychopharmacology, 4*, 263–267.

Wetzler, S., Asnis, G., Hyman, R., Virtue, C., Zimmerman, J., & Rathus, H. (1996). Characteristics of suicidality among adolescents. *Suicide and Life-Threatening Behavior, 26*, 37–45.

Whisman, M., & Pinto, A. (1997). Hopelessness and depression in depressed inpatient adolescents. *Cognitive Therapy and Research, 21*, 345–358.

Williams, J. (1988). A structured interview guide for the Hamilton Depression Rating Scale. *Archives of General Psychiatry, 45*, 742–747.

Windle, R., & Windle, M. (1997). An investigation of adolescents' substance use behaviors, depressed affect and suicidal behaviors. *Journal of Child Psychology and Psychiatry, 38*, 921–929.

Wolfgang, M. (1959). Suicide by means of victim-precipitated homicide. *Journal of Clinical and Experimental Psychopathology, 20*, 335–349.

Woods, E., Lin, Y., Middleman, A., Beckford, P., Chase, L., & Durant, R. (1997). The associations of suicide attempts in adolescents. *Pediatrics, 99*, 791–796.

Wozencraft, T., Wagner, W., & Pellegrin, A. (1991). Depression and suicidal ideation in sexually abused children. *Child Abuse and Neglect, 15,* 505–511.

Woznica, J., & Shapiro, J. (1990). An analysis of adolescent suicide attempts: The expendable child. *Journal of Pediatric Psychology, 15,* 789–196.

Woznica, J., & Shapiro, J. (1998). An analysis of adolescent suicide attempts: A validation of the expendable child measure. In A. Z. Schwartzberg (Ed.), *Adolescent in turmoil* (pp. 82–90). Westport, CT: Praeger.

Yoder, K. (1999). Comparing suicide attempters, suicide ideators, and nonsuicidal homeless and runaway adolescents. *Suicide and Life-Threatening Behavior, 29,* 25–36.

Yoder, K., Hoyt, D., & Whitbeck, L. (1998). Suicidal behavior among homeless and runaway adolescents. *Journal of Youth and Adolescence, 27,* 753–771.

Young, M., Fogg, L., Scheftner, W., Fawcett, J., Akiskal, H., & Maser, J. (1996). Stable trait components of hopelessness: Baseline and sensitivity to depression. *Journal of Abnormal Psychology, 105,* 155–165.

Zalsman, G., Netanel, R., Fischel, T., Freudenstein, O., Landau, E., Orbach, I., Weizman, A., Pfeffer, C., & Apter, A. (2000). Human figure drawings in the evaluation of severe adolescent suicidal behavior. *Journal of the American Academy of Child and Adolescent Psychiatry, 39,* 1024–1031.

Zlotnick, C., Donaldson, D., Spirito, A., & Pearlstein, T. (1997). Affect regulation and suicide attempts in adolescent inpatients. *Journal of the American Academy of Child and Adolescent Psychiatry, 36,* 793–798.

Zlotnick, C., Shea, T., Pearlstein, T., Simpson, E., Costello, E., & Begin, A. (1996). The relationship between dissociative symptoms, alexithymia, impulsivity, sexual abuse, and self-mutilation. *Comprehensive Psychiatry, 37,* 12–16.

Zlotnick, C., Wolfsdorf, B., Johnson, B., & Spirito, A. (in press). Impaired self-regulation and suicidal behavior among adolescent and young adult psychiatric inpatients. *Archives of Suicide Research.*

Zung, W. (1974). Index of Potential Suicide (IPS): A rating scale for suicide prevention. In A. Beck, H. Resnik, & D. Lettieri (Eds.), *The prediction of suicide* (pp. 221–249). Bowie, MD: Charles Press.

Appendix

Decision Trees for Choosing Instruments for Assessing Suicidal Behavior and Risk

The following decision trees are presented to help readers choose instruments that are appropriate to their needs. In most cases, the series of questions will help to direct the readers to a specific group of instruments. At that point, the reader should read the more detailed descriptions and the evaluative comments (e.g., regarding psychometric characteristics) of the instruments to choose among the various alternatives.

Do you want to select an instrument for (a) **screening purposes** [GO TO SECTION I BELOW], (b) **documentation of treatment outcome** [GO TO SECTION II BELOW], (c) **studies focused on the epidemiology or correlates of suicidal behavior** [GO TO SECTION III BELOW], (d) **description of clinical characteristics of suicidal behavior** [GO TO SECTION IV BELOW], or (e) **other purposes related to suicidal behaviors** [GO TO SECTION V BELOW]?

I. Do you want an instrument for (a) **detection purposes only** [GO TO SECTION IA], (b) **risk assessment purposes only** [GO TO SECTION IB], or **assessment of both detection and risk of suicidal behavior** [GO TO SECTION IC]?

IA. Do you want an instrument that assesses **suicidal ideation and behavior only** [GO TO SECTION IA1] or also **assesses other areas in addition to suicidality such as psychopathology** [GO TO SECTION IA2]?

IA1. At initial screening, do you want to use a **self-report questionnaire** [GO TO SECTION IA1a] or an **interview/clinician rating scale** [GO TO SECTION IA1b]?

IA1a. Do you want an instrument for use with **children** [GO TO SECTION IA1ai] or with **adolescents** [GO TO SECTION IA1aii]?

IA1ai. Consider the Suicidal Behaviors Questionnaire for Children (SBQ–C).

IA1aii. Consider the Beck Scale for Suicidal Ideation (BSI), the Suicidal Ideation Questionnaire (SIQ for older adolescents and SIQ–JR for younger adolescents), or the Suicidal Behaviors Questionnaire (SBQ–14).

IA1b. Consider the Lifetime Parasuicide Count (LPC) if you are interested in assessing suicidal and nonsuicidal self-harm behavior but not suicidal ideation. Consider the Risk of Suicide Questionnaire (RSQ) if you are specifically interested in an instrument for use in emergency room settings.

IA2. Do you want to use a **survey type instrument** [GO TO SECTION IA2a], **self-report questionnaire or behavior checklist** [GO TO SECTION IA2b], or **structured or semistructured clinical interview** [GO TO SECTION IA2c].

IA2a. Are you primarily interested in **screening surveys that have been used in high school and community samples** [GO TO SECTION IA2ai] or **surveys that have been used with special populations such as lesbian, gay, and bisexual youths, Native American youths, or homeless and runaway youths** [GO TO SECTAION IA2aii]?

IA2ai. Consider the Center for Epidemiologic Studies Depression (CES–D) Added Suicide Ideation Items or the DSM Scale for Depression (DSD) if you are interested in assessing suicidality primarily in the context of screening surveys for depressive symptoms. Consider the Middle Adolescent Vulnerability Study Survey if you are interested in assessing suicidal behaviors in the context of substance abuse. Consider the Youth Risk Behavior Survey (YRBS) if you are interested in assessing suicidality and a large number of other health-risk behaviors that has been used in national school-based epidemiologic studies.

IA2aii. Consider the Challenges and Coping Survey for Lesbian, Gay, and Bisexual Youth if you are interested in specifically working with lesbian, gay, or bisexual youths. Consider the Indian Health Service Adolescent Health Survey if you are interested in assessing suicidality and other risk and protective factors among Native American youths. Consider the Midwest Homeless and Runaway Adolescent Project Survey (MHRAP) if you are interested in assessing suicidal ideation and behaviors in a homeless or runaway population.

IA2b. Do you want to assess suicidality **primarily in the context of other depressive symptoms** [GO TO SECTION IA2bi] or **in the context of a variety of other symptoms or problems** [GO TO SECTION IA2bii]?

IA2bi. Consider the Children's Depression Rating Scale—Revised (CDRS–R) or the Hamilton Depression Rating Scale (HAM–D) if you are interested in screening for suicidality in the context of a clinician rating scale for depression. Consider the Beck Depression Inventory (BDI), Child Depression Inventory (CDI), or the Dimensions of Depression Profile for Children and Adolescents (DDPCA) if you are interested in screening for suicidal ideation in the context of self-report questionnaires for depression.

IA2bii. Consider the Adolescent Psychopathology Scale (APS or APS–SF for the short form) or the Achenbach Youth Self-Report (YSR) is you would like to screen for suicidality in the context of a broad-band self-report questionnaire. Consider the Achenbach Child Behavior Checklist (CBCL) or the Achenbach Teacher Report Form (TRF) if you would like to screen for suicidality in the context of a parent or teacher behavior rating scale, respectively.

IA2c. Are you interested in a more structured clinical interview that can be administered by trained laypersons or computer [GO TO SECTION IA2ci] or are you interested in a semistructured instrument that is more flexible but requires more clinical judgment [GO TO SECTION IA2cii]?

IA2ci. Consider the Dominic–R or the Pictorial Instrument for Children and Adolescents (PICA–III–R) if you are interested in using a pictorial-based instrument for younger children. Consider the Adolescent Suicide Interview (ASI or the Multimedia Adolescent Suicide Interview, the MASI) if you are interested in a nonpictorially based interview that assesses only suicidality and symptoms of major depression. Consider the Child and Adolescent Psychiatric Assessment (CAPA), the Children's Interview for Psychiatric Symptoms (ChIPS), the Diagnostic Interview for Children and Adolescents (DICA), or the Diagnostic Interview for Children (DISC) if you are interested in a nonpictorially based interview that assesses both suicidality and symptoms of a variety of psychopathology.

IA2cii. Consider the Interview Schedule for Children and Adolescents (ISCA), the downward extensions of the Longitudinal Interval Follow-Up Evaluation (K–LIFE and A–LIFE), or one of the School-Age versions of the Schedule for Affective Disorders and Schizophrenia (K–SADS–E, K–SADS–L, K–SADS–P IVR, or K–SADS–PL).

IB. In screening for risk for suicidal behavior, do you want to use a **self-report questionnaire** [GO TO SECTION IB1] or an **interview/clinician rating scale** [GO TO SECTION IB2]?

IB1. Are you interested in using the instrument(s) with **children** [GO TO SECTION IB1a] or with **adolescents** [GO TO SECTION IB1b]?

IB1a. Are you interested in assessing a **specific construct theoretically related to risk of suicidal behavior** [GO TO SECTION IB1ai] or are you interested in a **less theoretically based assessment of suicidal risk or**

propensity or an assessment based on multiple risk factors [GO TO SEC-TION IB1aii]?

IB1ai. Consider the Hopelessness Scale for Children (HPLC).

IB1aii. Consider the Child Suicide Risk Assessment (CSRA) or the Child–Adolescent Suicide Potential Index (CASPI).

IB1b. Are you interested in assessing a **specific construct theoretically related to risk of suicidal behavior** [GO TO SECTION IB1bi] or are you interested in a **less theoretically based assessment of suicidal risk or propensity or an assessment based on multiple risk factors** [GO TO SECTION IB1bii]?

IB1bi. Consider the Beck Hopelessness Scale (BHS), the Firestone Assessment of Self-Destructive Thoughts (FAST), the Life Attitudes Schedule (LAS), the Multi-Attitude Suicide Tendency Scale for Adolescents (MAST), or the Reasons for Living Inventory (RFL or the RFL–A for Reasons for Living Inventory for Adolescents or BRFL–A for Brief Reasons for Living Inventory for Adolescents).

IB1bii. Consider the Child–Adolescent Suicide Potential Index (CASPI), the Millon Adolescent Clinical Inventory (MACI) Suicidal Tendency Scale, the Suicide Risk Screen (SRS), or the Zung Index of Suicide Potential (IPS or the Israeli Index of Potential Suicide, IIPS) for a focus on risk but not protective factors associated with suicidality. For a focus on protective factors, consider the Positive and Negative Suicide Ideation (PANSI) Inventory (which includes a focus on both risk and protective factors) or the Suicide Resilience Inventory (SRI–25).

IB2. Consider the clinician-rated Adapted SAD PERSONS scale, the Expendable Child Measure, or the PATHOS. The Adapted SAD PERSONS scale was developed for screening in school settings, and the PATHOS was developed for screening in emergency departments.

IC. Are you interested in using a **single assessment instrument** [GO TO SECTION IC1] or a **two-staged assessment of suicidality and risk** [GO TO SECTION IC2]?

IC1. Are you interested in using a **self-report questionnaire** [GO TO SECTION IC1a] or a **clinician-rating scale** [GO TO SECTION IC1b]?

IC1a. Consider the Harkavy Asnis Suicide Scale (HASS) if you are interested in a self-report questionnaire that assesses suicidal behaviors as well as demographic factors and substance abuse behaviors thought to be associated with higher risk of suicidal ideation. The Inventory for Suicidal Orientation (ISO–30) and the Suicide Probability Scale (SPS) both yield information not only about suicidal ideation (referred to as critical items) but also about hypothesized suicide risk.

IC1b. Consider the Child Suicide Potential Scales (CSPS), which assess both severity of suicidality (with the Spectrum of Suicidal Behavior [SSB] scale) and other potential risk areas.

IC2. Consider the Evaluation of Suicide Risk Among Adolescents and Imminent Danger Assessment if working with populations already thought to be at risk or if there is a preference for a first-stage screener that is individually administered. Consider using the Suicidal Ideation Questionnaire (SIQ) followed by the Suicidal Behaviors Interview (SBI) if interested in a first-stage screener that focuses specifically on suicidal ideation and thoughts of death (rather than including queries about other risk factors) and does not have to be individually administered. Consider using the Columbia Teen Screen followed by the DISC–IV or the High School Questionnaire/Suicide Risk Screen (SRS) followed by the Measure of Adolescent Potential for Suicide (MAPS) if interested in a first-stage screening procedure that does not need to be individually administered and includes a focus on risk factors for suicidal behaviors.

II. Do you want to assess the effects of an intervention on **suicidal ideation** [GO TO SECTION IIA], on **suicide attempts** [GO TO SECTION IIB], or on **indicants of risk of suicidal behavior** [GO TO SECTION IIC]?

IIA. Consider the Beck Scale for Suicide Ideation (BSI) if you want to assess outcomes weekly or the Suicidal Ideation Questionnaire (SIQ) if you want to assess outcomes monthly or less frequently.

IIB. Any of the diagnostic interviews designed for or used previously in longitudinal studies should suffice for assessing suicide attempts at intervals following entry into a treatment study. Consider the Child and Adolescent Psychiatric Assessment (CAPA), the Interview Schedule for Children and Adolescents (ISCA), the various School-Age versions of the Schedule for Affective Disorders and Schizophrenia (K–SADS–E, K–SADS–L, K–SADS–P IVR, and K–SADS–PL), or the Child or Adolescent version of the Longitudinal Interval Follow-Up Evaluation (K–LIFE and A–LIFE).

IIC. Consider the Beck Hopelessness Scale (BHS), Hopelessness Scale for Children (HPLS), the Inventory of Suicidal Orientation (ISO–30), or the Israeli Index of Potential Suicide (IIPS), a modification of the Zung Index of Potential Suicide.

III. Any of the "Detection" instruments should be appropriate for determining the presence/absence or severity of suicidal ideation or behavior in research studies. The most commonly used structured diagnostic interviews in suicidality research are the Diagnostic Interview Schedule for Children (DISC) and the Diagnostic Interview for Children and Adolescents (DICA). The most commonly used semistructured diagnostic interviews in suicidality research are the Interview Schedule for Children and Adolescents (ISCA) and the Schedule for Affective Disorders and Schizophrenia, School-Age Epidemiologic Version (K–SADS–E). The most commonly used self-report questionnaire for assessing severity of suicidal ideation is the Suicidal Ideation Questionnaire (SIQ and SIQ–JR). The Youth Risk Behavior Survey (YRBS) has been used in more published suicidality research than any other survey-based instrument.

IV. Do you want to use an instrument that assesses **medical lethality of suicide attempts** [GO TO SECTION IVA], **intentionality of suicide attempts** [GO TO SECTION IVB], **or both medical lethality and intent** [GO TO SECTION IVC]?

IVA. Consider the Lethality of Suicide Attempt Rating Scale, the Risk-Rating Rescue Scale, or the Self-Inflicted Injury Severity Form (SIISF).

IVB. Consider the Beck Suicide Intent Scale (SIS) or the Pierce Suicidal Intent Scale.

IVC. For brief assessment of both medical lethality and subjective intent, consider the suicide attempt clinical characteristics questions of the Child and Adolescent Psychiatric Assessment (CAPA), the Interview Schedule for Children and Adolescents (ISCA), or the various School-Age versions of the Schedule for Affective Disorders and Schizophrenia (K–SADS–E, K–SADS–L, K–SADS–P IVR, and K–SADS–PL). Consider the Suicide Circumstances Schedule (SCS) if you want to use a compilation of instruments assessing aspects of suicidal behavior including intent and lethality.

V. Are you interested in assessing **attitudes about suicide and suicidal behavior** [GO TO SECTION VA], **exposure to suicide** [GO SECTION VB], **circumstances regarding completed suicide** [GO TO SECTION VC], or the **reasons for nonlethal suicidal behavior and/or the "pain" associated with suicidal behavior** [GO TO SECTION VD]? Are you interested in **clinical history form or interview outline for assessing suicidal behavior** [GO TO SECTION VE]? As a complement to assessing suicidal behaviors, do you want to assess **nonsuicidal self-injurious behaviors** [GO TO SECTION VF]?

VA. Consider the Attitudes Toward Suicide List, the Attitudes Toward Suicide and Suicidal Ideation instrument, or the Suicide Attitude Vignette Experience (SAVE).

VB. Consider the Characteristics of Exposure to Death (CED) instrument if you are interested in assessing only exposure to a particular suicidal incident.

VC. Consider the Completed Suicide Event Interview if you are interested in a more comprehensive assessment of a completed suicide. The

Suicidal Circumstances Schedule (SCS) has been used to assess characteristics of both nonlethal suicide attempts and completed suicides.

VD. Consider the Reasons for Suicide Attempts and Reasons for Overdose scales if interested in the reasons for suicidal behavior. Consider the Psychological Pain Assessment Scale (PPAS) if interested in a projective assessment instrument assessing the "pain" and unmet needs associated with suicidal behavior.

VE. Consider the Columbia/Ruane Initial Evaluation Form for Child and Adolescent Suicide Attempters/Ideators or the Suicidal Behavior History Form.

VF. Consider the Self-Injury Inventory (SII) if interested in an instrument assessing only nonsuicidal self-injurious behavior. Consider using the Lifetime Parasuicide Count (LPC) if interested in assessing specific incidents of both suicidal and nonsuicidal self-injurious behavior. Consider using the queries of the Child and Adolescent Psychiatric Assessment (CAPA), the Interview Schedule for Children and Adolescents (ISCA), or any of the School-Age versions of the Schedule for Affective Disorders and Schizophrenia (K–SADS–E, K–SADS–L, K–SADS–P IVR, K–SADS–PL) if you are interested in using a diagnostic interview that includes queries assessing both suicidal and nonsuicidal self-injurious behavior.

Index

About the Author

David B. Goldston received his PhD in clinical and developmental psychology from the University of Iowa in 1988. He completed his clinical psychology internship at the David Geffen School of Medicine at the University of California, Los Angeles, and later worked with Dr. Maria Kovacs in her longitudinal studies of youths with depression and with diabetes at the University of Pittsburgh School of Medicine. Dr. Goldston joined the faculty of the Department of Psychiatry at Wake Forest University School of Medicine in 1989 as an associate professor and served as the director of research. He was the recipient of a Faculty Scholar Award from the William T. Grant Foundation and has been conducting an ongoing longitudinal study focused on risk for suicidal behavior over the last 10 years. Dr. Goldston is currently an associate professor in the Department of Psychiatry at Duke University School of Medicine.